PSYCHE OF INDIAN WOMEN

About the Editor

Aradhana Shukla, is Professor of the Department of Psychology and Campus Dean (Faculty of Arts) at Kumaun University Campus Almora. She pursued her studies from Gorakhpur University and served as Asstt. Research Officer at Department of Paediatrics, BHU and Post Doctoral Fellow (UGC) at Gorakhpur University. She has been serving in Kumaun University since Twenty six years. She has authored ten books and completed seven research projects along with two in progress. Many of her research papers have been presented in national and international journals and seminars. She is in the editorial board of many journals and delivered key note address in two national seminars.

Psyche of Indian Women

Edited by

Aradhana Shukla

CONCEPT PUBLISHING COMPANY PVT. LTD.
NEW DELHI-110 059

ISBN-13: 978-81-8069-974-0

First Published 2013

Published and Printed by

Concept Since 1974

Concept Publishing Company Pvt. Ltd.
A/15-16, Commercial Block, Mohan Garden
New Delhi-110059 (India)
T: 25351460, 25351794, *F*: 091-11-25357109
E: publishing@conceptpub.com, W: www.conceptpub.com
Editorial Office: H-13, Bali Nagar, New Delhi-110 015, India.

Cataloging in Publication Data--Courtesy: D.K. Agencies (P) Ltd. <docinfo@dkagencies.com>

Psyche of Indian women / edited by Aradhana Shukla.
p. cm.
Contributed articles.
Includes bibliographical references and index.
ISBN 9788180699740

1. Women—Employment—India. 2. Women employees—India—Psychology. 3. Women employees—India—Social conditions. 4. Women employees—Family relationships—India. I. Shukla, Aradhana.

DDC 331.40954 23

Preface

Socio-psychological attempts to examine issues is related to Indian Women's entry into the employment market has caught direct at ention to important but the limited range of topics. More importantly, these attempts reflect genders' views of employment. As man's provided role is both socially accepted and valued, their employment is not seen to be in conflict which their homemaking and socializing roles and, therefore, their involvement outside the home is considered deviant behaviour, a problem and a source of stress in domestic life. Consequently, researchers mainly concern themselves with questions like how does women's employment status affect their performance of familial roles and quality of marital life? How does fulltime employment of the mother influence children's psychological development and academic performance? How do working women combine their so-called "traditional" roles of homemaker and earner and with impact does it have on their stress levels clearly, the focus is on studying the effects of employment and less attention is paid to examining work related aspects of employed women. In short, researchers have continued to study working women in their roles as "wives" and "mothers" rather than as "workers" in gainful employment. Keeping this scenario and Indian Womenhood in consideration this editorial volume was planned and captioned as "Psyche of Indian Women".

This editorial volume is comprised of seventeen chapters which are written by various eminent signatories of India. In first chapter "Women in New Horizon" Aradhana Shukla has shed light on the condition of women from Vedic period till now. She has also emphasized the existing responsibilities of working women at both platforms, i.e., home and office.

Amrita Deb and Meenakshi Arora in their article, "Resilience and Women : Changing Roles, Risks and Protective Factors" have derived that when faced with adversity, even the seemingly ordinary women is capable of showing extraordinary resiliency skills. The third chapter "Marital Happiness : An Attitude" written by Sunita Dwivedi and P.C. Mishra reflects the happiness pattern of Indian marital couples and it is found that for self-discloser husband and wife need to have a healthy and strong psychology to accepting each other with full confidence, affection and love. We again emphasize that the psychology of a woman is more strong and confident enough to start with. "Culture and Climate Supportiveness : A Developmental Analysis" is an empirical chapter which is written by Aradhana Shukla and Shraddha Joshi. In this empirical chapter they have presented the pattern of climate experiences of women in Uttarakhand.

The fifth chapter is entitled "Women Manager in Indian Organizations". It is a qualitative interpretation of Dr. H.L. Kaila and he has made few suggestions to make women's life easier in organizations such as compressed working week, creches at the workplace, employee counselling at workplaces flexitime, compulsory periodical medical examination providing the facility of working from home, *yoga* for improved physical and mental health. Nishi Tripathi in "Understanding the Real Story of Women's World: An Indian Scene" has shed light on the real profile of Indian Women in present-day society. Aradhana Shukla and Ruchhi Kakkar in "Developmental Analysis of Deprivational Experiences in Rural and Urban Kumauni Women" have shown the pattern of developmental experiences and personality profile of Kumauni urban and rural women. Anubhuti Dubey has described "Psychosocial Determinants of Health of Women in India" and stated that women's health is a mixture of physical, emotional, social and spiritual well-being.

Gyan Mudra and V. Suresh Babu have made a joint endeavour to describe "Marketing and Rural Women" and said that women entrepreneurs have created a variety of new ventures and contributed to develop the range of services and products. "Religiosity and Well-being of Pregnant Women" is written by Shobhna Joshi and Shilpa Kumari. They have concluded that religiosity facilitates well-being. Urmila R. Srivastava and Shamini Srivastava have presented issues and challenges for working women in tally commuting and work family life. They have stated that although work family interface is an important phenomena and telecommunicating can have effects on various dimensions of work family interface. In "Glass Ceiling" Poona Midha has stated that this glass ceiling comes to criple working women the most.

Rakesh Srivastava and Madhu Seth have written an article on "Attitudes of Married Women Towards Birth Restraints and Family Size in Relation to Personality". They have concluded that personality characteristics are found to influence the attitudes of males and females. Aradhana Shukla and Shraddha Joshi have attempted "Experiencing Satisfaction in Life: A study on paid and unpaid women" and they have suggested that age variation, family type and job status influence the pattern of life satisfaction and well-being. Neetu Jain, Nov Rattan Sharma and Amrita Yadav have shed light on "Mental Health of Adolescent School Girls in Relation to Anger". Akanksha Lall and Aradhana Shukla in their article have shed light on "Impact of Cultural Variation, Age and Climateric Variation on Emotional Disurbance."

Last but not the least is the paper of Punam Midha entitled "Gender Equality and Equity" in which she has expressed her views about the equality of males and females.

I hope that this collection of ideas will help the researchers of women psychology and provide them new visions to go ahead.

Aradhana Shukla

Acknowledgements

While preparing this volume the editor received help and encouragement from many sources of which I am thankful to them. The editor is extremely grateful to all the contributors who made this volume easy by their valuable thoughts. Assistance given by Ms. Shraddha Joshi cannot be denied. In spite of thanking, I wish bright and prosperous future for her. The editor is thankful to Mr. Abishek Yadav for the organization of the manuscript through computer. The publication has been undertaken by Concept Publishing Company Pvt. Ltd., New Delhi, with active interest and supervision of Shri Ashok Kumar Mittal to whom I am thankful.

Aradhana Shukla

Contents

Preface v

Acknowledgements *viii*

List of Contributors *xi*

1. **Women in New Horizon** **1**
—*Aradhana Shukla*

2. **Resilience and Women : *Changing Roles, Risks and Protective Factors*** **18**
—*Amrita Deb* and *Meenakshi Arora*

3. **Marital Happiness : *An Attitude*** **57**
—*Sunita Dwivedi* and *P.C. Mishra*

4. **Culture and Climate Supportiveness : *A Developmental Analysis*** **78**
—*Aradhana Shukla* and *Shraddha Joshi*

5. **Women Managers in Indian Organizations** **93**
—*H.L. Kaila*

6. **Understanding the Real Story of Women's World : *An Indian Scene*** **111**
—*Nishi Tripathi*

7. **Developmental Analysis of Deprivational Experiences in Rural and Urban Kumauni Women** **127**
—*Aradhana Shukla* and *Ruchi Kakkar*

8. **Psychosocial Determinants of Health of Women in India** **141**
—*Anubhuti Dubey*

9. **Marketing and Rural Women** **157**
—*Gyanmudra* and *V. Suresh Babu*

10. **Religiosity and Well-being of Pregnant Women** 181
—*Shobhna Joshi* and *Shilpa Kumari*

11. **Telecommuting and Work-Family Conflict : *Issues and Challenges for Working Women*** 210
—*Urmila R. Srivastava* and *Shamini Srivastava*

12. **Glass Ceiling** 235
—*Punam Midha*

13. **Attitudes of Married Women towards Birth Restraints and Family Size in Relation to Personality** 249
—*Rakesh K. Srivastava* and *Madhu Seth*

14. **Experiencing Satisfaction in Life: *A Study on Paid and Unpaid Women*** 263
—*Aradhana Shukla* and *Shraddha Joshi*

15. **Mental Health of Adolescent School Girls in Relation to Anger** 283
—*Nitu Jain, Nov Rattan Sharma* and *Amrita Yadav*

16. **Impact of Cultural Variation, Age and Climateic Variation on Emotional Disturbance** 301
—*Akanksha Lall* and *Aradhana Shukla*

17. **Gender Equality and Equity** 322
—*Punam Midha*

Index 331

List of Contributors

Akanksha Lall, Research Scholar, Department of Psychology, Kumaun University, S.S.J. Campus, Almora.

Amrita Deb, Research Scholar, Department of Psychology, Banaras Hindu University, Varanasi.

Dr. Amrita Yadav, Professor, Department of Psychology, Maharshi Dayanand University, Rohtak.

Anubhuti Dubey, Associate Professor, Department of Psychology, DDU, Gorakhpur University, Gorakhpur.

Aradhana Shukla, Professor, Department of Psychology, Kumaun University, S.S.J. Campus, Almora.

Gyanmudra, Associate Professor, CHRD, National Institute of Rural Development, Hyderabad.

H.L. Kaila, Head of Department, SNDT Women's University, Mumbai.

Madhu Seth, Principal, K.R. Girl's P.G. College, Mathura.

Meenakshi Arora, Professor, Department of Psychology, Banaras Hindu University, Varanasi.

Nishi Tripathi, Assistant Professor, College of Business Studies, Allahabad Agricultural Institute, Allahabad.

Nitu Jain, Department of Psychology, Maharshi Dayanand University, Rohtak.

Nov Rattan Sharma, Professor, Department of Psychology, Maharshi Dayanand University, Rohtak.

P.C. Misra, Professor, Department of Psychology, Lucknow University, Lucknow.

Punam Midha, Professor, Department of Psychology, Maharshi Dayanand University, Rohtak.

Rakesh K. Srivastava, Associate Professor, Department of Psychology, Post-Graduation College, Malikpura, Ghaziabad.

Ruchi Kakkar, Visiting Personnel, Department of Psychology, Kumaun University, S.S.J. Campus, Almora.

Shamini Srivastava, Department of Psychology, Banaras Hindu University, Varanasi.

Shilpa Kumari, Department of Psychology, Banaras Hindu University, Varanasi.

Shobhna Joshi, Associate Professor, Department of Psychology, Banaras Hindu University, Varanasi.

Shraddha Joshi, Research Scholar, Department of Psychology, Kumaun University, S.S.J. Campus, Almora.

Sunita Dwivedi, Associate Professor, Department of Psychology, Navyug Kanya Vidyalaya, P.G. College, Lucknow.

V. Suresh Babu, Assistant Professor, CTPM, National Institute of Rural Development, Hyderabad.

Urmila R. Srivastava, Associate Professor, Department of Psychology, Banaras Hindu University, Varanasi.

1

Women in New Horizon

Aradhana Shukla

It is the most common view among scholars that the best way to evaluate nations' progress is to find out the status of women there. Position of women in a society is the true index of its cultural, intellectual and spiritual attainments because nobody can deny her unavoiding graceful role in society (Asthana, 1974; Majumdar, 1967). Sengupta (1971) has also accepted her role in society as the measuring rod in assessing the standard of culture of any age. If we want to study the status of women in society we must study the complexity of rules which women perform in society and in the socio-economic, cultural, religious, cultural and political fields. It is also important to find out that how they understand these domains of society and act against them.

The role of women differs from society to society and from time to time. In several societies women enjoyed higher status than men and in some societies they enjoyed equal status to men. If we examine societies where women had enjoyed higher status, we may see that they had complete, or at least major role over economic activities. Westermack (1914) has stated that "the position of women is exceptionally good in tribes that live upon fish and roots which the women procure with a degree of expertness equal to that of the men, whereas it was among tribes that live by the chase or by other means in which women can be of little service, that we find the sex most oppressed. Again, women among hunters and pastoral tribes had low status but among the agricultural group, the position of female was generally higher."

In Vedic period women enjoyed equal status and rights along with men. Aryans, as new settlers has to face the antagonistic natives. Their women had important role not only, as the potential source of population growth but as individuals preparing war materials and looking after civilian jobs. They enjoyed equal shares in learning Vedas and in the performance of religious rituals, as Vedic religion required propitiating supernatural powers and the rituals demanded performance of them jointly by husband and wife. During this period widows were permitted to remarriage, as expansion of the numbers of the race was important to make up the loss of men in war with natives and also to add number in the natives in terms of population. In *Rigveda*, words like "Paraparva" and "Dhidista" refer to women having second husband and "second husband of the women", respectively.

In the post-Vedic period, i.e. the period of *Ramayana, Mahabharata* and the birth and spread of Jainism and Buddhism Aryan men took to hypergamy, i.e. the marriage of Aryan men to indigenous women. In the Aryan caste system, the natives were assigned the last rank in the hierarchy. Therefore, non-Aryan wives did not enjoy equal status with Aryan wives. Moreover, they could not perform the Aryan ritual roles. This resulted in the stopping of participation of women, as a whole in religious ceremonies. Also, they were deprived from the participation in the economic sphere, and were left merely as a source of progeny.

For the Indo-Aryans ceremonial purity was very important. The biological phenomenon of menstural period, childbirth etc. were viewed as the marks of impurity in women. They were also regarded as more susceptible to pollution.

In aforesaid period, the condition of widows was not very good. Their remarriage and divorce were becoming unpopular, but the need to have a son was very important. They were permitted to marry dead husbands' brother strictly for the purpose of bringing forth a male child.

Afterwards, the treatment of women became worse. It was instructed to widows to lead a miserable life. They were also instructed to give up adorning their hair, applying perfume, chewing betel nuts, etc. During this period, along with celibacy of women, idea of *Sati* was also gaining ground. It was stated that widow should observe celebacy and should accept the funeral pyre of her husband.

As a result, Jainism and Buddhism arose as revolt against the situationism of Hinduism, in general. Strangely, instead of helping these religious movements in the uplift of women, indirectly, helped Hinduism to degrade women. To fight against Jainism and Buddhism, Hinduism tightened up its ethical and religious codes which particularly affected women. Following Buddhistic practices, widows were instructed to shave their hairs. The age of marriage of girls was also reduced and child marriage became the order of the day.

During Muslim rule in India further deterioration in the treatment of women took place. During this period women were compelled to use *purdah* to cover their face so that they should be prevented from men from seeing them. Menon (1981) has stated that the *purdah* or seculsion was looked upon as a symbol of respectability. It was a great dishonour for a family when a wife is compelled to uncover herself. *Purdah* system isolated these women from the outer world and confined them to the boundaries of their homes (Ojha, 1961). The *Purdah* system snatched the freedom of movement of women. In addition to it, negligence on the part of parents and administration was also visited in this regard.

The other important factor which hampered the development of education of Muslim women was the institution of early marriage. It resulting to which they had to experience early motherhood. The only aim of these women was centred to their households and they had restricted to take interest for literary pursuits.

The economic factor was also responsible for the denial of education to women during Mughal period. The economic inequalities prevalent in these days prevented women of lower sections of society from acquiring even fair amount of literacy. The poor families of that period could hardly produce women of great repute in the realm of education or learning. So, it is surely fair to say that economic factor must have blocked the educational progress of the Muslim women of poor families during Mughal period.

As a whole, we find that the position of women during Mughal period was definitely inferior. "The women were not generally considered full persons whose advise was to be sought and experience relied upon, and conclusions were drawn from this belief by men according to their temperament and culture" (Mujeeb, 1967).

Contrary to this view some supporting evidences have also been found. Choudhary has stated that the education of Muslim women was confined mostly to the women belonging to royal and aristocratic sections of the society. In general, there were no separate schools for Muslim women. They received primary education with boys. As soon as they grew up they were separated from the boys. There were *maktabs* in houses for the education of Muslim girls where *Quran, Gulistan* and *Bostan* were taught to them. When the girls finished the reading of *Quran,* a special assembly was invited to celebrate the occcasion. Generally, it was thought as the educational end of mediocre Muslim women. But high level of attention was paid on the education of royal Muslim ladies. Muslim ladies like Gullbadan Begum, Sati-un-Nisa, Jahanara, Hifiza Maryan were well-educated and highly accomplished ladies. The curriculum of their education generally included the study of Persian language and literature besides memorizing the Arabic religious texts, chiefly the *Holy Quran*. Apart from this, the coverage of education was also consisted of singing, instrumental music, riding, shooting, embroidery etc. The royal lady like Nurjahan was highly skilled in embroidery. She was thoroughly versed in Persian language and Arabic literature and it was she who carried on the administration of Government during the lifetime of her husband.

Jahanara Begum, daughter of Shahjahan is memorable in Mughal history for her vast knowledge and cultural accomplishments. She patronized and encouraged many learned men and scholders of her fathers' court? In addition, Zeb-un-Nisa, the eldest daughter of Aurangzeb had achieved mastery in literature, mathematics, astronomy and other difficult sciences. Also, she had achieved great success in the art of calligraphy.

It has also been evidenced that the education under the great Mughals was a branch of religion and it was mainly in the hands of learned Brahmim and the Ulema of the century. There was a department in the Government to look after the educational institutions of the state. When the states were engaged in wars and conquests they felt inability to facilitate these institutions. Such policies of Government did not encourage the education of Muslim women. Thus, we see that there was no systematic and conscious move on the part of the state to ameliorate their condition.

During British period increasing attention was being paid to women's education. Rawat (1970) has pointed out that "if we see the picture of household dynamics in relation to women's employment distribution of housework is considered the acid" or litmus test of couples' attitude towards gender equality. There are not many studies on this aspect and the few that are available generally report that women's employment and educational status are of little consequence as far as sharing of domestic labour is concerned (Bharat, 1992; Rao, 1990). Many sociological studies such as those by Ramu (1989), and Radha Devi and Ravindran (1985) report similar findings. Women, whether employed or not, and whether in professional or non-professional jobs, continue to shoulder maximum household responsibilities of kitchen work, home management, looking after guests, etc.

Where men share responsibilities, they do so for less taxing and masculine tasks like repairs and keeping monthly accounts (Bharat, 1992). Rao (1990) also found that husbands' participation was higher in nuclear families and in families where spouses expressed more companionship in their relationship. Significantly, marital happiness was reported to be greater in households where women received assistance from their husbands, implying that companionship and husbands' support was greatly valued by women engaged in paid work.

Psychological Well-being of Women in Employment

There are a considerable number of sociological works (see reviews by Krishna Raj, 1986; Ramu, in press) which examine the disproportionate level of stress and anxiety experienced by employed women in comparison to both—employed women and men. A major source of this stress and anxiety is in the conflict between job and familial responsibilities. Psychological studies on the individual consequences of women's employment include adjustment problems, stress and strain, anxiety and depression, and anger expression.

Bhattacharjee and Bhatt (1983) compared family adjustment of 76 Gujarati-speaking middle class married working women and 70 non-working women. It was hypothesized that the double role burden of employed women contributed to differences in familial adjustment, neuroticism, and psychological conflicts between the two groups of women. Although the differences were not statistically significant, on the basis of trends in the data, the authors noted that married working women were better adjusted, more stable and experienced less psychological conflicts compared to non-employed married women. Without citing additional evidence, the authors "concluded" that the adjustment of an educated, married woman, whether employed or not, "is a function of her own personality traits, aspirations and expectations and perceptions of her own roles combined with the attitudes and expectations of her husband and other family members."

In several sociological researches, both Western and Indian, difficulty in coping with the competing demands of work and family are shown to produce guilt feelings, fatigue, role conflict, stress and strain among women. In a study of 50 professional and 50 non-professional men and women Tarabadkar and Ghadially (1985) noted that work family conflict was expressed in 63 per cent of the TAT (Thematic Apperception Test) stories written by women whereas men's stories did not reflect this conflict. However, in a later study, Ghadially and Kumar (1989) neither found family-work conflict nor identified role overload as a major stressor among women, a majority of whom were employed as university teachers or researchers. Instead, inadequate pay and underutilization of skills ranked high as stressors. As the authors explained, the absence of stress due to role overload and/or work—family conflict among women in their sample was perhaps due to a better social support network—elderly relatives, domestic servants in these families and because of flexible working hours of women in the teaching profession. This finding is in sharp contrast to some sociological findings which report both role conflict and role overload among working women. The composition of the sample may be one factor contributing to these contradictory findings. It is possible that family related stresses are experienced more often by employed women who cannot afford domestic help or whose working hours are inflexible and demanding. Major strains reported by the subjects in Ghadially and Kumar's study were tension, fatigue and physical complaints, although the areas of tension or the nature of physical problems were not described. Women sought to cope with their problems by reading for acquiring knowledge, planning and goal setting, and seeking and building social support. They used both individual centred and interpersonal coping strategies. Comparing their data with Taiwanese and American samples, Ghadially and Kumar (1989) noted that the three cultures differed on stressors (in the US conflict with colleagues, and in Taiwan work overload and job-family conflict were the major stressors) but not on strains. Further, the samples in the two Asian countries were similar in terms of coping styles (both used limited strategies) as well as in the probability of sickness (lower chances of sickness), as compared to the American sample. Since no comparable groups of non-professional and non-employed women were studied, it is difficult to state to what extent the stresses, strains and coping styles of professional women differed from those of non-professional women, that is, women in lower ranking jobs like clerks, and from those of women who are full-time housewives. Unlike male employment, women's employment is necessarily viewed in the context of their social, marital and familial roles and relationships. When women cross the threshold of their homes to enter the world of paid work, their employment is seen as intruding upon their primary responsibility of home making. They are expected to reorganize their "traditional" roles of wife, mother and homemaker in order to accommodate their "non-traditional" role as earner. A fair amount of sociological research exploring the work-family interface in the case of employed women is available. Two major lines of enquiry are discernible. First, explores the balancing of roles and the accompanying role conflict, role perceptions, and role burden of employed women. Second, examines the impact of women's earner role on their status within the family in terms of their decision-making power, sharing household labour, etc. In comparison to sociological literature, psychological research on these aspects is limited, though insightful.

In traditional Indian homes the husband is considered to have greater power in decision-making and the wife is merely expected to execute those decisions. In the context of women's involvement in paid work, the question arises "Do women gain more power, at home when they are gainfully employed outside?" Shukla (1987) compared the decision making patterns single (N 47) and dual career couples (N 54) residing in a north Indian city. A decision-making scale with statement; covering different decision areas like finance and home decoration was used. The wives were employed as government officers, doctors, bank officers and lecturers. As hypothesized, employed women enjoyed more power than non-employed women and on the whole dual career couples were more egalitarian than single career couples leading to the conclusion, "since wives' employment is significantly associated with their marital power, their employment may be regarded as an important resource variable in the Indian context" (p. 628).

A sociological analysis of dual earner couples by Ramu (1989) also revealed the positive impact of wives' employment on their decision making power at home. Employed wives had significantly greater power than non-employed wives. However, these findings are partly at variance with Western findings that show that although employed wives have more power, they still have less power than their husbands (Scanzoni & Polonka, 1980). In the light of this, decision areas in which working wives enjoy power are worth examining. Shukla (1987a) reported that employed wives enjoyed power in economically significant areas like insurance and investments. A study by Bharat (1992) with career (N 190) and non-career women (N 136) revealed that even if women employed in high placed jobs gained power, they did so in seemingly less crucial areas like menu making or home decoration while decisions on matters involving finances were generally made by husbands.

In the only study of women entrepreneurs, Surti and Sarupria (1983) found that Ahmedabad based women in business (N 40) experienced role stress because of lack of time to attend to their various other roles. This also gave them the feeling of being less involved in their entrepreneurial role and having less control over the results, this was especially true of married women entrepreneurs. If women were part of a joint family set-up, they experienced less role stress. Personality factors were also important. For example, women high on external locus of control and fear of success experienced greater role stress and result inadequacy. Further, a majority used individual centred coping styles supporting Ghadially and Kumar's (1989) findings on this aspect. This means that more women tended to rely on self to solve problems.

Jobs create additional stresses for women in the form of promotions and appreciation. Since promotions mean additional responsibilities, greater commitment in terms of time, and very often transfers, women experience depression even on account of these "positive life changes" (Khanna, 1992). Such findings are often interpreted to mean low job commitment and involvement on the part of women. However, what such findings probably indicate is that for women wage earners, family and job spheres are intimately linked such that job related changes, even positive changes, result in depression because of an increase in responsibilities.

There is some evidence that the parental status of working women is crucial for their mental health status. Shukla and

Verma (1986) found that the presence of children in the age groups 6-12 years and/over 12 years was more strongly associated with poor mental health and least favourable home role and employment role attitudes of employed mothers. Women in the "empty nest" and those who did not have any children, on the other hand, enjoyed overall good health. Similar findings were reported by Rao Gupta and Ganguli (1982) with regard to school age children and mothers' adjustment to multiple.

The preoccupation of employed women with their multiple roles is believed to interfere with their psychological adaptation to physiological changes. They are, therefore, expected to be more prone to emotional outbursts. Sailaja and Swaminathan (1992a; 1992b) investigated anger expression and state and trait anxiety among employed and non-employed pregnant women. While anxiety is normally associated with pregnancy, the focus on anger expression is not clear; why would pregnant women, employed or not, experience anger? The sample included 110 pregnant women, 61 of whom were non-working. Withhout providing adequate justification, the authors hypothesised that employed women would manifest more trait and state anxiety as compared to non-employed pregnant women (Sailaja and Swaminathan, 1992b) and the two groups would significantly differ on anger expression (Sailaja & Swaminathan, 1992a). Using Spielberger's scales for assessing trait and state anxiety and anger, the authors found support for both the hypotheses. Working pregnant women scored higher on trait and state anxiety, as well as on the anger dimension. These results implied that pregnancy induced more stress among employed women resulting in anxiety and anger, and underlined the importance of counselling for women to cope with physiological changes. However, the study did not probe into the specific factors that caused anxiety and anger among pregnant women who performed dual roles.

It is obvious that the studies reviewed here do not reveal a clear picture of the stresses and strains experienced by women who work outside the home. There is a vast difference in the social background of the women who were studied—some belonged to professional groups (Ghadially and Kumar, 1989), others were from a non-professsional background (Khanna, 1992) therefore it is difficult to compare the findings. An important variable is the personality factor which predisposes employed women to approach their situation with a certain frame of mind. Women who are internally-oriented and who adopt an individual centred coping style seem more in command and less stressed. Another aspect that has not been adequately explored but is probably a crucial factor in the well-being of earning women is the support available at home and the quality of their relationships with significant others. Significantly, the presence of young children is an important variable to be considered in future research.

Work Aspects of Women in Employment

The non-work aspects of employed women's lives have attracted greater attention of researchers than their work related aspects. Research studies on women as workers in their own right—job motivation of women workers, their career choices and career growth, job satisfaction and performance—are few and far between. As a result it has neither been possible to appreciate and understand women in relation to their job environment nor acknowledge their contribution to the world of work.

Tarabadkar and Ghadially (1985) examined achievement motivation and job satisfaction among 50 professional and 50 non-professional men and women through the TAT (Thematic Appereption Test) and Burke's job description method respectively. As hypothesized, men in general and professional men in particular, were more achievement-oriented than women. Contrary to expectation, professional women were lower on need for achievementnAch as compared to professional men. The authors attributed this to "fear of success" among women. As mentioned earlier, success in career often has negative consequences for women in terms of transfers or increased job responsibilities. Therefore, they seem to fear and avoid success. This is in line with Khanna's (1992) observations that positive life changes like promotions were associated with depression in working women. However, further analysis of data revealed that women in traditionally feminine professions (teaching and nursing) were low on nAch whereas those in male dominated careers (engineering) were high on nAch. In other words, it would be incorrect to conclude that women as a group were not achievement-oriented; those who opted for male-oriented professions did so because of their high nAch levels. Also, work-family conflict due to non-cooperation from husbands for sharing household chores perhaps dampened their need for achievement at work. A supportive home environment may help women in expressing and realising their need for achievement in a comparative study of need achievement among 50 women employed as teachers and doctors. Das and Mathur (1992) observed that work related obstacles and conflicts "possibly channel a specific type of women into the working world who possess typical characteristics of n-achievement such as high competitiveness and drive to succeed" (p. 21). While demonstrating that nAch was a major characteristic of working women, this study failed to explain the reality of women who were forced to work despite low nAch or those who were unable to work even if they were high on nAch.

Sastry and Pandey (1992) provided further evidence in support of the observation that achievement and career motivation are related to gender orientation rather than to sex *per se*. They noted higher sex role conflict among feminine sex role-oriented executives (both males and females) compared to executives (males and females) with masculine or sex orientation androgynous. With respect to job satisfaction, the nature of job was important: professional women behaved very much like men (both professional and non-professional). All these three groups attached greater importance to intrinsic factors while non-professional women were driven more by extrinsic factors like monetary benefits. Other studies concluded that women in general worked for primarily economic gains. Aleem and Khandelwal (1988; 1989) found that women engaged in different types of jobs (banks, hospitals) and across income levels attached more value to the extrinsic (economic security) aspects of their jobs. Men, in contrast, rated intrinsic values (responsibility) higher. Success in job or career was more salient for men. Whereas non-work aspects like performance of multiple roles, and integration of family and work were more important for women. It would seem that work is the only channel available to men for achieving a sense of well-being, whereas there are several other routes open to women. This was seen in the case of career-oriented wives as well. They reported spending less time on the job and being less involved in pursuing a career on the other hand, husbands exhibited greater job involvement in making a career, and experienced less role stress (Aleem and Khandelwal, 1989). Sekaran (1984), however, reported contrary findings. Both men and women in her sample (N 123) drawn from several Bombay based organisations (banking, transport, insurance), regarded their career as equally salient. Two correlates of career salience were (a) planning for a dual career family, and (b) self-esteem derived from work. Sekaran concluded that if couples planned for a dual career family lifestyle before entering matrimony and if organisations helped employees in deriving self-esteem from work, career salience would be enhanced. Shukla (1987b) found that women's education and marital status were significant for their work involvement and job satisfaction. Single, highly educated, employed women experienced greater work satisfaction and work involvement. Married educated women also expressed work involvement but they preferred housework to their job. Two important observations made in the study were (a) even if women were working they experienced greater satisfaction in doing their household work, and (b) non-working women were not necessarily a bored lot, thus belying the stereotypical notion of unhappy and depressed housewives (Shukla, 1987b).

For women in the management sector (N 600), Parikh and Shah (1994) analyzed their career paths and identified organizational and internal barriers to their career growth. Dividing women's career path into three phases of 15 years each, the authors demonstrated that there has been a gradual transition of women from being job-oriented to career-oriented to profession-oriented. During this transition, women managers sought to transform organizational and internal barriers into opportunities and attempted to integrate social identity with professional identity. The attitude of the top management and the visibility of senior women professionals as role models were crucial in facilitating the growth of women of the second generation in the corporate world. At the level of the family and society, the supportive role of family members and broadening of social attitudes were significant in enabling women to overcome barriers. However, the internal barriers imposed by gender biased socialization hampered women's efforts to secure greater mobility and flexibility in working hours.

In nearly all the studies reviewed here, there has been a tendency to explain women's job motives and lower job performance in terms of their personality disposition-achievement motivation, extrinsic orientation, etc. Structural conditions, family situation or job environment as the context within which women work and live have rarely been investigated. The only context that has been mentioned is the family wherein non-participation of husbands in domestic work, inadequate child care arrangements, and lack of support have been identified as factors contributing to women's low job motivation and poor career mobility. The job situation, in particular, has been ignored in analysis. The problem, according to Krishna Raj (1986), is that the job environment is seen as given and hence not in need of examination. In reality, however, several features of the work context like inflexible working hours, lack of child care facilities, and male oriented job policies may operate as greater impediments for women in wage labour. Some other macro aspects are also important such as the size of the organization, nature of management, and type of work activity.

The few studies that have examined the job aspects of women have used concepts like job involvement, motivation, and achievement. These are derived from male behaviour patterns and the practice is to evaluate women against the criteria employed for male success. If the household remains the primary responsibility of women alone, then it is hardly surprising that their priorities are different from those of men. The problem lies in the failure to appreciate that what constitutes success and satisfaction among men may not constitute the same in the case of women. If heading a business gives satisfaction to a man why cannot making a home be satisfying to women? Why and how are women's and men's behaviour patterns valued differently?

Another problem is that employed women are treated as a homogeneous group. At different age levels and family phases. women's involvement and attitude towards their job may vary. As some studies have indicated, career salience may be low for women who have younger children but it may be high for those with fewer child related responsibilities.

Conclusion

Studies reviewed under the theme of women and work are based on the premise that women's work constitutes a "deviant" behaviour and hence is likely to have multifarious (negative) effects on individual family members and on the dynamics of the family. Broadly speaking, the findings are analyzed from the limited perspective of role theory and role conflict paradigm. Feminists have critiqued the static and a historical tendencies of the role theory approach and its emphasis on individual socialization rather than on the social structural processes (Ferree, 1990). In the Indian context, for example, role theory ignores class, caste, educational imbalances, and economic forces that influence work choice and job patterns.

There is non-clarity and inadequacy regarding definitions of key concepts and terms such as career couples and job involvement. There is a need to arrive at a consensus on these. For instance, what is a non-traditional profession? Which of the professions can be considered as non-traditional? Will the job of a "hotel chef" be traditional or non-traditional for men and for women? Even within the category of professional jobs, the social value attached to them and the size of the pay packet ought to be considered. It would be erroneous, for example, to equate lecturers with computer engineers in terms of job value or income level. With increasing specialisation and diversification of professional opportunities, there is an urgent need to develop research frameworks that take into account these complexities.

The exclusive concern with urban, large city based working women needs to be corrected in future research work as women in smaller towns are also entering the organized labour force in large numbers. The socio-political and economic environment of smaller towns is likely to impart a different meaning to the work, status of women in employment. Although studies are increasingly considering the working couple as a unit of analysis, the inclusion of significant others (in-laws, children) into the research design will offer a wholistic picture.

Scales, inventories, personality tests and similar other tools are the most commonly preferred measures used in psychological research on women and work. Most of these tools suffer from social desirability effects. Future research may improve the quality of data by using qualitative methods in combination or independently like in-depth interview, observation, case study, and focus group discussion.

One of the drawbacks of majority of the studies is that they fail to go beyond the mere statement of results. No efforts are made to draw implications for action or provide practical suggestions for overcoming women's problems, a need voiced by women in employment (see Narasimhan and Iyer, 1990).

While in-depth analysis is required to explain the household/family mechanisms that preclude women from using their employment status as a resource, the focus itself needs to shift from family to the job context and to the analysis of the linkages between the two. As the number of working women is steadily increasing, researchers are required to focus on both the macro and micro structures of the work-family system as in need of reform (Moen, 1989). Further, researchers are expected to move beyond conceiving the employed women's family and work as separate spheres and focus on the "evolving women"—women who are creating wider spaces for themselves despite multiple demands and challenges.

So, I have no hesitation to say that women at some place have proved themselves as superior to men by virtue and by deeds. On the one side of coin they are progressing highly and on the other side they are being exploited by the males physically as well as mentally and in sum, it can be said that women should be aware about their grace and importance in society. They should also know their self-esteem then their education will be practically utilized and they in real sense will be treated as equal segment of society like men.

REFERENCES

Asthana, P. (1974). *Women in India.* Delhi. Vikas Publishers.

Chaudhary, I.K. (1976). "Education of Muslim Women under Great Mughals". *The Journal of Bihar Research Society* 12, i-iv, 154-161.

Majumdar, D.N. (1961). *Races and Cultures in India.* Bombay, Asia Publishing House.

Menon, M.I. (1981). *Status of Muslim Women in India.* Delhi, Uppal Publishing House.

Ojha, P.N. (1961). *Some aspects of North Indian Social Life,* Patna. Nagari Prakashan Pvt. Ltd.

Sengupta. S. (1971). *A story of Women of Bengal,* Calcutta, Indian Publications Monograph Series.

Shanmugam, I.E. (1987). *Community Psychology,* Madras.

2

Resilience and Women
Changing Roles, Risks and Protective Factors

Amrita Deb and *Meenakshi Arora*

Introduction

Vulnerability is something all mortals are endowed with (Handmer, 2003). Hence throughout life, individuals run the risk of encountering events that are challenging, difficult, and threaten to affect their homeostasis. Such disruptions cause a change in one's intact world paradigm and may result in perceived negative or positive outcomes (Richardson, 2002). According to Zimmerman and Arunkumar (1994), vulnerability refers to the individual's predisposition to develop varied forms of psychopathology or behavioural ineffectiveness. In other words, it is typically conceptualized as a predispositional factor, or set of factors, that makes possible a disordered state (Ingram and Luxton, 2005). We live in turbulent times, on the edge of uncertainty (Walsh, 1998) and hence it is important for us to be able to overcome ambiguity and adapt to stress. This ability to successfully cope with change and misfortune is known as resilience (Wagnild and Young, 1993). Dyer and McGuinness (1996) state that resilience evokes the promise of something good resulting from misfortune, hope embedded in adversity. According to Masten (2001), it refers to good outcomes in spite of serious threats to adaptation or development. Brendtro and Larson (2004) cite the use of terms like "courage" and "discouragement" to express similar ideas (Adler, 1930), to mean the same thing, long before the terms "resilience" and "risk" came into common use. The American Psychological Association (2004) defines resilience as " ... the process of adapting well in the face of adversity, trauma, tragedy, threats, or even significant source of stress—such as family and relationship problems, serious health problems, or workplace and financial stressors ..." (p. 2). This definition goes on to reflect on the more human aspect of the term by mentioning that being resilient does not mean that a person does not experience difficulty or distress. Resilient people don't walk between the raindrops, they have scars to show for their experience; in other words, it is not the ability to escape unharmed but a process by which one moves towards a goal beyond themselves, transcending pain and grief by perceiving bad times as a temporary state of affairs ("Psychology Today", 2008). Walsh (1998) points out how most cultures breed intolerance for personal suffering; encouraging the individual to "cut their losses" (p. 5), get instant closure and simply move on, without looking back to draw meaning from the experience, coming to terms with it and finally heal from it. She warns against misconstruing this as a capacity for resilience, which includes suffering as well as courage, struggling yet functioning. In the words of Higgins (1994), the active process of self-righting and growth in resilient individuals characterizes those who negotiate significant challenges and do more than merely get through difficult emotional experiences.

Some researchers have defined resilience as a trait of individuals while others view it as a process (Jacelon, 1997). Resilience essentially is understood to be a construct that has to be derived from finding an interactive effect (M. Rutter, Personal Communication, April 19, 2007). Bartlett (1994) asserts that the concept of resilience is relational. That is, it should be examined in reference to—a subjective experience of stress, an inventory of resources, and a biography of success or failure. Arrington and Wilson (2000) further explain that resilience is inferred when a person exceeds the expectations that is warranted by an individual or community's biographical field. An important point here is the emphasis of resilience theory on strengths rather than deficits, focusing on how one can succeed instead of why they fail. In this context, mention maybe made of the 'damage-model' that highlights life experiences and behaviours from a negative perspective and the 'challenge-model' which takes a positive stance for the same (Wolin and Wolin, 1993). According to Utesch (n.d.), a strengths-based approach is characterized by its emphasis upon capacities, competencies, and resources that exist within and outside of the individual, family, or community. In doing so, it shifts focus from viewing distressed families and individuals as damaged to seeing them as challenged affirming their potential for repair and growth (Walsh, 1998).

Over the years, resilience has come to be used as an umbrella term covering many different aspects of overcoming adversity and adapting to one's environment (McCubbin, 2001). Kirby and Fraser (1997), (as cited in Ungar, 2008) clarify that the term resilience maybe used to explain multiple meanings. First, it maybe a description of a set of characteristics children are understood to possess when despite being born into disadvantaged environments, they grow up successfully that is, they exhibit better than expected developmental outcomes. Secondly, resilience may refer to competence when under stress. Thirdly, it maybe used to indicate positive functioning as in recovery from trauma. Ungar (2008) points out that, whether resilience is understood to demonstrate developmental outcome, set of competences or coping strategies, there appears to be much overlap between these conceptualizations; however, what the definitions share in common is that they all agree, that resilience occurs in the presence of adversity.

Adversity or risk factors in the context of resilience

Although the study of resiliency first began with case studies of individuals who survived major world traumas, the construct is now being seen, as having broader applicability in many typical life situations. What constituted a 'hard knock' earlier is no longer viewed as something akin to war atrocity but is now understood to include issues as common as divorce, emotional disorders, or learning disabilities (Weiss, 2008). Richardson (2002) cites that being offered a new job or suddenly being courted by a romantic interest maybe regarded as disruptive events in one's life because they represent change.

According to Howard, Dryden, and Johnson (1999), risk refers to environmental factors that either singly or in combination renders an individual's failure to thrive, more likely. In the words of Rutter (1988), risk is an important predictive variable that can be seen as acting in concert with vulnerability. No one single factor is, in itself, sufficient to pose a significant risk to development and behaviour (Condly, 2006). Life events, minor stressors, specific high-risk factors, low SES, or any other combination of factors (Luthar and Zigler, 1991) build up over time resulting in a cumulative effect (Ungar, 2004). Masten, Neemann and Andenas (1994) cite that cumulative risk or adversity maybe attributed to both non-independent events and independent events. The former include—being expelled from school, breaking up with a boyfriend and other events related to a person's own behaviour whereas death of a parent falls within the realm of an independent event. In this context, Rende and Plomin (1993) have distinguished between proximal and distal risk factors. The former are experienced directly by the individual, whereas the latter are those that arise from the individual's context, but are mediated through more proximal processes. An abusive parent is an example of proximal risk because the abuse directly affects the child, whereas parental lack of education would be considered a distal risk because it affects family income, kinds and amounts of reading material, and the like which then affect the child (as cited in Condly, 2006).

Women's experience of risk factors

Resilience research has revealed that there are varied adversities that women have successfully overcome. These include teenage pregnancy, academic challenges, body image confusion, miscarriages, postpartum difficulties, children with mental disorder, single-parenthood status, schizophrenic parent, physical abuse, alcoholic husband, infidelity in marriage, breast cancer, and divorce (Boon, 2005; Bowen, Morasca, and Meischke, 2003; Choate, 2005; Hung, 2004; Rogers, 2000).

Werner and Smith (1992) on the basis of their Kauai longitudinal study concluded that for girls between the ages of two and ten, serious risk factors include—death of mother, long-term absence of father and severe conflict between parents. They also found that girls are more vulnerable than boys in the second decade of life, as compared to the first. In the words of Turner, Norman, and Zunz (1995), adolescence takes "a terrible toll" on the self-esteem and self-efficacy of American girls (p. 29). Siqueira and Diaz (2004) agree that despite changing roles and greater equality of women in recent decades, girls today often fall into traditional patterns of low self-image, self-doubt and self-censorship of their creative and intellectual potential and thus emerge from adolescence with reduced expectations of themselves and lesser confidence in their abilities than do boys. According to Rutter (1984), as girls become subjected to gender and traditional values and expectations, they become more and more subdued and unsure of themselves; for society tolerates active, assertive and courageous girls, but this kind of behaviour is deemed inappropriate when they reach adolescence. Gilligan, Lyons, and Hanmer (1990) observe that by the age of 13 or 14, girls come to realize that it is not considered feminine to be assertive and full of confidence (as cited by Turner, Norman, and Zunz, 1995). Thus, the remarkable psychological resilience of girls in the childhood years turns into a liability as they enter adolescence (Brown and Gilligan, 1993; Chatham-Carpenter and DeFrancisco, 1998, Frydenberg and Lewis, 2000). Female adolescents experiencing more stress than males could be explained by the fact that the social and emotional demands on the former are much more as compared to the latter. Kula (2003) researching Jewish women's experiences of the

Holocaust found that it was women who were better able to cope with Nazi persecution, than men. Bacalla (2005) observed similar consequences of the tsunami in Banda Aceh, Indonesia where the women as per society's expectations, quickly reverted back to the role of the traditional caregivers in Aceh, and continued to perform the household chores. On further inquiry, she discovered that these women had turned into victims of physical violence, wielded by men who were bored or frustrated because they were unable to practice their usual means of livelihood. Bacalla (2005) questions why women, who endured the same conditions as men, did not react in the same way and instead were made to bear the brunt of the men's pent-up emotions. The answer lies in the difference in socialization process in males and females. According to the differential exposure hypothesis, women are exposed to higher levels of demands and obligations in their social roles, as well as more stressful life events than men (de Vries and Watt, 1996; Turner and Avison, 1987). Almeida and Kessler's (1998) observation of 166 married couples who kept a diary of their daily stressors for 42 days revealed that women did not hold onto their stress more; rather, they experienced more episodes of being stressed. Also, women maybe more willing to admit that they find a scenario stressful. It is more socially acceptable for women to show emotions and to admit they find situations stressful than it is for men (Thompson and Walker, 1989). Maginness (2007) reported an interesting pattern that emerged from the interviews of the female participants (versus male participants) in her study. Unlike their male counterparts, they acknowledged that their ability to be resilient was not constant over time and that they experienced emotional ups and downs, which they believed to be part of the experience and life in general. McDonough and Walters (2001) support that women react differently than men to the social determinants of health. There are also important gender differences in perceived control and in self-esteem, with women reporting lower levels of both resources than men (Mirowsky and Ross, 1989; Turner and Roszell, 1994). This in turn makes them more vulnerable to stressors and less capable of fighting adversity. Misra, West,

Russo, and McKean (2000) have suggested that it may not be the number and type of stressors exposed to men and women but the latter's perception of stressors that result in negative outcomes among them.

According to the differential vulnerability hypothesis, women have greater vulnerability to the effects of chronic stressors (Denton, Prus, and Walters, 2004). This is in accordance with the findings of Voges and Romney (2003) who concluded on the basis of their study of risk and resilience factors in post-traumatic stress disorder that, only being female and perceiving a threat to one's life were significant predictors of the disorder. A few studies have found that adolescent girls tend to experience more interpersonal stress such as those related to social networks whereas boys report more non-interpersonal or school-related stress (Gore, Aseltine, and Colten, 1993; Rudolph and Hammen, 1999). This is because girls value their relationships more (Rudolph, 2002) whereas school is a domain boys value more (Sund, Larsson, and Wichstrom, 2003). The Living Out Loud Programme, a five-year demonstration project serving female adolescents aged 14-21 with learning disabilities and/or physical disabilities that was aimed at building resiliency in disabled girls so they would not use drugs, found that the most widely implicated risks for substance abuse among adolescent girls include poor body image, the desire to "fit in" with peers, be accepted by boys and a desperate need of role models (Ferreyra, 2001). Studies conducted on adult women have found that they tend to report higher levels of chronic and daily stressors as compared to men (Hogan, Carlson, and Dua, 2002; Ptacek, Smith, and Zanas, 1992; Tamres, Janicki and Helgeson, 2002). Wang *et al.* (2007) subjected 16 females and 16 males—to FMRI (Functional Magnetic Resonance Imaging) scans before, during and after they underwent an arithmetic task (serial subtraction of 13 from a 4 digit number), under pressure. Measurement of heart rate, cortisol levels, subjects' perceived stress levels throughout the experiments, and regional Cerebral Blood Flow (CBF), which provides a marker of regional brain function, revealed that men as well as women's limbic system (primarily involved in emotion) was activated under stress and this activation lasted beyond the stress task for both. However, the lasting response in the female brain was stronger (Wang *et al.*, 2007). Although there is little evidence that women are vulnerable to job strain (Roxburgh, 1996), they are more likely to list family and health-related events as stressors as compared to men (Matud, 2004; McDonough and Walters, 2001). Hamermesh and Lee (2003) found that "time stress"—an absence of sufficient time to accomplish all their tasks is greater among women than men. The perception of stress in women was more when they had additional housework and pre-school children to attend to. Although most researchers agree that women experience more interpersonal and episodic stress than men (Hankin and Abramson, 2001; Nolen-Hoeksema and Girgus, 1994; Rudolph, Hammen, Burge, Lindberg, Herzberg, and Daley, 2000) there appears to be some discrepancies as to who among them experiences more stress overall. Shih, Eberhart, Hammen, and Brennan (2006) suggest that additional studies are needed to elucidate the social, psychological and physiological processes that underlie the sex differences in stress reactivity.

The changing role of women over the years

Of the many transformations that have taken place since the 1960s, one of the greatest is the change in lives of women (Rogers, 2000). Women born during the 1930s and 1940s were part of a transitional group and were pivotal in establishing new multiple role patterns. These women were part of the generation raised with the traditional values of the 1950s and grew up expecting to play traditional roles as homemakers and volunteers (Giele, 1993). They entered adulthood in the mid-1960s known as the "era of transition" when expectations for women were undergoing significant change (Schuster, 1993). However, Schuster (1993) notes that the majority of these women continued to seek the conventional lifestyle envisioned for them in the 1950s because the effects of the women's movement and civil rights were not yet widespread and hence there continued to be an absence of role models for envisioning careers. Also, there was a lack of husbands who would be supportive of working wives. In fact, even the studies undertaken with women who were young adults in the 1960s were based on the notion that "women would be most comfortable and effective in family-centred functions and those who deviated from these conventional roles were described as prone to depression, neurosis, or alienation during adulthood" (Schuster, 1993, p. 21). In the face of rapid social change, women's lives underwent a major upheaval as they were challenged to juggle multiple roles (Hulbert and Schuster, 1993). If adaptation in the past was "achieved by a woman molding herself to cultural narratives", those narratives were now being re-examined "to construct a new sense of self" (Labouvie-Vief, 1994, p. 160). For women awakening to fresh possibilities in middle age, new attitudes and courage were required to grasp "the opportunity to reverse their most cherished principles of femininity" (Heilbrun, 1988, p. 124). This transformation also revealed how women exhibited the potential for adaptability and resilience in the face of such changes (Hulbert and Schuster, 1993). For today's modern woman, juggling multiple roles, coping with a sinking economy, inundated with government colour alerts and the constant threat of terrorist attacks, the idea of relaxing for even a minute from the bone-crushing weight of stress they operate under, may seem as difficult as achieving world peace ("Women: Chronic Stress, and Resilience", 2003). Thus, it is not surprising that nearly 93 per cent of those who participated in the National Women's Health Resource Centre Web-based survey on stress described the level of stress in their daily life as moderate or higher ("Women: Chronic Stress, and Resilience", 2003). Holly (n.d.) adds that under such demanding circumstances, if a woman has successfully quit smoking, lost weight, run a mile, got a promotion, started a business or survived a divorce and yet maintained love for life and sense of humour, then it would be correct to presume that she has achieved greatness. Antonucci and Akiyama (1997) note that women seem to have drawn advantage from multiple roles, especially employment outside the home that offer external gains—the same from which men have benefited for many years. The investigators believe that although this additional role may have created stress, it has also helped women find and profit from the more diverse multioptioned pathways that have opened up by resulting in a sense of competence and independence outside of family that proves to be a buffer for negative experiences and interactions. Rogers (2000) expresses confusion over the reality of life for women, but at the same time highlights the extraordinariness of ordinary women who have often endured much by mid-life.

Recent researches in the area

Not many recent researches in the area of resilience have focused solely on women survivors and their struggle with adversity. The studies that came up during the review of literature maybe categorized under the following heads:

Women's health

Many researches have been conducted in the area of women's health; however most of the earlier attempts have been based on the pathological approach. Resiliency research in the area of women's health has sought to identify resiliency factors that assist the recovery process instead of focusing on factors that make them prone to succumbing to the disease. Moreno and Simoni (1997) studied stress and resilience among Latina women infected with HIV. Information gathered using qualitative tools such as focused group methodology and individual interviews revealed that coping mechanisms included spirituality, non-traditional healing cures, therapeutic support groups relevant to their culture, gender and current situation and the presence of significant others. Bowen, Morasca, and Meischke (2003) examined several aspects of resilience including optimism and life attitude and related them to personal perceptions of breast cancer risk and worry about cancer in 357 women. Stojanovska (2004) conducted an investigation with the aim of improving resilience in menopausal women so as to smoothen the transitional process. This study attempted to discover the mechanisms, or coping tools that made some women more resilient and able to positively adapt to a major life event such as menopause. After conducting interviews on peri- and post-menopausal women to identify the meaning of resilience and coping mechanisms, psychological factors that contribute to resilience, and differences between these factors; it was concluded that women who coped with life's adversities and challenges generally were able to cope with the challenges of menopause as well; whereas those who displayed little or no resilience in life matters also displayed little or no resilience with the experience of menopause. Choate's (2005) examination of body image resilience in women, led to the finding that there is a normative discontent that women experience with regard to their body. Buchanan, Fischer, Tokar and Yoder (2008) emphasize on the cultural contributions to understanding resilience in such women. Zautra, Johnson, and Davis (2005) assessed demographic data, health status, and personality traits of a sample of 124 women with osteoarthritis or fibromyalgia, or both and after interviewing them on pain, stress, negative affect, and positive affect, concluded that positive affect was a source of resilience in women suffering from pain.

Education and profession

LePage-Lees (1997) in tracing the path traversed by disadvantaged girls to becoming successful women, described the life stories of 21 women between the ages of 24 and 54. All of them had advanced degrees, had been raised in low-income homes, were first-generation college students, and had faced stress as children. In-depth interviews, questionnaires, and school records were used to gather information. The findings revealed that their circumstances at home led them to seek out reinforcement in other places, and they did this by excelling in school. Their achievement can be attributed to a great extent to their belief in their intellectual abilities and motivation to succeed. In an investigation on successful women graduates' academic resilience and their personal strategies for doctoral success, Culpepper (2004) found that these women viewed working on the degree as personally fulfilling, believed that they possessed a strong sense of academic confidence, self-discipline, saw themselves as a role model and were motivated by a personal or career goal. The roadblocks along the doctoral journey were overcome by personal fortitude and strong self-efficacy. In addition to this, they also acknowledged the support they received from families, peers, and their professors. African-American women from low-income communities seeking college education, were convinced that they had the power to resist the negative influences of their communities and were strongly motivated to reach their desired goal even in the absence of external confirmation and support (Matthews-Armstead, 2002). Similar results were reported by the participants of Morales' (2008) study on academic resilience and gender in higher education in African-American and Hispanic participants. He found that although females faced more resistance than males in the pursuit of their career goals, they were more strongly motivated by these goals than were males. They accomplished their objectives by either working harder at home and outside, or by dismissing and disregarding their families' expectations to concentrate on their personal ambitions, even if it meant strained relationships between the participants and her parents. Suarez-Mccrink (2002) points out how throughout a considerable time in history, even after having gained the right to literacy, women were not allowed to enter the male-dominated purview of certain disciplines. "Intense mental pursuit was considered unnatural for women and at least potentially damaging to women's reproductive organs" (Crocco, and Davis, 1999, p. 8) whose proper sphere was believed to be home and "foremost role was to be a wife and a mother" (Suarez-Mccrink, 2002, p. 239). It is for this reason, that many "women college graduates often remained unmarried because many people, male and female, believed intellectual and familial responsibilities for women to be incompatible" (p. 9). This sentiment is reflected in author and feminist Virginia Woolf's satirical illustration of women who gain a university education, enter the professions and then form a 'Society of Outsiders' (as cited by Brown and Gilligan, 1993). Some of the black women participants in O'Connor's (2002) study described how they cut down drastically on social engagements and lived "like a hermit" (p. 894) in order to concentrate purely on meeting the academic challenge before them. In resiliency studies, little attention has been paid to higher education, and even less scholarship has regarded women in higher educational administration (Christman and McClellan, 2008). The investigators in exploring the professional lives of women administrators in educational leadership programmes found that resilient women leaders often embrace or disclaim one gender norm for another to varying degrees in order to sustain their administrative roles. According to Christman and McClellan (2008), these women have to fight the traditional norms of leadership that put them at odds with their own gender. Hence, they concluded that women leaders must be willing to traverse conventional borders. This is consistent with the findings of Elliott and Stead (2008) who have investigated the experiences of leading women in different sectors.

Family and relationships

In an investigation of 18 women between the ages of 40 and 60 years who had experienced adult challenges or adversity and developed resilience to rise above them, Rogers (2000) found a good diversity in the ethnicity, socio-economic, cultural and educational levels of the participants. Comprehensive interviews with them revealed that their stories of challenge and resilience began at different points in the lifecycle. Most of these women had had difficult childhoods, strongly influenced by physical abuse, alcoholism, abandonment, poverty and lack of education that started them on what one participant described as "a lifetime of struggle." Even though these women had exhibited resilience to the adversities they faced, they recounted having experienced feelings of abandonment and isolation at some point of time in their lives.

This important detail was also reported by Boon (2005), on the basis of an in-depth study of 5 women having experienced divorce. She found that although they went on to overcome the situation and build productive lives, the most important feelings reported initially included emotional emptiness and disorientation following the dissolution of a significant love relationship. Gullo (1992) proposed that such women undergo an emotional course that occurs in the order of—shock, grief, blame, magnification, resignation, and renewal. Other than bitter feelings, family disapproval, and continued attachment with their ex-husbands, most women post-divorce reported difficulty in dealing with family reorganization, single parenthood, balancing career and home.

Recovery from abuse

Anderson and Danis (2006), cite Anderson (2006), whose research on adult survivors of incest investigated the strategies of resistance in childhood as leading to resilience. These protective strategies included resistance to being powerless, silenced, and isolated. Anderson's (2006) findings demonstrated how resilience may emerge as a result of the interplay between risk (feeling lonely, suicidal, confused, and helpless in childhood and struggling with problems elated to intimacy, mistrust, depression, anxiety and guilt in adulthood) and protective factors (strategies of resistance). This is a process that continues to develop throughout a person's life. Rutter and Quinton (1984) observed how some women, maltreated and institutionalized in childhood were later able to establish satisfactory marital relationships. Bogar and Hulse-Killacky's (2006) qualitative study aimed at discovering resiliency determinants and resiliency formation among 10 women who had experienced sexual abuse as children revealed 5 determinant clusters—interpersonal skills, competence, high self-regard, spirituality, and helpful life circumstances; and 4 process clusters—coping strategies, refocusing and moving on, active healing, and achieving closure. McClure, Chavez, Agars, Peacock and Matosian (2008) in their attempt to study risk and protective factors in 177 women who had experienced Childhood Sexual Abuse (CSA) evaluated the contribution of family characteristics (conflict and cohesion) and abuse characteristics (age, severity and relationship to perpetrator) to resilience (self-acceptance, ability to engage in positive relationships with others, and environmental mastery). The results indicated that family characteristics are critical in the prediction of resiliency among sexually abused women. Despite the debilitating effects of being in a violent relationship, Humphreys (2003) argued that battered women do possess the capacity for resilience. This was supported by Kubany, Hill, Owens, Iannce-Spencer, McCaig, and Tremayne (2004), who found that women with PTSD demonstrated decreased symptomatology in response to cognitive trauma therapy. The investigators emphasized on the need for more research in the area with the aim of developing suitable tools for building resilience in traumatized women.

Resilience in elderly women

Only recently has the concept of resiliency advanced into gerontological research. This new focus highlights the unique strengths of older adults (Nakashima and Canda, 2005) and shows that a view of the self as resilient can sustain women through the process of becoming older. It provides a buffer against the challenges of ageing, including deleterious changes in health status (Gattusc, 2003). Wagnild and Young (1990) conducted a qualitative study to identify and describe characteristics of successfully adjusted older women who had experienced a recent major loss and were considered successfully adjusted as evidenced by social involvement in a senior centre, a mid level to high level of morale and self-report. They identified five underlying themes: equanimity, self-reliance, existential aloneness, perseverance and meaningfulness. To determine resilient outcomes in the sample of older women relocated from their own homes to a retirement community or apartment, Ryff, Singer, Dienberg Love, and Essex (1998) found that the respondents' lives were full of both positive and negative life events, which supports the theoretical stance that resilience is affected by both cumulative advantage as well as adversity. They operationalized resilience in terms of overall well-being, stability of well-being, and physical health and found social comparison, self-appraisal, and self-perceptions of behaviour to be the determinants of resilience. Felten and Hall (2001) used the metaphor of a coiled wire enclosed within a box similar to a jack-in-the-box situation, to symbolize resilience in female subjects aged above 85. According to the investigators, important factors within the box were frailty, determination, previous experience with hardship, access to care, health beliefs, family support, self-care activities, caring for others, and functioning like efficiently working machines. LeRoy, Walsh, Kulik and Rooney (2004) in their exploratory study interviewed 29 Irish and American older women with intellectual disabilities. Demographics, economic and personal safety nets, health, social roles, and well-being were assessed. It was found that although these women had very limited resources, social networks, and opportunities, they reported good health and happiness. Kinsel's (2005) interview of seventeen women between the ages of 70 and 80 revealed that the paths to resilience in their lives were variously affected depending on developmental, socio-structural, historical, and individual life story influences. Internal resources—including a head-on approach to challenge, curiosity, maverick (non-traditional) behaviour, spiritual grounding and moving forward with life, as well as external resources of social connectedness and extending self to others following adversity were found to facilitate resilience in these women. Morrissey's (1998) study on 17 women, above age 75 and living alone yielded similar results. He reported that acceptance of help from others in the surroundings without losing a sense of autonomy was a salient factor in the women's positive aging.

In view of researches conducted in the area, some common protective factors were found to play a significant role in the process of resilience in women.

Resilience in women: protective factors

Literature is replete with stories of women who go on to create highly successful futures despite having difficult pasts. While Helen Keller, Anne Frank and Aung San Suu Kyi are famous examples, many instances slip away unnoticed. Rogers (2000) believes that in order to comprehend the phenomena of resilience in women, it is important to find out how they make meaning of their challenges. The focus of attention Rutter (1987) suggests, should be on protective processes. Protection he wrote, resides " ... in the ways in which people deal with life changes and in what they do about their stressful or disadvantageous circumstances" (p. 329). Protective factors like risks seem to have the same cumulative effect (Epstein, Botvin, Griffin, and Diaz, 2001; Howard, Dryden, and Johnson, 1999). Hence, in order to deal with to adversity, women must cultivate a number of protective factors known collectively as resilience (Noble, Subotnik, and Arnold, 1999). These factors maybe studied under the following groups: internal and external assets.

Internal assets

Internal assets are those characteristics or personality traits within the individual that serve as protective factors in resilience (Howard, Dryden, and Johnson, 1999; Masten, Best and Garmezy, 1990). The attributes that consistently appear in literature include:

Perseverance: Walsh (1998) refers to it as a sense of tenacity that often appears to show itself in stubbornness, struggling well, bouncing back from failure, and finally finding pride in one's endurance. In this context, Poulter, Brooks, and Goldstein (2002, p. 1) cite Anne Frank who wrote in her diary, "... I don't think I shall easily bow down before the blows that inevitably come to everyone ..." (p. 260). This endurance comes from stubbornness and the need for survival which is so strong that it makes one do things that one had never attempted earlier in life. One of the participants in Rogers' (2000) investigation recounted how she had to take up a job working in a bar to support her young children, even though she had never even been to a bar before. Other researches have also identified determination as being a key source in helping individuals who were faced with adversity (Bachay and Cingel, 1999; Maginness, 2007).

A sense of identity and autonomy: Grotberg (1999) believes that autonomy and identity are among the 'building blocks' of resilience. Identity is "characterized by the nature of one's relations with others" (Franz and Stewart, 1994, p. 326) while autonomy is the capacity to be independent and to direct one's own life (Rogers, 2000). Researchers investigating resilience in women aiming for professional and academic achievement were found to be driven by the need to develop identity and autonomy through attainment of their goals (Culpepper, 2004; LePage-Lees, 1997).

Hope, optimism and humour: Resilient individuals often claim that hope, optimism and humour saw them through the toughest times. Wolin and Wolin (1993) describe this as finding the comic in the tragic. Maginness (2007) observed that much of the humour is in fact, attuned toward minimizing the negativity of the events without minimizing the event itseif. Resilient individuals often attribute their success to their optimism about life (Bachay and Cingel, 1999). Kaiser, Major and Mccoy (2004) confirmed that optimists are better able to counter prejudice and discrimination than are pessimists as the former are more likely to employ adaptive coping strategies such as cognitive restructuring and problem-solving to deal with the crisis, than the latter. Kinsel (2004) exploring the phenomenon of resilience in older women and Zautra, Johnson and Davis (2005) studying 124 women in chronic pain found that the participants in their respective investigations, continued to realize a strong investment in, and positive orientation towards life regardless of the challenges and losses they experienced.

Self efficacy: A woman's agency in the midst of constraint is what helps her to emerge successfully out of it (Franz and Stewart, 1994). While traditionally, self-efficacy has focused on a person's self-view of a specific challenge (Waaktaar, Christie, Borge and Torgersen, 2004); it has also been linked to resistance against both minor hassles as well as major disasters (Caprara, Scabini, Barbaranelli, Pastorelli, Regalia, and Bandura, 1998; Masten, Best, and Garmezy, 1990). Rivera, Anderson, and Middleton (2000) found that self-efficacy was instrumental in Mexican-American women's decision-making process about their choice of career. This sense of self-directedness and self-reliance was also a common sentiment shared by young college-bound African-American women from poor communities (Matthews-Armstead, 2002).

Internal locus of control: Resilient individuals possess the belief that the ability to influence one's life resides inside. oneself and can defeat the threatening forces outside (Wolin and Wolin, 1993). Maginness (2007) found the "non-victim perspective" (p. 92) to be a consistent theme in the experiences of 10 women who were deemed as resilient by their peers. They believed that "it was important to take responsibility for managing what had happened to them and to find the best way forward" (p. 92). Many researchers interviewing resilient individuals found that they accepted what they could not or did not choose to change, and mastered what they could change (Boon, 2005; Rogers, 2000).

Mastery or competence: Walsh (1998) discussed mastery or competence in terms of a process wherein although one "may not be able to control the outcome of events ... they can make choices and find meaningful ways to participate actively in the process of unfolding events" (p. 68). According to Werner and Smith (1992), females who were identified as resilient were better readers and could reason more effectively than could females who had more difficulty coping with life events. Resilient individuals described learning to be independent, resourceful, organized, and self-sufficient through the choices they made which often included education and hard work. This explains why personal fulfilment and a sense of accomplishment were reported to be strong driving factors in the pursuit and achievement of academic goals in women (Culpepper, 2004).

Additionally, attributes such as creativity (Rogers, 2000; Waaktaar, Christie, Borge and Torgersen, 2004), reconciliation and forgiving aspects of their own lives and choices (Boon, 2005), absence of blaming, empathy and belongingness (Maginness, 2007), active problem-solving (Wright, 1998) and spiritual beliefs—which is not often measured but is believed to be a significant factor in women's coping (Kinsel, 2004; Utsey, Bolden, Lanier, and Williams, III, 2007)—were all found to be important buffering variables. Religious beliefs enhance resilience by providing a basis for optimism (Barbarin, 1993). Waaktaar, Christie, Borge and Torgersen (2004) noted how centering groups around creative activities provided an opportunity for foreign language-speaking, traumatized youths to express themselves symbolically, though not necessarily verbally, through whatever modes preferred by them. They concluded that such knowledge about resilience factors could be used for intervention purposes in several ways.

Resilient women generally report improved self-esteem, greater independence and competence after they have been through a difficult experience (Bisagni and Eckenrode, 1995; Weitzman, 1985). Walsh proposed that resilience enables people to " ... heal from painful wounds, take charge of their lives, and go on to live fully and love well" (1998, p. 4). Studies have established that resilient persons became more substantial individuals because " ... they were sorely tested, endured suffering, and emerged with strength they might not have otherwise developed. They acquired a depth of experience and purposeful pursuits" (Walsh, 1998, p. 269). In other words, resilient women may eventually realize some positive growth as a result of the difficult experience, and ultimately, empowerment (Herman, 1992).

External assets

External assets are protective factors that have been described in relation to the systems in which the individual grows and develops (Howard, Dryden, and Johnson, 1999) such as family and community. Werner and Smith (1982) concluded on the basis of their longitudinal study that a warm positive relationship with a caring adult (parent, teacher, sibling or counsellor) helped most children grow up to be resilient adults. This maybe regarded as one of the single most important protective factors in a child's life because intimate attachments to other human beings are the nucleus around which a person's life revolves (Bowlby, 1980). Also, positive role models and good parenting skills lead to good coping skills in later life (Baumrind, 1991). Werner and Smith (1982) emphasize that having a cohesive, supportive family and parents who have high but realistic expectations for achievement and behaviour are important protective factors. They claim that girls who are raised in homes where they are not overprotected, and independence is encouraged grow up to be resilient women. Such protective factors serve as buffers in later life when the individual is exposed to adversity. Rak (2002) confirms that for many resilient individuals, a nurturing and supporting adult figure; that he refers to as "hero in the nursery" helps them to adapt and find inner strength to survive ordeals in the early years. According to Benard (1990), youngsters who are given the responsibility of family chores develop competence and a sense that they can contribute in some way. Grotberg (1999) confirms that such experiences in childhood help in establishing the building blocks of resilience, namely trust, autonomy, identity, initiative and industry. Positive school experiences and popularity with peers are also cited as important (Rutter, 1979).

For women dealing with stressors—be it major trauma or daily stressors—the emotional support derived from connectedness and relationships appear to play a major role in helping them overcome the adversity. Utsey, Bolden, Lanier and Williams III (2007) refers to this as collective coping—a group centred strategy whereby individuals rely on their family and social networks for managing risk and adversity. For example, Ramsey and Blieszner (1999) found that resilient individuals involved in an organized religious group were able to draw structure and meaning about their lives and transcend adversities through forgiveness and caring relationships. A sense of connectedness and significant relationships are believed to be most influential in women's sense of resilience in dealing with critical life events. The relationships that they consider to be important are a combination of marriage, family, their children, role models, and friends (Boon, 2005). Waters and Lawrence (1993) cited examples of women who emphasized how important it was to have someone to encourage them, "to continue the journey" (p. 99). Encouragement, Walsh (1998) believes provides women with an important sense of strength. This emotional support maybe derived from their spouses, friends, role models, mentors, therapy, and peer support groups. Women doctoral graduates interviewed by Culpepper (2004) acknowledged that apart from personal strategies for success, the importance of support—both personal and programmatic, was an important determinant in the successful completion of their degrees. Four out of five women in Boon's (2005) study reported to have been encouraged and comforted by their therapists while spousal support was another important source of encouragement, as conveyed by successful resilient women (Hansen and Hall, 1997; Roger, 2000; Ezzedeen and Ritchey, 2008). Cabrera and Padilla (2004) in their retrospective study on academic resilience reported that their subject, coming from a background of extreme impoverishment attributed her academic success to her mother. Herman (1992) from her observation of women who survived trauma, concluded that caring relationships have been found to facilitate healing and recovery following a sexual assault. McClure, Chavez, Agars, Peacock and Matosian's (2008) findings which suggest that family variables can contribute in significant ways to resilience in survivors of childhood sexual abuse, is highly encouraging because family environments are potentially modifiable. Social support was found to have an indirect effect on women suffering from postpartum stress as well (Hung, 2004). In studying pregnant women, Cameron, Wells and Hobfoll (1996) found that they draw resilience from external support; however the authors suggest that it is important to understand more fully the sources of resilience that they draw from their social networks.

Understanding resilience through the tend-and-befriend theory

An interesting observation by Taylor, Klein, Lewis, Gruenewald, Gurung, and Updegraff (2000) claims that although the human response to stress has been characterized both physiologically and behaviourally as "fight-or-flight" in women, the responses are different. Azar (2006) believes that one reason this difference in stress response has not previously shown up is that until recently women were markedly underrepresented in research studies. Taylor *et al.* (2000) propose that females' responses are manifested more through a pattern of "tend-and-befriend." Tending involves nurturing activities designed to protect the self and offspring, which promotes safety and reduces distress. Taylor *et al.* (2000) used neuroendocrine evidence to explain the biobehavioural mechanism that underlies the tend-and-befriend pattern. They suggested that secretion of oxytocin during stressful events is responsible for such behaviour. Oxytocin is related to caring and nurturing in both animal and human studies. This explains why Rogers (2000) found that surviving "for my children" was a very strong theme for many resilient women. The women in her study discussed the importance of focusing on goals and their beliefs in active mastery throughout their narratives. But it was for the sake of their children that they were most motivated to surmount their challenges. Nash (2007) in studying women's experiences with partner violence found that despite the fact, that many of them contemplated suicide more than once in their lifetime; for most of the survivors, the children's welfare was a decisive factor in their remaining alive. Three out of five women in Boon's (2005) study strongly emphasized on the role of their children in keeping them strong and focused.

Anderson and Danis (2006) in their interviews with daughters of battered women who grew up to be resilient adults found that even as children, they used strategies of resistance against the abuser (mother's partner/husband)—protecting and comforting their mothers and siblings; one participant even at the age of 3 years expressing to her mother that she wanted her to leave him. The investigators claim that this was so because the children felt a personal responsibility to keep their mothers and siblings safe. Befriending is the creation and maintenance of social networks that may aid in the coping process. Women find that social interaction tends to ameliorate stress and so they form coalitions (befriending) to respond to threats (Taylor *et al.*, 2000). They tend to call up their sisters when they are under stress (Azar, 2006). Pinker (2006) points out that even though it might look like a method of gossip but it really is a protective mechanism that damps down stress responses. This is consistent with the observation of Rogers (2000) who described how the participants' friendships with other women proved to be transformative for them as they shared a crisis experience. The emotional support they received from their women friends was significant to their resilience and corroborates what other studies have documented on the importance of friendship. An interesting example of such behaviour maybe found in personal narratives in popular women's magazines. McKay and Bonner (2002) note that the main point in illness narratives in such magazines is not to tell of the triumph of biomedicine, although medical success does underpin many of the stories; but rather to demonstrate the resilience of the human condition in a personal manner so that the sufferer can directly or indirectly draw meaning from their condition. The tend-and-befriend phenomenon is clearly evident in Klein and McCabe's (2007) study of resilience in women with children having disabilities. These women found meaning and purpose in being able to help other families. All the women reported that their change in role from being a mother to a disability professional, after having children with disabilities was rewarding.

Enhancing resilience in women: a focus on the future

While gender differences in susceptibility to and protection from situations of risk has been highlighted by many researches (Turner, Norman, and Zunz, 1995), Fine and Zane (1989) recommend that prevention programmers now study how survival and resistance strategies maybe developed in girls experiencing stress. The process maybe facilitated by introducing intervention at critical points specific to the individual and situation. For example, Frydenberg and Lewis (2000) emphasize on the need to intervene in the education of adolescents at approximately age 14, in order to improve coping behaviour and avert the development of non-productive strategies.

According to Flynn (2008), resilience results from a sustained commitment to four factors: robustness—to keep operating or to stay standing in the face of disaster, resourcefulness—skilfully managing the adversity by identifying options, prioritizing actions to control damage and to begin mitigating it, rapid recovery—getting things back to normal as quickly as possible after a disaster, and finally having the means to absorb the new lessons that can be drawn from the experience. Recently Miller (2005) outlined 12 qualities and some exercises for women that must be cultivated in order to increase one's resiliency in the face of adversity that include everyday and traumatic setbacks. These include: admitting vulnerability, handling the suffering that accompanies loss or illness, recognizing and using one's talents, and harnessing the saving grace of humour. The fact that women draw resilience, more from external supports than internal strengths has been established by many researchers (Grotberg, 1999; Hampel and Petermann, 2005; Khan, 1998; Sun, and Stewart, 2007). However, it is also important to help them to develop resilience by enhancing internal attributes such as self-esteem and self-efficacy. This could be made possible by encouraging them to engage in activities not narrowly sex-typed; for example, karate, judo and the like (Turner, Norman, and Zunz, 1995). Schultz (1990) asserts that playing sports helps girls get past resistance to science, mathematics and technological learning. Along with this, they also develop a sense of competitiveness and assertiveness which are traits that resilient individuals have been found to possess (Rutter, 1984; as cited by Turner, Norman, and Zunz, 1995). Also, Werner and Smith

(1982) have argued that the possession of androgynous traits leads to a greater sense of self-esteem and resilience. Other researchers have emphasized that protective factors that must be encouraged in adolescent girls include assertiveness, problem-solving skills and competence (Turner, Norman, and Zunz, 1995), self-efficacy, self-esteem (Colton and Gore, 1991), internal locus of control and a strong sense of identity (Rogers, 1990). Waaktaar, Christie, Borge and Torgersen (2004) through their clinical intervention project, sought to explore how resilience factors could be utilized in an intervention for young people from stressful backgrounds. The target resilience factors were: positive peer relations, self-efficacy, creativity, and coherence. 58 youths (mean age 12.3 years) of which 36.2 per cent were girls participated in the project. The selected factors were implemented through group activities with the aim of promoting positive chain reactions of resilience in the participants. Although the resilience factors were treated as distinct entities, the effect as the investigators were to discover later, was rather intertwined. Moreover, they reported the strength of the relationship between resources, risks and difficulties, to be yet unclear. Hence, it was proposed that in order to design resilience-enhancing processes with greater precision, one must first address the interplay between the positive and negative chain reactions in determining the outcome of stressful experiences (Waaktaar, Christie, Borge, and Torgersen, 2004). Also, there is a need to develop suitable intervention procedures for populations with specific problems. The findings of a study by Whittaker, Hardy, Lewis and Buchan (2005) raise the paradox of how Somali women refugees value support, yet also attach great importance to concealment and hence, fear disclosures. The researchers suggest that promoting well-being and resilience is more important here, rather than working specifically with distress. Literature generally defines juvenile delinquency in androcentric terms, often ignoring the specific need of girls (Joe and Chesney-Lind, 1995). McKnight and Loper (2002) cite that the contribution of females in the adolescent delinquent population has been underestimated by demographical and historical factors. Hence, the authors suggest that intervention programmes in this area should include components that foster academic competence, academic involvement, positive perception of school and environment, improve the quality of parent-child interactions and discourage substance abuse. Researchers have suggested the need for intervention in specialized areas as also for specific samples. The former includes: the area of educational resilience as an institutionally responsive (versus an individually determined) process (O'Connor, 2002), certain diagnostic categories where more women than men are positioned such as anorexia (Cosgrove, 2000), and mathematic, scientific and technological fields as careers for women (Zeldin and Pajares, 2000). Specific samples that demand attention are sexual minorities (Connolly, 2005; Heaphy, 2007), pregnant women (Cameron, Wells, and Hobfoll, 1996), women with HIV/AIDS (Hobfoll and Schröder, 2001), those affected by political violence (Barber, 2008), Muslim and (Bacalla, 2005), black women (Flynn, 2008; O'Connor, Lewis, and Mueller, 2007). A recent development in the area of resilience is the growing interest in the gene-environment interaction (Hanson, and Gottesman, 2007; Rutter, 2006). Waaktaar, Christie, Borge and Torgersen (2004) question that if those who develop symptoms in the face of stress are genetically different from those who do not, then would vulnerable and resilient people be helped the same factors. Rutter (personal communication, as cited by Waaktaar, Christie, Borge, and Torgersen, 2004) illustrates that people exposed to a high risk of getting a heart attack need one type of intervention if the aim is to avoid the heart attack and a very different one if a full-blown heart attack is already in progress. Hence, it maybe concluded that there is a need to design strategies specific to populations and as well conditions in the area of resilience, for women.

In view of the above literature, it maybe derived that when faced with adversity, even the seemingly ordinary woman is capable of showing extraordinary resiliency skills. Although women's life experiences in psychology have been articulated by many scholars, McIntyre (1998) recognizes that there still remains a need to expand our theorizing and extend research methodologies to include the less visible areas of women's lives—areas that are oftentimes left unnamed and underresearched. According to Hage (2006), the exceptional efforts of women to survive within the context of overwhelming difficulty, are often ignored by scholars and counselling professionals. That is, resilience in women is an area few investigators have chosen to explore in depth. The broad concepts from the resiliency theory need to be operationalized into psychotherapeutic principles and specific techniques (Waaktaar, Christie, Borge and Torgersen, 2004) in the context of women's issues to develop a clinically focused theory. Further research is required in the direction of design and implementation of intervention programmes pertaining to different areas that women of all ages can benefit from.

REFERENCES

Adler, A. (1930). *The problem child.* New York: Capricorn Books.

Almeida, D.M., and Kessler, R.C. (1998). Everyday stressors and gender differences in daily stressors [Abstract]. *Journal of Personality and Social Psychology,* 75, 670-680. Retrieved April 3, 2005 from http://stress.about.com/gi/dynamic/offsite.htm?zi=1/XJ&sdn=stress&cdn=health&tm=28 &gps=273 1239 1276 528&f=00&su=p674.5.336.ip &tt=2&bt=0&bts=0&zu=http%3 A//www.ncbi.nlm.nih.gov/pubmed/9781406%3Fordinalpos%3D66%26itool%3DEntrezSystem2.PEntrez.Pubmed.Pubmed ResultsPanel.Pubmed RVDocSum

American Psychological Association (2004). *The road to resilience.* Washington DC: APA. Retrieved December 12, 2005 from http://apahelpcenter.org/dl/the road to resilience.pdf

Anderson, K.M. (2006). Surviving Incest: The art of resistance. *Families in Society, 83,* 409-116.

Anderson, K.M., and Danis, F. (2006). Adult daughters of battered women: Resistance and resilience in the face of danger. *Affilia, 21,* 419-432.,

Antonucci, T.C., and Akiyama, H. (1997). Social support and the maintenance of competence. In S.L. Willis, K.W. Schaie, and M. Hayward (Eds.), *Societal mechanisms for maintaining competence in old age* (pp. 182-206). New York: Springer.

Arrington, E., and Wilson, M., (2000). A Re-examination of risk and resilience during adolescence: Incorporating culture and diversity. *Journal of Child and Family Studies, 9,* 221-230.

Azar, B. (2006). A New Stress Paradigm for Women. APA Monitor, July/ August 2000. Retrieved March 18, 2008 from http://mentalhealth.about.com/cs/womensmentalhealth/a/tendbefriend.htm

Bacalla, T. (2005). *Women and Disaster: Resilience amid Ruin.* PCIJ Report, Issue No. 4 Retrieved March 18, 2008 from http://www.pcij.org/i-report/4/aceh-women.html

Bachay, J.B., and Cingel, P.A. (1999). Restructuring Resilience: Emerging Voices. *Affilia, 14,* 162-175.

Barbarin, O. (1993). Coping and resilience: Exploring the inner lives of African-American children. *Journal of Black Psychology, 19,* 478-492. Retrieved April 3, 2005 from http://jbp.sagepub.com/cgi/reprint/19/4/478

Barber, B.K. (2008). Contrasting portraits of war: Youth' varied experiences with political violence in Bosnia and Palestine. *International Journal of Behavioural development, 32,* 298-309. Retrieved September 9, 2008 from http://jbd.sagepub.com/cgi/reprint/32/4/298

Bartlett, D.W. (1994). On resilience: Questions of validity. In M. C. Wang, and E.W. Gordon, (Eds.). *Educational resilience in inner-city America: Challenges and Prospects,* pp. 97-108, Hillsdale, NJ: Erlbaum.

Baumrind, D. (1991). The influence of parenting style on adolescent competence and substance use. *Journal of Early Adolescence, 11,* 56-95.

Benard, B. (1990). Youth service: from youth as problems to youth as resources. *Illinois Prevention Forum 10,* 6-14.

Bisagni, G.M., and Eckenrode, J. (1995). The role of work identity in women's adjustment to work. *American Journal of Orthopsychiatry, 65,* 574-583.

Bogar, C.B., and Hulse-Killacky, D. (2006). Resiliency Determinants and Resiliency Processes among Female Adult Survivors of Childhood Sexual Abuse. *Journal of Counselling and Development, 84,* 318-327.

Boon, C. (2005). Women after divorce: Exploring the psychology of resilience. (Doctoral dissertation, *University of South Africa, 2005).* Retrieved July 10, 2008 http://etd.unisa.ac.za/ETD-db/ETD-desc/describe?urn=etd-03032006-105612

Bowen, D.J., Morasca, A.A., and Meischke, H. (2003). Measures and correlates of resilience [Abstract]. *Women* and *Health, 38,* 65-76. Retrieved April 12, 2007 from http://www .ncbi.nlm.nih. gov/pubmed/14655795

Bowlby, J. (1980). *Attachment and loss: Loss, sadness and depression.* Vol. 3. New York: Basic Books.

Brendtro, L., and Larson, S. (2004). The resilience code: Finding greatness in youth. *Reclaiming Children and Youth. Cultivating Resilience, 12.* Retrieved December 12, 2005 from www.cyc-net.org/Journals/rcy-12-4.html

Brown, L.M. and Gilligan, C. (1993). Development meeting at the crossroads: Women's psychology and girls. *Feminism Psychology, 3,* 11-35. Retrieved December 12,2005 from http://fap.sagepub.com/cgi/reprint/3/l/11

Buchanan, T.S., Fischer, A.R., Tokar, D.M., and Yoder, J.D. (2008). Testing a culture-specific extension of objectification theory regarding African-American women's body image. *The Counselling Psychologist, 36,* 697-718. Retrieved September 9, 2008 from http://tcp.sagepub.com/cgi/reprint/36/5/697

Cabrera, N.L., and Padilla, A.M. (2004). Entering and succeeding in the "Culture of College": The story of two Mexican heritage students. *Hispanic Journal of Behavioural Sciences, 26,* 152-170.

Cameron, R.P., Wells, J.D., and Hobfoll, S.E. (1996). Stress, social support and coping in pregnancy: taking gender and ethnicity into account. *Journal of Health Psychology, 1,* 195-208.

Caprara, G.V., Scabini, E., Barbaranelli, C., Pastorelli, C., Regalia, C., and Bandura, A. (1998). Impact of adolescents' perceived self-regulatory efficacy on familial communication and anti-social conduct. *European Psychologist, 3,* 125-132.

Chatham-Carpenter, A., and DeFrancisco, V. (1998). Women construct self-esteem in their own terms: A feminist qualitative study. *Feminism Psychology, 8,* 467-489.

Choate, L.H. (2005). Toward a theoretical model of women's body image resilience. *Journal of Counselling* and *Development, 83,* 320-330.

Christman, D., and McClellan, R. (2008). Living on barbed wire: Resilient women administrators in educational leadership programmes. *Educational Administration Quarterly, 44,* 3-29. Retrieved August 28, 2008 from http://eaq.sagepub.com/cgi/content/abstract/44/1/3

Colton, M.E., and Gore, S. (1991). *Gender differences in stress and coping behaviours among late adolescents.* Washington, DC.: National Institute for Mental Health.

Condly, S.J. (2006). Resilience in children: A review of literature with implications for education. *Urban Education, 41,* 211-236.

Connolly, C.M. (2005). A qualitative exploration of resilience in long-term lesbian couples. *The Family Journal, 13,* 266-280.

Cosgrove, L. (2000). Crying out loud: Understanding women's emotional distress as a symptom of anorexia nervosa. *Feminism and Psychology, 6,* 505-521.

Crocco, M.S., and Davis, O.L. (Editors). (1999). *Bending the future to their will: Civic women, social education, and democracy.* Lanham, Boulder, New York, Oxford: Rowman and Littlefield Publishers, Inc.

Culpepper, A. S. (2004). Women graduates' academic resilience and their personal strategies for doctoral success. (Doctoral dissertation, *Florida International University, 2004).* Retrieved August 17, 2008 from http://proquest. umi.com/pqdlink?vinst= PROD&attempt= 1&fmt=6&startpage=-l&ver=l&vname=PQD&RQT=309& did=885616731&exp=09-06-2013&scaling=FULL&vtype=PQD& rqt=309&cfc= 1 &TS= 1220779326&clientId=62557

de Vries, B., and Watt, D. (1996). A lifetime of events Age and gender variations in the life story, *International Journal of Aging and Human Development, 42,* 81-102.

Denton, M., Prus, S., and Walters, V. (2004). Gender differences in health: A Canadian study of the psychosocial, structural and behavioural determinants of health. *Social Sciences and Medicine, 58,* 2585-2600.

Dyer, J.G., and McGuinness, T.M. (1996). Resilience: analysis of the concept. *Archives of Psychiatric Nursing, 10,* 276-282.

Elliot, C., and Stead, V. (2008). Learning from leading women's experience: Towards a sociological understanding. *Leadership, 4,* 159-180.

Epstein, J.A., Botvin, G.J., Griffin, K.W. and Diaz, T. (2001). Protective factors buffer risk factors on alcohol use among inner-city youth. *Journal of Child and Adolescent Substance Abuse, 11,* 77-90.

Ezzedeen, S.R., and Ritchey, K.G. (2008). The man behind the woman: A qualitative study of the spousal support received and valued by executive women. *Journal of Family Issues, 29,* 1107-1135. Retrieved September 9, 2008 from http://jfi.sagepub.com/cgi/reprint/29/9/1107

Felten, B.S. and Hall, J.M. (2001). Conceptualizing resilience in women older than 85: Overcoming adversity from illness or loss. *Journal of Gerontological Nursing, 27,* 46-53.

Ferreyra, N. (March-April, 2001). Living out loud: Building resiliency in adolescent girls with disabilities. *Disability World, 7,* Retrieved September 9, 2008 from http://www.disabilityworld.org/03-04 01/ women/lol.shtml

Fine, M., and Zane, N. (1989). Being wrapped too tight: When low-income women drop-out of high-school. In L. Weis, E. Farrar, and H. Petrie (Eds). *Dropouts from school.* (pp. 23-53). Albany: State University of New York Press.

Flynn, S.E. (2008). America—The resilient: defying terrorism and mitigating natural disasters. *Foreign Affairs, 87.* Retrieved July 10, 2008 from http://www.foreignaffairs.org/20080301 faessay87201/ stephen-e- flynn! america-the-resilient.html ?mode=print

Franz, C.E., and Stewart, A.J. (1994). *Women creating lives: Identities, resilience and resistance.* Boulder, CO: Westview Press.

Frydenberg, E., and Lewis, R. (2000). Teaching coping to adolescents: When and to whom? *American Educational Research Journal, 37,* 727-745.

Gattuso, S. (2003). Becoming a wise old woman: resilience and wellness in later life. *Health Sociology Review, 12,* 171-177.

Giele, J.Z. (1993). Women's role change and adaptation, 1920-1990. In K. D. Hulbert and D. T. Schuster, (Eds.), *Women's lives through time: Educated American women of the twentieth century* (pp. 32-60). San Francisco: Jossey-Bass.

Gilligan, C., Lyons, N.P., and Hanmer, T.J. (1990). *Making connections: The relational worlds of adolescent girls at Emma Williard School,* Cambridge, MA: Harvard University Press.

Gore, S., Aseltine, R.H., and Colten, N.E. (1993). Gender, social-relational involvement and depression. *Journal of Research on Adolescents, 3,* 101-125.

Grotberg, E. (1999). Countering depression with the five building blocks of resilience. *Reaching Today's Youth, 4,* 66-72.

Gullo, S. (1992). *Divorce shock: Perspectives on counselling and therapy.* Philadelphia: Charles Press.

Hage, S.M. (2006). Profiles of women survivors: the development of agency in abusive relationship. *Journal of Counselling and Development, 84,* 83-94.

Hamermesh, D.S., and Lee, J. (2003). Stressed Out on Four Continents: Time Crunch or Yuppie Kvetch? Retrieved April 9, 2008 from http://www.melbourneinstitute.com/hilda/conf/conf2003/pdffiles/DHamermesh.pdf

Hampel, P., and Petermann, F. (2005). Age and gender effects on coping in children and adolescence. *Journal of Youth and Adolescence, 34,* 73-83.

Handmer, J. (2003). We are all vulnerable. *The Australian Journal of Emergency Management, 18,* 55-60.

Hankin, B.L., and Abramson, L.Y. (2001). Development of gender differences in depression: An elaborated cognitive vulnerability-transactional stress theory. *Psychological Bulletin, 127,* 773-796.

Hansen, J.B., and Hall, E.G. (1997). Gifted women and marriage. *Gifted Child Quarterly, 41,* 169-180.

Hanson, D.R., and Gottesman, I.I. (2007). Choreographing genetic, epigenetic, and stochastic steps in the dances of developmental psychopathology. In A. S. Masten (Ed.), *Multilevel dynamics in developmental psychopathology: Pathways to the future* (pp. 27-43). Mahwah, NJ: Erlbaum.

Heaphy, B. (2007). Sexualities, gender and ageing: Resources and social change. *Current Sociology, 55,* 193-210.

Heilbrun, C. (1988). *Writing a woman's life.* Ballantine, New York.

Herman, J.L. (1992). *Trauma and recovery.* New York: Basic Books.

Higgins, G.O. (1994). *Resilient adults: Overcoming a cruel past.* San Francisco, CA: Jossey-Bass.

Hobfoll, S.E., and Schroder, K.E.E. (2001). Distinguishing between passive and active prosocial coping: Bridging inner-city women's mental health and AIDS risk behaviour. *Journal of Social and Personality Relationships, 18,* 201-217.

Hogan, J., Carlson, J., and Dua, J. (2002). Stressors and stress reactions among university personnel. *International Journal of Stress Management, 9,* 289-310.

Holly (n.d.). Adversity. Retrieved July 10, 2008 from http://www.booksofletters.com/pdfs/adversity.pdf

Howard, S., Dryden, J. and Johnson, B. (1999) Childhood resilience: review and critique of the literature, *Oxford Review of Education, 25,* 307-323.

Hulbert, K.D. and Schuster, D.K. (1993). *Women's lives through time: Educated American women of the twentieth century.* San Francisco: Jossey-Bass.

Humphreys, J. (2003). Resilience in sheltered battered women. *Issues in Mental Health Nursing, 24,* 137-152.

Hung, C. (2004). Predictors of Postpartum Women's Health Status. *Journal of Nursing Scholarship, 36,* 345-351.

Ingram, R.E., and Luxton, D.D. (2005).Vulnerabilty-Stress Models. In J. Albela (Ed.). *Development of Psychopathology; Stress-Vulnerability Perspectives.* New York: Sage.

Jacelon, C.S. (1997). The trait and process of resilience. *Journal of Advanced Nursing, 25,* 123-129.

Joe, K., and Chesney-Lind, M. (1995). Just every mother's angel: An analysis of gender and ethnic variations in youth gang membership. *Gender and Society, 9,* 408-431.

Kaiser, C.R., Major, B., and McCoy, S.K. (2004). Expectations about the future and the emotional consequences of perceiving prejudice. *Personality and Social Psychology Bulletin, 30,* 173-184.

Khan, S., (1998). Moderator variables in vulnerability to anxiety, social support and resilience. (Doctoral dissertation, *University of Karachi, 1998*). Retrieved April 9, 2008 from http://eprints.hec.gov.pk/620/1/273.html.htm

Kinsel, B.I. (2004). Older women and resilience: a qualitative study of adaptation. (Doctoral dissertation, *Ohio State University, 2004).* Retrieved April 9, 2008 from http://www.ohiolink.edu/etd/send-pdf.cgi/Kinsel%20Beth%20I.pdf?osul092707347

Kinsel, B.I. (2005). Resilience as Adaptation in Older Women. *Journal of Women and Aging, 17,* 23-39.

Kirby, L.D. and Fraser, M.W. (1997). Risk and resiliency in childhood. In Fraser, M. W. (Ed.), *Risk and Resiliency* (pp. 10-33). Washington, DC: NASW Press.

Klein, S.M., and McCabe, H. (2007). From mother to disability professional: Role change, resilience, and rewards. *Journal of Early Intervention, 29,* 306-319.

Kubany, E.S., Hill, E.E., Owens, J.A., Iannce-Spencer, C., McCaig, M.A., and Tremayne, K.J. (2004). Cognitive trauma therapy for battered women with PTSD (CTT-BW). *Journal of Consulting and Clinical Psychology, 72,* 3-18.

Kula, A. (2003, September 27). Resilience and courage: Women, men and the Holocaust. *The Age.* Retrieved July 10, 2008 from http://www.theage.com.au/articles/2003/09/25/1064083123976.html?from= storyrhs

Labouvie-Vief, G. (1994). *Psyche and eros: Mind and gender in the life course.* Cambridge University Press, New York (1994).

LePage-Lees, P. (1997). *From disadvantaged girls to successful women: Education and women's resiliency.* Westport, CN: Praeger.

LeRoy, Walsh, Kulik and Rooney (2004). Retreat and resilience: Life experiences of older women with intellectual disabilities. *American Journal on Mental Retardation, 109,* 429-441.

Luthar, S.S., and Zigler, E. (1991). Vulnerabilty and competence: A review of research on resilience in childhood. *American Journal of Orthopsychiatry, 61,* 6-22.

Maginness, A. (2007). The development of resilience—a model. (Doctoral dissertation, *University of Canterbury, 2007).* Retrieved July 10, 2008 from http://digital-library.canterbury.ac.nz/data/collection3/etd/adt-NZCU20071206.163903/01front.pdf

Masten, A.S. (2001). Ordinary magic: Resilience processes in development. *American Psychologist, 56,* 227-238.

Masten, A.S., Best, K.M., and Garmezy, N. (1990). Resilience and development: Contributions from the study of children who overcome adversity. *Development and Psychopathology, 2,* 425-444.

Masten, A.S., Neemann, J., and Andenas, S. (1994). Life events and adjustment in adolescents: The significance of event independence, desirability, and chronicity. *Journal of Research on Adolescence, 4,* 71-97.

Matthews-Armstead, E. (2002). And still they rise: College enrollment of African-American women from poor communities. *Journal of Black Studies, 33,* 44-65.

Matud, M.P. (2004). Gender differences in stress and coping styles. *Personality and Individual Differences, 37,* 1401-1415.

McClure, F.H., Chavez, D.V., Agars, M.D., Peacock, M.J. and Matosian, A. (2008). Resilience in sexually abused women: Risk and protective factors. *Journal of Family Violence, 23,* 81-88.

McCubbin, L. (2001). *Challenges to the Definition of Resilience.* Paper presented at the Annual Meeting of the American Psychological Association (109th, San Francisco, CA, August 24-28, 2001).

McDonough, P. and Walters, V. (2001). Gender and health: Reassessing patterns and explanations. *Social Science* and *Medicine, 52,* 547-559.

McIntyre, A. (1998). A kaleidoscopic view of women's development. *Journal of Adult Development, 5,* 141-143.

McKay, S., and Bonner, F. (2002). Evaluating illness in women's magazines. *Journal of Language and Social Psychology, 21,* 53-67.

McKnight, L. and Loper, A. (2002). The effect of risk and resilience factors on the prediction of delinquency in adolescent girls. *School Psychology International, 23,* 186-198.

Miller, B. (2005). *The woman's book of resilience: 12 qualities to cultivate.* York Beach, ME: Conari Press.

Mirowsky, J., and Ross, C. E. (1989). Explaining the social patterns of depression: Control and problem-solving — or support and talking. *Journal of Health and Social Behaviour, 30,* 206-219.

Misra, R., West, S., Russo, T., McKean, M. (2000). Academic stress of college students: comparison of student and faculty perceptions. *College Student Journal, 34,* 236-245.

Morales, E. (2008). Exceptional female students of colour: Academic resilience and gender in higher education. *Journal of Hispanic Higher Education, 7,* 228-248.

Moreno, C.L., and Simoni, J.M. (1997, May). *Latina women and HIV: coping and resilience.* [Abstract] National Conference on Women and HIV, *May 4-7.* Retrieved April 3, 2007 from http://www.aegis.com/aidsline/1997/dec/M97C/1199.html.

Morrissey, S. (1998). Resources and characteristics of elderly women who live alone. *Health Care for Women International, 19,* 411-421.

Nakashima, M., and Canda, E.R (2005). Positive dying and resiliency in later life: A qualitative study. *Journal of Aging Studies, 19,* 109-125.

Nash, S.T. (2007). Teaching African American women's experiences with intimate male partner violence: Using narratives as text in gender violence pedagogy. *Journal of Transformative Education, 5,* 93-110.

Noble, K.D., Subotnik, R.F., and Arnold, K.D. (1999). To thine own self be true: A new model of female talent development. *Gifted Child Quarterly, 43,* 140-149.

Nolen-Hoeksema, S. and Girgus, J.S. (1994). The emergence of gender differences in depression during adolescence. *Psychological Bulletin, 115,* 424-443.

O'Connor, C. (2002). Black women beating the odds from one generation to the next: How the changing dynamics of constraint and opportunity affect the process of educational resilience. *American Educational Research Journal, 39,* 855-903.

O'Connor, C., Lewis, A., and Mueller, J. (2007). Researching "black" educational experiences and outcomes: Theoretical and methodological considerations. *Educational Researcher, 36,* 541-552.

Pinker, S. (2006, September 23). Women naturally 'tend and befriend.' *The Globe and Mail,* Retrieved May 17, 2007 from http://www.susanpinker.com/docs/2006 2309 tend befriend.pdf

Poulter, S.B., Brooks, R., and Goldstein, S. (2002). *Raising resilient children: Fostering strength, hope, and optimism in your child.* McGraw.

Psychology Today. (2008, June 17). Learning the art of resilience. *PsychCentral.* Retrieved August 17, 2008, from http://psychcentral.com/lib/2008/learning-the-art-of-resilience/

Ptacek, J.T., Smith, R.E. and Zanas, J. (1992). Gender, appraisal, and coping: A longitudinal analysis. *Journal of Personality, 60,* 747-769.

Rak, C.F. (2002). Heroes in the nursery: Three case studies in resilience. *Journal of Clinical Psychology, 58,* 247-260.

Ramsey, J.L., and Blieszner, R. (1999). *Spiritual resiliency in older women: Models of strength for challenges through the life span.* Thousand Oaks, CA: Sage.

Rende, R., and Plomin, R. (1993). Families at risk for psychopathology: Who becomes affected and why? *Development and Psychopathology, 5,* 529-540.

Richardson, G.E. (2002). The metatheory of resilience and resiliency. *Journal of Clinical Psychology, 58,* 307-321.

Rivera, A.A., Anderson, S.K., and Middleton, V.A. (1999). A career development model for Mexican-American women. *Journal of Career Development, 26,* 91-106.

Rogers, L.P. (2000). Women recreating their lives: Challenges and resilience in midlife. (Doctoral dissertation, *Virginia Polytechnic Institute and State University, 2000).* Retrieved July 10, 2008 from http://scholar.lib.vt.edu/theses/available/etd-04192000-09580054/unrestricted/etd.pdf

Roxburgh, S. (1996). Gender differences in work and well-being: Effects of exposure and vulnerability. *Journal of Health and Social Behaviour, 37,* 265-277.

Rudolph, K.D. (2002). Gender differences in emotional responses to interpersonal stress during adolescence. *Journal of Adolescent Health, 30 (Supp.),* 3-13.

Rudolph, K.D., and Hammen, C. (1999). Age and gender determinants of stress exposure, generation, and reactions in youngsters: A transactional perspective. *Child Development, 70,* 660-677.

Rudolph, K.D., Hammen, C., Burge, D., Lindberg, N., Herzberg, D., and Daley, S.E. (2000). Toward an interpersonal life-stress model of depression: The developmental context of stress generation. *Development and Psychopathology, 12,* 215-234.

Rutter, M. (1979). Protective factors in children's responses to stress and disadvantage. In M.W. Kent, and J. E. Rolf (Eds.), *Primary prevention of psychopathology, Social competence in children.* Hanover, NH: University Press of New England.

Rutter, M. (1984). Resilient children. Why some disadvantaged children overcome their environments and how we can help. *Psychology Today, 3,* 57-65.

Rutter, M. (1987). Psychological resilience and protective mechanisms. *American Journal of Orthopsychiatry, 57,* 316-331.

Rutter, M. (1988). Longitudinal data in the study of causal processes: Some uses and some pitfalls. In: M. Rutter, Editor, *Studies of psycho-socio risks: the power of longitudinal data,* (pp. 1-28). Cambridge University Press, New York.

Rutter, M. (2006). How does the concept of resilience alter the study and understanding of risk and protective influences on psychopathology? *Annals of the New York Academy of Sciences, 1094,* 1-12.

Rutter M., and Quinton, D. (1984). Long-term follow-up of women institutionalized in childhood: Factors promoting good functioning in adult life. *British Journal of Developmental Psychology, 18,* 225-234.

Ryff, C.D., Singer, B.H., Dienberg Love, G., and Essex, M.J. (1998). Resilience in adulthood and later life. In J. Lomrantx (Ed.), *Handbook of aging and mental health: An integrative approach* (pp. 69-99). New York: Plenum Press.

Schultz, D. (1990). *Risk, resiliency, and resistance: Current research on adolescent girls.* New York: National Council for Research on Women.

Schuster, D.T. (1993). Studying women's lives through time. In K.D. Hulbert and D.T. Schuster *(Eds.), Women's lives through time: Educated American Women of the Twentieth Century* (pp. 3-31). San Francisco: Jossey-Bass.

Shih, J.H., Eberhart, N.J., Hammen C. and Brennan, P.A. (2006). Differential exposure and reactivity to interpersonal stress predict sex differences in adolescent depression. *Journal of Clinical Child and Adolescent Psychology, 35,* 105-115.

Siqueira, L.M., and Diaz, A. (2004). Fostering resilience in adolescent females. *The Mount Sinai Journal of Medicine, 71,* 148-154.

Stojanovska, L. (2004). *Coping in the face of life adversity: A model of resilience for menopausal women.* Paper presented at The 8th Australian Menopause Society Congress, 23-25 September 2004, Perth. Retrieved September 1, 2008 from http://www.eurekalert.org/pub_releases/2004-09/jhf-mwm0921 04.php

Suarez-Mccrink, C. (2002). Hispanic women: Building a room for self-efficacy. *Journal of Hispanic Higher Education, 1*, 238-250. Retrieved January 17, 2008 from http://jhh.sagepub.com/cgi/reprint/1 /3/238

Sun, J., and Stewart, D. (2007). Age and gender effects on resilience in children and adolescents. *The International Journal of Mental Health Promotion, 9*, 16-25.

Sund, A.M., Larsson, B., and Wichstrom, L. (2003). Psychosocial correlates of depressive symptoms among 12-14-year-old Norwegian adolescents. *Journal of Child Psychology and Psychiatry, 44*, 588-597.

Tamres, L., Janicki, D., and Helgeson, V. S. (2002). Sex differences in coping behaviour: A meta-analytic review. *Personality and Social Psychology Review, 6*, 2-30.

Taylor, S.E., Klein, L.C., Lewis, B.P., Gruenewald, T.L., Gurung, R.A.R. and Updegraff, J.A. (2000). Biobehavioural responses to stress in females: Tend-and-befriend, not fight-or-flight. *Psychological Review, 107*, 411-429.

Thompson, L., and Walker, A.J. (1989). Women and men in marriage, work, and parenthood. *Journal of Marriage and the Family, 51*, 845-872.

Turner, J.R., and Avison, W.R. (1987). Gender and depression: Assessing exposure and vulnerability to life events in a chronically strained population, *Journal of Nervous and Mental Diseases, 77*, 443-455.

Turner, S.T., Norman, E., and Zunz, S. (1995). Enhancing resiliency in girls and boys: A case for gender specific adolescent prevention programming. *The Journal of Primary Prevention, 16*, 25-38.

Turner, R.J., and Roszell, P. (1994). Psychosocial resources and the stress process. In: W. Avison, (Ed.). *Stress and mental health: Contemporary issues and prospects for the future*, (pp. 179-205). Plenum Press, New York.

Ungar, M. (2004). A constructionist discourse on resilience: Multiple contexts, multiple realities among at-risk children and youth. *Youth and Society, 35*, 342-65.

Ungar, M. (2008). Resilience across cultures. *British Journal of Social Work, 38*, 218-235.

Utesch, W.E. (n.d.). *From a glass half empty to a glass half full: A review of the Transition from Deficit to Strength-Based approaches.* Retrieved January 17, 2007 from http://archives.zinester.com/8583/93725/139832 UteschArticle.pdf

Utsey, S.O., Bolden, M.A., Lanier, Y., and Williams, III, O. (2007). Resilient outcomes in African-Americans from high-risk urban examining the role of culture-specific coping as a predictor of communities. *Journal of Black Psychology, 33*, 75-93.

Voges, M., and Romney, D. (2003). Risk and resiliency factors in post-traumatic stress disorder. *Annals of General Hospital Psychiatry, 2*. Retrieved March 18, 2007 from http://www.annals-general-psychiatry.com/content/pdf/1475-2832-2-4.pdf

Waaktaar, T., Christie, H.J., Borge, A. and Torgersen, S. (2004). Building adolescents' resilience within a psychiatric outpatient setting: Results from a clinical intervention pilot project. *Psychological Reports*, 94, 363-370.

Wagnild, G., and Young, H.M. (1990). Resilience among older women. *Journal of Nursing Scholarship, 22*, 252-255.

Wagnild, G.M., and Young, H.M. (1993). Development and psychometric evaluation of the resilience scale. *Journal of Nursing Measurement, 1*, 165-178.

Walsh, F. (1998). *Strengthening family resilience.* New York: Guilford Press.

Wang, J., Korczykowski, M., Rao, H., Fan, Y., Pluta, J., Gur, R.C., McEwen, B.S., and Detre, J.A. (2007). Gender difference in neural response to psychological stress. *Social Cognitive and Affective Neuroscience, 2*, 227-239. Retrieved September 9, 2008 from http://www.cfn.upenn.edu/perfusion/stress. pdf

Waters, D. and Lawrence, E. (1993). *Competence, courage, and change.* New York: Norton.

Weiss, L. (2008). Toward the mastery of resiliency. *Canadian Journal of School Psychology, 23*, 127-137.

Weitzman, L.J. (1985). *The Divorce Revolution.* New York: Free Press.

Werner, E.E., and Smith, R.S. (1982). *Vulnerable but invincible. A study of resilient children.* New York: McGraw-Hill.

Werner, E.E., and Smith, R.S. (1992). *Overcoming the odds. High risk children from birth to adulthood.* Ithaca: Cornell University Press.

Whittaker, S., Hardy, G., Lewis, K., and Buchan, L. (2005). An exploration of psychological well-being with young Somali refugee and asylum-seeker women. *Clinical Child Psychology and Psychiatry, 10*, 177-196.

Wolin, S.J., and Wolin, S. (1993). *The Resilient Self: How Survivors of Troubled Families Rise Above Adversity.* New York: Villard Books.

Women, Chronic Stress and Resilience (2003, June). *National Women's Health Report*, 2003. Retrieved January 17, 2008 from http://findarticles.com/p/articles/mi moNKT/is 3 25/ai 106233553/print?tag=artBody;c 011

Wright, M. O. (1998). Resilience and women's health. In E.A. Blechman and K.D. Brownell (Eds.). *Behavioural Medicine for Women: A comprehensive handbook,* (pp. 151- 161). New York: Guilford.

Zautra, A.J., Johnson, L.M., and Davis, M.C. (2005). Positive affect as a source of resilience for women in chronic pain. *Journal of Consulting and Clinical Psychology, 73*, 212-220.

Zeldin, A. and. Pajares, F. (2000). Against the odds: Self-efficacy beliefs of women in mathematical, scientific, and technological careers. *American Educational Research Journal, 37*, 215-246.

Zimmerman, M.A., and Arunkumar, R.F. (1994). Resiliency research: Implications for schools and policy. *Social Policy Report, 8*, 1-19. Retrieved July 7, 2007 from http://www.srcd.org/documents/publications/SPR/spr8-4. pdf

3

Marital Happiness
An Attitude

Sunita Dwivedi and *P.C. Mishra*

Marriages are made in heaven. The nuptial knot is tied in this world. Man and woman Nature's two most creative partners, build up a lasting personal relationship through love and mutual cooperation and coexistence. The joint years pass by and glide away in the blissful status of trust and love for each other. This is the significance of marriage. The course of love and life is hardly straight. In this uneven journey through life, faith, fortitude and devotion, displayed by two souls towards each other, could only see the married couple through various ups and downs. Marriage may be all happiness, if strict vigil is maintained in interactions of senses, feelings, affection and various other sentiments that are to rise in the close liaison that marks the husband and wife's married life.

Few relationships are more complex than the relationship between husband and wife. It carries within it the fires of hell as well as the soothing shades of heavenly abode. The book "How to be Happy though Married" must have shared the uneasy feelings of an immense majority of men and women about the gamble of a married life. More man than woman want to keep out of it. This must necessarily be so. Besides the biological necessity common to both, a woman is an engine of nature's reproductive function. In the background of social and moral set-up, sex disorderliness is more throwned upon her than upon the male. Under these compelling conditions, she is groomed to enter marriage willy-jilly. It has become her life time job to explore the pitfalls in the path of married happiness. This search begins from the period of unmarried adulthood; with marriage, she has to fight on several fronts. In some cases, her commander-in-chief, her husband, wavering in his needs between her and those who do not take kindly to her. It is during her years of married life that she gathers the secrets of how to be happy though married. There is no instant recipes for a happy marriage. Many a time two distinctly different individuals have to work towards creating a successful marriage. It is not necessary to get what you had wanted out of marriage. Striking the right balance between reality and expectations is something every couple has to work at. One may not have been involved in choosing one's partner, but one can certainly have to be actively involved in creating an enjoyable, fruitful and successful relationship with him or her and thus drive the marital happiness.

Marriage is an institution which cannot be successful one until both of the partners derive a sort of happiness in it. Happiness is an ambiguous term. "Happiness" of what? Marriage and emotions are related to such an extent that one cannot get a marital happiness without it. Because emotions are the force which compels both of the partners nearer to each other. Tagore was with the opinion—"a real romance starts on the altar of the marriage." Thus marriage is not a contract between the two people rather it is a lifetime happiness. Of course! if the couple tries to get it. Harlow (1958) survived with the thought that "marital happiness can better be written by poets and novelists." Therefore "marriage" refers to the ceremony through which a male and a female start to live together. Of course! one of the several reasons is—reproduction. So sex is indirectly related and involved with marriage and therefore sexual happiness can said to be the base of marital happiness. Everyone, who is married, wants to maximize his/her happiness and marital happiness has always been vital in shaping individual's lifestyle. Every individual born and blessed are perceived happy and satisfied in so many ways. In our society, life is evaluated worthy mainly on the basis of the happiness which he/she gets from his/her marital relationship.

A young man and a young woman are joined in wedlock, they take the vow to belong to each other body and soul, and that is how, with this glorious aim and vision they begin their journey in life. Of all the institutions in our civilized society, marriage is the most respected and the most acclaimed one. Customs and religions in different countries may be different, but the common factor in marriage remains and that is to seeking souls meet to build up a nest, an abode, a shelter for them, where body and their personalities are allowed by society to reach the highest level of fulfilment. For the young bride, marriage is a myriad of sweet and sensitive expectations that would spring from the actions of the husband, to sweep her completely off her feet, and to stamp her as his very own forever.

And she as his bride and wife, would happily submit to his claims to become one with him in all the trials and tribulations of life. On the other hand, the young groom may also have his expectations about his new wife, a term he is yet to get used to, but the very utterance of it souls thrills of charming ripples that make determined to carry on his responsibility in the spirit of love and protection of his newly acquired life's partner. These grand sentiments and expectations meet in the bridal chamber at the nuptial bed when according to the traditions of some countries, the groom removes the veil of the bride and looks at her radiant beauty with wonder and heavenly joy and thus starting of marital happiness. "They married, and lived happily ever after." This is the way how most fairy tales end. But then, that's all they are; fairy tales. Marriage is not a fairy tale. People are conditioned from early childhood to look upon marriage as nature's solution to the search for happiness. Such a view of marriage is two dimensional. On one dimension, it is natural to romanticize weddings. But on the another dimension it should be viewed realistically. "The function of the marriage is not to lift people 'up to the stars'. Marriage is not a substitute for divine ecstacy and it can give people, a new recognition of what they are already, in themselves."

Marital happiness should not be approached as a beautiful but motionless painting. Rather, it should be viewed "as an opportunity forever—further growth and development". It should be recognized as a challenge and an opportunity to make someone else happy, rather than pursue selfishly throughout life one's own happiness. Marital happiness should be undertaken creatively, as an art. Couple, should seek fresh ways everyday to express their love for one another, and to bring out the best in each other, and in themselves.

"Creativity" is a key word for marital happiness, for marriage is not, in itself, a solution. It simply provides new opportunities for finding solutions to life's problems. Any couple who think to live "happily ever after" once the wedding bells have stopped ringing are destined for a rude awakening. Thus, for real happiness in marriage, what people entering marriage must do is "stop dreaming" and face their joint adventure not only hand in hand, but open-eyed. Perfection in marriage, as in everything else in life, should be seen not a still photograph, and not as a plateau, but as continuous movement in a forever unfolding direction—movement accompanied sometimes by struggle, sometimes by tensions and sometimes by pain but ultimately lead to the marital happiness. So in marriage 'SHE' includes 'HE'—this should always be remembered. Then it is useless to fight in marriage rather fight for marriage. Marriage like all human relationships, has its ups and downs.

If one really wants to derive marital happiness, one must be self-honest. Every selfish desire must be recognized for the "black hole" in marriage, it should be chiselled away like an ideal sculptor. Marriage, in order to reach at the top of happiness, must be based on free sharing, not on a mutual sense of obligation. Obligations are bondage in marriage. When married people look at each other with the thought, "what is in it for me" love flies out of the window. Unfortunately, people are not even raised to think expansively. There is rather, a growing tendency in society these days to think in terms of what the world owes us, rather than what each of us, personally, can do for others, and for the world, to make it a better place to live in.

There is a common confusion about marriage. It is unrealistic to expect love, considered purely as an emotion to continue unchanged through years of married life. 'Dry periods' come frequently. If dryness can occur in a saint's relationship with God, how much more so is it bound to occur in the fluctuations of feeling that are normal to male and female relationships. One must think of marriage as normal human condition, not as a special condition separate from normal life. In other words, to become a successful human being, it is essentially what it takes to become a successful marriage partner. The real basis of marital happiness is not sex appeal, but those simple human consideration which make for happy unions of all kinds. For those persons, especially, who aspire to increase their understanding, marriage should be viewed as a doorway to self-expansion. For the basic purpose of marriage is not to enroll two egos in a "mutual admiration society". It is to contribute to the fundamental purpose of life, which is to expand the limitations of human consciousness towards universal awareness. The further purpose of marital relations is self-knowledge and self-understanding. Living in close proximity to another human being affords an objective proving ground for personal development. So, in order to derive marital happiness, every selfish desire must be recognized as unproductive. There should be free sharing in marriage and there must be free opportunity for self-knowledge and self-understanding. In order to be maritally happy, the couple must understand the fact that both of them are basically different on behaviour patterns. The lady must not except the same feelings and behaviour from her partner as hers. The couple must realize that even boy and girl babies behave differently from one another. To claim otherwise would be to try to squeeze reality. In men, "reason is uppermost; feeling is kept hidden." Whereas in women, "feeling is uppermost, reason is kept hidden." These differences in no way indicate that men have not as great a capacity for feeling, or women as great a capacity for reason. A specific man maybe capable of deeper feeling, and greater love, than most women, and a specific woman may be capable of reasoning more clearly than most men. Each of these, however, in his own nature, is likely to depend more on reason, if a man, and more on feeling, if a woman. It is only in saints that we find these two attributes perfectly balanced. So for right happiness in marriage husband and wife must know this fact. Both of them must try to balance between reason and feeling. Because if the husband is overanalytical and less in feelings towards his wife, it is painful for her. On the other hand, feeling, when it is not guided by reason, falls into a welter of emotions. So feeling must be kept in a state of calm reason, reason must be inspired by calm feeling that leads to happiness in marriage. Feeling and reason, both, are important and both equally so. Women and men therefore need to learn to live in harmony together, with ever depending appreciation for those qualities in each other which complement their own only by mutual respect and appreciation can marriage become truly a delight. And only by mutual respect and appreciation can marriage also give its participants the opportunity for mutual growth and happiness, which is its highest potential.

A good motto in marriage is "People are more important than things." Circumstances change, but our deeper commitments remain. Outsiders come and go, but those who are close to us remain. Marriage is a long-term investment. Respect and consideration are the simple kindness in human relationships that, like oil keep the machinery of life flowing smoothly. Marriage should be rooted in respect and courtesy. Without these, love never grows to become a healthy plant, capable of surviving the storms of life and of shifting fortunes. Couple who treat each other too familiarly imply, by look, word and gesture, that there can be no further depths in the other person waiting to be explored. There is always an opportunity for each other to explore. For marriage is to be an ever expanding experience. It must be creative. Passively marriage is like a slow-acting poison. Creating is a tonic. Marriage should be treated as an art. To be kept forever interesting, forever new, it must be based on giving—on loving mutual service. The energy in marriage is like flowing water: As long as there is creative input, it will retain its freshness. But if it remains idle for too long, the marriage will grow stagnant. Hence, again, marriage should be ever-expansive. There are two ways for couples to grow together. One is—by intertwining themselves, like twin creepers. But such relationship is suffocating, for it implies total interdependence, not creativity in sharing. No one; if locked in such a union, can reach out expansively towards a larger reality. The other way is—by accepting the simple fact that perfect union is achieved not only physically or mentally, but above all in soul-union. True marital happiness is possible only if each partner assumes personal responsibility for their growth together. Mutual growth is possible only from the soil of mutual respect and respect flourishes best when a degree of distance, mutually agreed upon, is maintained. It is good even in the intimacy of marriage, for couples to appreciate each other's need for privacy. For everyone needs some space of his own. Couples need some time to themselves—both as a couple, and also apart from one another.

Only in the state of inner privacy and freedom can we preserve that happiness which is the highest promise of marriage. Love is a sharing, a giving; it isn't a taking. Marriage is such a sensitive relationship that if in anyway one tries to coerce one's partner there is a risk of damaging the relationship irretrievably. True love is based on mutual giving. It never makes demands. Marriage is such a sensitive relationship that there should be respect for one another's freewill instead of issuing emotional commands. Partner should offer his/her suggestions, kindly even humbly for the free consideration of husband or wife. Respect for one another should include giving each other the freedom to grow and to change, each at his own pace. Woman who expects a second ideal or God for a husband would better not to marry and men who want perfection in their wives might as well marry a statue. Men who demand their wives to be like Sita, must be like Rama himself. Because the basic rule in life is to work with things as they are, not as we wish they were. This rule applies universally and certainly no less so to relationship and to marriage. One must not be the teacher of one's partner, never criticize him or her. Husband or wife must offer their ideas—tentatively, as a friend—mentally leaving the other person entirely free to accept or reject them. One more thing should be checked in marriage—strong emotions abhor reason so one should never speak under influence of emotions. To be maritally happy, the couple should plan to talk their differences. However, no goodwill come from suppressing them. But speak when both of the partners are calm. The important thing in happy marriage is to give "strength" to one another. This is to say that if one partner is found upset, the second partner should serve as peacemaker. Because situations, or things or anything else isn't that much important in marriage as love and respect for one another is. Marriage is or should be, a lifelong commitment. That means it should be taken with lifelong goals in mind. Responsibilities in marriage seems very important because wife and husband both are shared career couple now-a-days.

Apart from satisfaction level and level of tension, marital adjustment too is an important aspect of marital happiness. Marital adjustment has been defined as the presence of such characteristics in marriage as tendency to avoid or resolve conflicts, feeling of satisfaction with each other, sharing of common interests, activities and sex feeling and lastly, but not the least, fulfilling of marital expectations of husband and wife. Hicks and Platt (1970) conducted research on marital happiness and marital stability. They derived a conclusion that at least two basic marital types exist in the present-day society. Each of these type contain different aspects of behaviour and expectations from each other (couple). These two basic marital types are (i) Institutional Marriage, (ii) Companionship Marriage. In the institutional marriage, traditional role specifications are most significant to the success of marriage or marital happiness. These traditional role specifications are between husband and wife. The husband's role is held to be the more instrumental, the wife's role is said to be more traditional. In this marital type, the wife is more accommodating and the husband, more rigid in role needs. Marital happiness is more a function of the husband's possession of the expected instrumental needs and capacities. While in companionship marriage, greater emphasis is placed on the emotional aspect of the relationship. Variables such as esteem, sexual enjoyment, companionship and communication are significant to marital happiness. Buerkle *et al.* (1961) have taken altruism as a general factor in marital happiness. Emphatic behaviour too was taken as a satisfying factor in happy marriages by Cottrell (1992). Though the exact role of personality in marital happiness is yet not clear. The similarity theory (developed by Newcomb, 1961) suggests that individuals tend to marry those of similar education, S.E.S., race: religion, age, culture, attitudes and even physique and physical attractiveness, whereas complementarily theory (by Winch, 1954-58) suggests that individuals who are paired on the basis of need complementarily (having different traits or having different levels of the same trait) should experience greater happiness and adjustment in their marriage than those who are not. Choosing right person to marry is important not only for adjusting to all the social roles associated with marriage but also important because marriage is an art of living with another person, who is not as same as 'you'. Therefore, 'the partner' must develop emotional intimacy and must communicate his/her feelings to the better half to be maritally satisfied.

The concept of 'Intimacy' is in fact often equated with closeness. It may be taken as involving greater intensity or romantic involvement (Parks and Floyd, 1996). Hinde (1979) used intimacy as synonymous with self-disclosure. Tillman, Frelick, Russell and Weisz (1980) interviewed a random sample of adult, in the general population about their views on intimacy. These interviews revealed that most people identified—"sharing private thoughts, dreams, attitudes, beliefs and fantasy" as important for intimacy. Researchers called these elements of self-disclosure as "Expressiveness". Other findings show that (a) sexuality is a part of intimacy, (b) anger argument, and criticism are not the part of intimacy, (c) self-knowledge and self-esteem (identity) is important for intimacy, and (d) childhood exposure to intimacy, usually through parents, is important. Chelune, Waring, Vosk, Sultan and Ogden (1984) found that disclosure was significant means through which marital couples expressed intimacy. Thus, it can be said that intimacy is a hidden aspect of self-disclosure because the second leads to the first. The results suggested that the content of the disclosure was important. Positive disclosure statements about the self were positively associated with intimacy. While negative statements about one's self are inversely related to intimacy. Waring, Me El rath, Mitchell and Derry (1981) in their studies strongly reveal that there is an association between intimacy and relational adjustment. They are of the opinion that disclosure is more likely to emerge in certain types of relational environment and subsequently it enhance those relational environments. Thus, self-disclosure and relationship are mutually transformative.

Relationship and the intimacy develops over-time. People meet, talk, separate, talk to others, meet again, talk again and so on. This all happens in the due course of time. There are some features of relationships that only time can put in perspective. Knapp and Vangelisti (1991) considered 'time' as a 'string'. In the same line social penetrating theory developed by Altman and Taylor (1973) presents an analysis of how time influences disclosure and the lifecycle of a relationship. It is based on the assumption that relationships intensify gradually and in an orderly fashion, paralleling the development in message exchange from superficial to intimate topics and from a narrow to a broad range of topics. If both the couple are willing to reciprocate, self-disclosure helps in building trust and intimacy between them, according to Altman and Taylor (1973). Thus, beads on their string of time may be few, but they are very important. Relational events occur over time, some are affected by self-disclosure and some are not. Social penetrating theory also suggest that self-disclosure and close relationships do not necessarily develop over time in a parallel, incremental and continuous fashion. Another transformation agent, the third one; is Attributional Processes in self-disclosure. According to Duck (1982) people are not the passive receivers of information about their partners. Rather they make attributions regarding the message which has been disclosed. People tend to make one or two types of attributions about another person's disclosure, (a) One is dispositional attributions, (b) another is situational attributions, and (c) interpersonal attributions are also used sometimes when the relational environment is multilayered and complex because of shared experiences and intertwined goals. According to Taylor (1981), the attributions we use to explain why someone is telling us something intimate or revealing an important part of what the self-disclosure will mean to the relationship. When the person builds the attribution that disclosure considers 'me' to be special and that is why I am getting this disclosure message, this attribution feeling tends to increase the feeling of attraction for that individual and thus the person feels special emotional relationship with him or her, according to Baile (1984). The most important thing in the attributional process is that if one wants to intensify a relationship, one must concentrate on positive attributions about self-disclosure, because negative attributions sustain the established relationship. Shimanoff (1987) found that when one receives negative information about others this may create the attribution of closeness. On the contrast, when one gets positive information about others, this may be a threatening attributional process. She further states that when marital couples communicate negative emotional disclosure about their partners, these messages result in negative attributions and feelings. Often, the emotional disclosure may be communicated in the form of a complaint. And this also, according to Shimanoff's (1987) research, may be considered as negative attributions such as vulnerability or hostility.

Albert (1988) explored few complaint messages in the form of attributional process towards one's partner. She compared maritally adjusted and maladjusted couples. These couplès were married for 6 months. She found that both differ in several issues. The maritally adjusted couple tend to offer more behavioural complaints than maladjusted couples. While maladjusted couples offer more personal complaints. The adjusted couples used more positive affect while delivering these complaints. For the adjusted couples, the receiving partner responded with more agreement responses while maladjusted couples responded with more counter-complaints. At the most general level, if we feel attracted towards the person, we are more likely to reciprocate the disclosure and thus intimacy and liking increases. So, disclosure leads to liking as the fourth transformation agent of developing close relationship. Because most people are most comtortable around the people they know, than the people they do not know, according to Berger (1987).

Intimacy is a feeling laying behind the self-disclosure. It may be called abstract while self-disclosure in activity may be visible. In fact, intimacy can be the hidden motive behind self-disclosure. Self-disclosure need social support. The social benefits of self-disclosure derive from the reactions that others provide. Wills (1985, 1990) suggested four types of social support that help in self-disclosure, (a) First type of social support needed for self-disclosure is "esteem support". When one discloses one's self, he or she needs the feeling of acceptance, love and value even though one is having difficulties. The sense of acceptance that occurs can reduce a person's anxiety about troubling events. Esteem support may occur when a disclosure target listen attentively, shares similar personal experiences, avoids criticism or offer sympathy (b) second type of social support is "informational support" that is disclosure target can offer information, advice and guidance in coping with a problem, (c) "instrumental support" is the third type of social support which contains such as "helping" when he or she is needed. If a person who need assistance cannot or will not tell others, instrumental support will not be available because it is the most tangible form of assistance, and (d) problems takes their own time and way to get resolved. People around us can only provide "motivational support" which is said to be the fourth type of social support. Even if problems are not easily resolvable, other people can offer encouragement and inspiration to stand against the odds. Motivational support can help the individual in coping with upsetting situations in which the ordinary tendency might be to give up and become depressed. Coyne, Wortman and Lehman (1988) said that on the contrast if motivational support is sarcastic in nature, it might be unhelpful rather than helpful by the depressed person.

To walk on this way of life, partners have to ride side by side, talking to each other, disclosing to each other and thus coming closer and closer. Because self-disclosure, loosely defined as what individuals verbally reveal about themselves to others (including thoughts, feelings and experiences), plays a major role in close relationships. It is hard to imagine how a relationship might get started without such self-disclosure. When two persons are near to each other (married), they would obviously like to know about each other, in turn, one must be willing to share more information about oneself. They begin to talk about attitudes, feelings and personal experiences. In brief, people start to disclose the personal information. In fact, self-disclosure is an important component of the development of a close relationship. When one wants to disclose one's feeling that shows that the feeling of trust is created. We may feel closer to that person because we know he or she trusts us and values our responses.

Early theories of self-disclosure suggest that self-disclosure is synonymous with a close relationship. It contributes in developing a close relationship and maintaining it too. In fact, self-disclosure may serve different functions or goals in a relationship (Archer, 1987; Miller and Read, 1987). It also serves the purpose of social validation, getting feedback from others about our thoughts or feelings or getting help with problems in our lives. On the other side, it also helps for social control selectively presenting information about ourselves to create a good impression. It further helps in providing personal goals. Coupland, Giles and Wieman (1988) told that it is important in successful relationships, partners negotiate what they talk about with one another, and decisions about self-disclosure are not made in isolation by individuals. As Holtgraves (1990) perceptively wrote: "It is misleading to consider self-disclosure as an individual phenomenon, rather, the emphasis is on the joint contributions of the interactants through the give and take of a conversation. In the end, both what is disclosed, and its significance, are to be viewed as a collective, emergent phenomenon." However, particularly in a close relationship in which individuals have a high investment and commitment, individuals may also negotiate what to talk about and in what manner. Both the disclosurer and the disclosure recipient may avoid talking about certain topics what might prove too threatening to them, e.g., any negative feeling. To protect one another, relationship partners also may encourage and accept disclosure messages what are stated "indirectly" instead of "directly".

Morton (1976, 78) said that the content of self-disclosure might be descriptive or evaluative as well, (a) Descriptive self-disclosure contains the information and facts about oneself that might be more or less personal while (b) evaluative self-disclosure is the expression of personal feelings, opinions and judgments. Self-disclosure can further be classified as personal self-disclosure and relational self-disclosure. P.S.D. (Personal self-disclosure) is the disclosure about oneself while (RSD) Relational self-disclosure is that has as its referent one's relationship with another person or one's interaction with others. Self-disclosure can have multiple effects. Because it cannot be said that self-disclosure always cause a relationship to develop or that relationship development always cause self-disclosure. In fact, self-disclosure is "mutually transformative" means that self-disclosure and relationships are dynamic and subjective. Self-disclosure messages transform the nature of the relationship and the nature of relationship transforms the meaning and consequences of the self-disclosure. Knapp (1984) have proposed that relationships follow a lifecycle through different stages of development.

According to Mark Knapp, these stages are characterized by certain patterns in behaviour, feelings, thoughts and communication. According to the author, in early stages, uncertainty may be high and communication might be awkward, stylized, impersonal and non-judgmental. In later stages, uncertainty is low and communication might become smoother, more spontaneous, more personal, more judgmental and taken of affection might be exchanged. Knapp and Vangelisti (1991) suggested that relationships develop through two complementary processes—coming together and coming apart, (a) "Coming together" contains five stages that help in the development of relationship—initiating, experimenting, intensifying, integrating and bonding. During 'initiating' relationship starts from small talks, during experimenting, the relationship holder asks questions about the preferences, activities and other informations regarding similarities and common interests, while at the third stage (intensifying) self-disclosure, depth increases and commitment is expressed verbally and symbolically. During integrating, self-disclosure continues to increase and thus the social network comes to see the relationship partners as 'couple'. Last and fifth stage is called "Bonding" and this stage is marked by public rituals as marriage. These five stages, no matter in romantic couples or in business partners, work actively in creating self-disclosure and thus developing intimate relationship.

Knapp and Vangelisti (1991) also proposed five stages for the "coming apart" process that is disengagement from the relationship. These five stages are made of—differentiating, circumscribing, stagnating, avoiding and terminating. During the first stage, the couple begins to separate themselves from their joint identity and present themselves as individuals in front of social network. They stress on their differences rather than on similarities. The second stage contains the avoidance of important topics while at the stagnating stage physical and psychological distance is so pronounced that even conflict is unlikely. Avoiding additional interaction follows and finally termination of relationship occurs.

Knapp and Vangelisti (1991) argued that even couples who may skip stages eventually will have to recycle and progress through earlier stages. According to them, some relationship neither progress nor decline beyond a certain point, they simply continue to exist where they are. This is 'Empty marriage' concept where relationship is stagnated but has not eliminated through formal divorce. Though Baxter (1990) had the opinion that intimate relationships may have cyclical movements in relationships of togetherness and separateness.

There are many factors which help in mutual transformation process that is in building certain relationship. These factors are called transformation agents. They include relational definition, time, attributional process, liking, reciprocity and goals. Though pattern of self-disclosure varies across the relationships. That is with whom one is disclosing himself or herself that matters. Tardy *et al.* (1981) noted that perhaps friends and family members are providing different functions regarding disclosure. Thus, the relational definition may influence our disclosure. Relational definition means that when people disclose in certain way, the recipient may be expected or be forced, to define the nature of the relationship differently. A study by Rosenfeld and Welsh (1985) examined that disclosure differ from dual-career to single career marital couples. They found that for dual-career couples, the patterns of disclosure are more equal than those for single career couples. Wives of single career husbands reported that they disclose more than their husbands in regard to breadth, depth and amount of disclosure. Dual-career spouses did not differ on anything except depth. Rosenfeld and Welsh suggested that such findings focus on relational definition that includes role equality that both the couple have careers so they must share the responsibilities of household as well. This pattern of self-disclosure violates traditional sex role expectations bad on female expressively and male inexpressively. Disclosure also maybe one means by which relationship qualities such as intimacy are manifested and reinforced. According to Waring (1987) "Self-disclosure is one aspect of how close a couple feels towards one another and thus a factor that could increase the couple's intimacy."

Achary and Surender (1996) said that role of husband and wife communication not only directly effects the quality of relationship but through the decision making regarding family planning. He conducted his data in Bihar and Tamil Nadu (India). Indralal Desilve (1994) conducted data on husband-wife communication in Sri Lanka. He conducted that spouses who communicated on matters related to sex have favourable attitudes to family planning and marital happiness. Sai-Sujatha and Murthy (1993) collected data on two sets of Brahmins of Andhra Pradesh (India) and found that wife's educational level seemed to affect the inter-spousal self-disclosure. Dobbins Lee (2006) (net) says that every marriage suffers times of trial but in today's society, it is so easy to simply walk away without trying to fix things. Sadly, most of us want to stay married but many lack the knowledge of what to do to keep the marriage going. He further says that one way to help get your marriage back on track is to properly communicate with your spouse. When talking to your spouse, honesty is the best policy. However, one must be mindful of two important procedures when being honest. The first, be sure to speak truth in love. At times honesty will be painful, therefore one should consider saying what needs to be said with tenderness and compassion. One should always take into consideration of the one you are speaking with Dobbins contains the opinion that 'put yourself in their shoes'. How would you feel if you were the one being told what you are about to tell them. The seemed issue to consider is this: determine if what you are going to say is necessary some things can go without being said and it will not hurt anyone. Dobbins' idea is that, yes! it does not hurt anyone. The other aspect of communicating is listening. It is just as important to be a good listener of your feelings and you need to make an effort to really hear what your spouse is saying. It will be difficult, at times, to listen without reacting, but you can always make a try. Further Randy Siegal, 2006 (The Power of self-disclosure - net) carries the opinion that communicaing without disclosing self is like trying to play tennis without a ball. Though according to Randy Siegal, there is no set formula for how much we should disclose about ourselves, it changes from person to person and situaton to situation. Still, the larger the open self piece, the more likely we are more close to self-disclosure. The question arises 'should you reveal your true self to your spouse?' Different people contain different attitudes (ToI, Sunday April 23, 2006). This is Mars *Vs* Venus Controversy. Is a white lie better than a black truth? Should one tell all or act with tact? These queries have individual answers. Perhaps honesty of relationship is not hidden in the quantity you are disclosing to your partner rather in the quality of disclosure. Film Director Mahesh Bhatt says that intimacy is about sharing yourself, not about sharing every single particle of yourself that comes through your heart and your mind. According to him "you are what you hide. In spite of all the poppy cock about true intimacy, the truth is that in the sub-terranian region of one's being, there hides a beast called the 'real you'. Which never comes out in the open to reveal its inadequate self, because if he did so, it would shatter the image on which the sacred bond of marriage is built, and all the King's men of culture and marriage counsellors will not be able to put this Humpty Dumpty together again." While on the other hand, Shobhaa De, the author and columnist is of the opinion that there are some things best left hidden, best left to the imagination while integrity is key in any relationship, be it with a spouse, business-colleagues, lover or child, the whole idea of "total-transparency" is a load of rubbish. According to her "one hundred per cent true" is baloney. Even in the best of relationships there is a small level of hypocrisy and play acting involved, and that is essential for the health of relationship.

We personally believe that marital happiness of the couple, their level of intimacy and amount of disclosure between them—this all is based on attitudinal psychology of man and woman in a particular relationship.

A feminine gender is taken as a special creation of nature. As natural things have a lot of attraction and everything in abundance, woman also have qualities of extreme opposite things in nature, action and behaviour of thoughts. Shyness and sometimes quite outspoken, serious and folly, it is not easy to judge a woman only by action and appearence to her inner core. She likes to respect others of her choice and be respected by all. She cannot waste money on others and may spend lacs for her maintenance and satisfaction of ego. She sacrifices for the family and remains disturbed in herself for children, their education and growth. As a diplomat, she creates an atmosphere for her betterment and silently changes the mind working of man. Havıng a good quality of an actress to appear as she wishes and gets her work done behind the curtain. CERTAINLY SHE IS A FOUNTAIN OF PLEASURE ON EARTH.

Women of old times were not well-educated, but were keeping a correct concept of submission to God, husband, children and family. Now-a-days, education had made their life prosperous and complicated both in hankering self-ego-satisfaction so simplicity of heart and feeling of generosity are deteriorating. Even today we find that extremes are playing in their life. In duty and learning, though man fails to defeat a woman, but costs are being paid. Virtually, divineness is bestowed in woman. Tolerance, adjustments and bearance are divine qualities. Action, reaction, tit for tat are the worldly qualities. To be ambitious and prosperous are human qualities—all are bestowed in a woman. All these qualities of a woman makes married life intimate and happy. Her affection towards children, husband and family is important for society and human growth. Total pleasure of human life is centralized marital, sex is a natural phenomenon as described in ancient times to modern ages. A man is more outspoken, fearless and maintains himself physically strong than a woman, but woman is a centre of real power. Psychologically, woman is a stronger sex. She is able to bear the majority of responsibilities and therefore we personally believe that for the intimate marital happiness, woman is more responsible because she is more efficient to handle these responsibilities. As far as Indian culture is concerned, shyness, submissiveness, softness and less exposed system of living is the beauty and grace. These qualities create the atmosphere of pleasure and happiness. As you sow, so you reap formula applies in an attempt of pleasure and happiness in one's life. The input of feelings and sensitivity is essential to get the output of happiness. We find that women have the power of this input and thus the whole relationship of the family enjoys the output of happiness. In marital happiness, more important point is a true relationship and self-disclosure which brings the couple closure and closure. In action and behaviour, a woman is more intelligent in getting a man exposed of his ideas, attitudes, thoughts, feelings etc. In other words, a woman has a quality to compel the other person disclose himself and thus the process of self-disclosure gets start and intimacy develops and thus marital happiness is increased.

Now-a-days, due to globalization, economic growth structure and advancement, women also go for education and career. They have also started imposing the equal share in responsibilities and economics and expects the man to share their domestic affair too. The expectation of a woman to share the responsibility is not wrong as she also shares the economic world too. But she gets disturbed when she does not get the proper support from the spouse. In the home, when appears to be a 'progressive man' becomes traditional, the rift starts. So in order to achieve marital happiness—intimacy is required. For intimacy—self-disclosure is required. For self-disclosure, husband and wife need to have a healthy and strong psychology to accept each other with full confidence, affection and love. We again emphasise that the psychology of a woman is more strong and confident enough to start with.

REFERENCES

Altman and Taylor (1973): *Social Penetration: The development of interpersonal relations*. New York: Holt, Rinchart and Winston.

Albert, J. (1988) : An Analysis of Couples' Conversational Complaints. *Communication Monographs, 55*, 184-197.

Archer, R.L. (1987) : *Self-disclosure: Theory, research and therapy*, pp. 323-324, New York : Plenum.

Acharya, A. and Surender, S. (1996): *The Journal of Family Welfare*, Vol. 42, 4. Dec. pp. 5-10.

Buerkle, *et al.* (1961) : Altruism: Role conflict and family adjustment. *Marriage and family living*, 1961.

Berger C.R (1987) : Communicating under uncertainty in M.E. Reloff and Miller *Interpersonal Process* (pp. 39-62), Newbury Park, Saga.

Baxter, L.A. (1990) : Dialectional Contradictions in relationship development. *Journal of Social and Personal Relationships, 7*, 69-88.

Cottrell, N. (1992) : Inhibiting effects of reciprocation wariness on interpersonal relationships. *Journal of Personality and Social Psychology, 62*, 658-668.

Chelune, Waring, Vosk, Sultan, Ogden (1984) : Self-disclosure and its relationship to marital intimacy. *Journal of Clinical Psychology, 40*, 216- 219.

Coyne, J.C., Wortman, C.B. and Lehman, D.R (1988), *The other side of support: Emotional Overinvolvement and Miscarried helping*, pp. 305-330, Newbury Park-Saga.

Coupland, J., Giles, H. and Wieman J. (1988): My life is in your hands: process of self-disclosure in Intergenerational talk. *Styles of self-disclosure*, pp. 201-253. London: Croom Helm.

Duck, S.W. (1982) : A topography of relationship disengagement and dissolution in S.W. Duck. *Personal Relationships, 4,* 1-29, New York Press.

Dobbins, L. (2006) : Communicating for a better marriage wwwxy article.com

Hinde, R.E. (1979): *Relationships: A Dialectical Perspective.* Psychology Press. Taylor and Francis Ltd. (UK).

Hicks and Platt (1970) : A Marital Quality - A Review, *A Journal of Marriage and Family* (NOV).

Harlow, H.F. (1958) : Affectional responses in the infant monkey. *Science 130,* 421-432.

Holtgraves, T. (1990) : The Language of self-disclosure. *Handbook of Language and Social Psychology,* pp. 191-207, Chichester, UK, John Wiley.

Indralal W, Desilva (1994): *The Journal.of Family Welfare,* Vol. 40, June 1994, 1-13.

Knapp, M.L. and Vangelisti, A.L. (1991) : *Family Secrets.* Unpublished manuscript, Univ. of Texas, Austin.

Morton, T.L. (1976): *Two-dimensional Scoring System: training manual,* Unpublished manuscript. Univ. of Utah, Salt Lake City.

New Comb, Y. (1961) : *The acquainatance process.* New York: Holt, Rinehart and Winston.

Park, M.R. and Floyd, K. (1996) : Meaning for closness and intimacy in friendship. *Journal of Social and Personality Research, 13,* 85-107.

Rosenfield, L.B. and Welsh, S.M. (1985): Differences in Self-disclosure in Dual Career and Single Career Marriage. *Communication Monographs, 52,* 253-263.

Randy, Siegal (2006): *The Power of Self-Disclosure,* www.xyArticles.com

Shimanoff, S.B. (1987) : Types of emotional disclosure and request compliance between spouses. *Communication Monograph, 54,* 85-100.

Sai Sujatha, D. and Murthy, M.S.R. (1993), *The Journal of Family Welfare.* Vol. 39, 4, Dec. 26-30.

Taylor, D.A. (1981): Effects of Personalistic Self-disciosure. *Personality and Social Psychology Bulletin, 7,* 487-492.

Tardy, C. *et al.* (1981): Disclosing Self to Friends and Family: A re-examination of initial questions. *Communication Quarterly, 29,* 263-268.

Times of India, Sunday, April 23, 06: Should you reveal your true self to your spouse?

Waring, E.M. (1987) : Self-disclosure in Cognitive marital therapy in V.J. Derlega and J.H. Berg, *Self-disclosure: Theory, Research and Therapy.* pp. 283-301, New York: Plenum.

4

Culture and Climate Supportiveness: *A Developmental Analysis*

Aradhana Shukla and *Shraddha Joshi*

One of the significant dimensions of educational climate is climate supportiveness. By climate supportiveness we refer to a positive affect which members have towards an organization and its functioning. Feelings of supportiveness or unsupportiveness can be considered as attitudinal dispositions for home and for the academic and non-academic pursuits in the school.

The factors responsible for the perception of the school and home climate as supportive could be both, inherent in the perceiving individual and also in the specific features of his environment. Factors peculiar to the individual that influence perception of school climate are his value structure, personality and needs. An important environmental factor related to the perception of a lack of support is the behaviour of teachers and peers in school and parents in the home. Parental teacher expectancy and peer group acceptance have been particularly found significant in determining the supportiveness of the perceived climate. These concepts, therefore, need to be discussed in some detail.

Family Climate

The term climate has been regarded as providing a network of forces and factors which surround, engulf and play on the individual (Bloom, 1968). According to Stott (1974), the term environment in its usual sense, emcompasses all of the influencees upon development which come from outside the individual. Good (1973), Biswas and Aggrawal (1971) and Wolman (1977) have also given similar definitions to the term environment.

Different authors have also defined the home or family. Murdock (1949) states that "the family is a social group characterized by common residence, economic co-operation and reproduction, it includes of both sexes, who maintain a socially approved sexual relationship and one of more children, own or adopted of the sexual co-habituating pair." *The International Dictionary of Education* mentions that "family is a primary social group of parents, offspring's and possibly other members of household."

Three terms have been used in respect to the type and quality of environment prevailing in home. These are authoritarian, democratic and permissive; these terms have been used in relation to both home and school environments and defined in behavioural terms by different authors. Platt *et al.* (1962) states that authoritarian control employed by parents. This continuum stems from parents who are restrictive and coercive, permitting the child little freedom of child or range of activity, to the parents who are lax and ineffectual and unable to control the child. Between these two extremes are the parents who allow the child freedom but who is capable of asserting authority when and where desired. According to Shah (1982) "Authoritarian parents rely too heavily on one's means to enforce obedient. For this purpose they use many repressive restraints. They hold a strong concretion that child must obey and that it is the responsibility of parents to mark children to obey their parents. Authoritarian parents take advantage of child's weakness to secure complaints even subservience."

In this study an attempt was made to find out the pattern of home climate and school climate. It is the first study and the objectives and hypotheses are given separately.

- The first objective of this study was to classify the participants on the basis of their scores on family climate scale. It was hypothesized that there would be difference in participants in relation to their scores on family climate scale.
- The second objective of this study was to classify the participants on the basis of their scores on school climate scale. It was assumed that there would be differences in participants in relation to their scores on school climate supportiveness scale.
- The third objective of this study was to find out the relationship between the areas of family climate scale among different cultures. It was hypothesized that a close relationship would be manifested by the participants in the areas of family climate by the participants of different cultures.
- The fourth objective of this study was to find out the area-wise relationship between school climates among different cultures. It was expected that a close relationship would be evinced by the areas of the school climate supportiveness scale by the participants of different cultures.

Keeping these objectives in consideration this study was planned in factorial perspective.

Method

Sample

A large number of children (N=900) in the age group of 8-13 years was taken. They were hailed from various schools of Almora, Haldwani, Khatima and Ramnagar of Uttarakhand. The schematic presentation of experimental design is as follows:

Table 4.1(a): Schematic presentation of experimental design used in this study

A					
A1		A2		A3	
B		B		B	
B1	B2	B1	B2	B1	B2
150	150	150	150	150	150

Legends: A—Chronological Age   B—Types of Cultural Variation

A1—8-9 years   B1—Tribal (Tharu, Buxa)

A2—10-11 years   B2—Non-Tribal

A3—12-13 years

On a large sample (N=900) the measures of home climate and school climate were administered and then 480 participants were taken. In this way, 20 participants were taken in consideration. The detail of sample selection is mentioned in preceding section however, the schematic presentation of design after sample selection is as follows:

Table 4.1(b): Schematic presentation of experimental design after first phase of sample selection

A											
A1				A2				A3			
B				B				B			
B1		B2		B1		B2		B1		B2	
C		C		C		C		C		C	
C1	C2	C1	C2	C1	C2	C1	C2	C1	C2	C1	C2
45	45	45	45	45	45	45	45	45	45	45	45

Table 4.1(c): Schematic presentation of experimental design after second phase of sample selection

	A											
	A1				A2				A3			
	B				B				B			
	B1		B2		B1		B2		B1		B2	
	C		C		C		C		C		C	
	C1	C2	C1	C2	C1	C2	C1	C2	C1	C2	C1	C2
D1	20	20	20	20	20	20	20	20	20	20	20	20
D2	20	20	20	20	20	20	20	20	20	20	20	20

Legends: A—Chronological Age B—Types of Cultural Variation
A1—8-9 years B1—Tribal (Tharu, Buxa)
A2—10-11 years B2—Non-Tribal
A3—12-13 years
C—Types of Climateric Variation
C1—Home
C2—School
D—Level of climateric Supportiveness
D1—Low level of Climateric Supportiveness
D2—High level of Climateric Supportiveness.

Measures: The description of the measures is given below:

Home Environment Scale

In order to assess the patterns of family climate, the HES was employed. Constructed by Dhaundiyal (1993) this measure has 7.4 items and it deals with ten dimensions, namely 1—Attention and care, 2—facilities, 3—impartiality, 4—parental approval of adolescents' activities, 5—sharing of ideas, 6—trust, 7—confidence, 8—decision making, 9—parental support and encouragement and 10—harmony among family members. It is a questionnaire of True-False items. Two scores are given for the true items and one score for false item. Thus, the score ranges between 74-148. Low score indicates supportive family climate and high *vice versa*. Split half reliability is .79 and test retest reliability is .70.

The School Climate Supportiveness Scale

In order to measure the pattern of scholastic climate supportiveness in children, a measure was constructed by Shukla and Mishra (1993). It was developed on the lines of Garg (1975). This measure consists of forty-five items and deals with physical environment of the school, teachers' behaviour, teachers' expectancy, peer group behaviour and peer expectancy. The scores range between 40-200. Low score indicates supportive school climate and high scores *vice versa.*

Procedure: At first the investigators made a close perusal of the universe selected already and also mentioned in sample selection [see Table 4.1(a)]. Two types of universe were taken in consideration. One was concerned with tribals and the next was related with the non-tribals. Ramnagar and Khatima of Uttarakhand were taken for Buxas and Tharus and non-tribals were taken from Haldwani and Almora. After the selection of the universe, the researcher contacted the "Mukhias" or "Gram Pradhans" of the village to get the knowledge about the families of the target age group of tribal sample then she made rapport with the families. It was followed by the administration of home environment scale on 450 children at Ramnagar and Khatima. A close observation of the home was also made while administering the home environment scale. In such a way, the home environment scale was administered on non-tribals children at Haldwani and Almora. There were 450 participants of the target age and they were selected by the help of school. In this way, the universe taken was of 900 participants i.e. 150 per cell. The home environment scale was administered at their homes along with the observation of their family environment. After this exercise, the data were sequentially arranged according to the research design and following the extreme group strategy method 45 participants were placed in each cell and the sample of 900 reduced to 540. [*see* Table 4.1(b)]. On this sample, the school climate supportiveness scale was administered either in the school or at the home. Similar to the data of home environment scale, the data of school climate supportiveness scale were also subjected to extreme group strategy method and 20 participants were placed in each cell. Through this placement only 480 participants were selected [*see* Table 4.1(c)] and they constituted the final sample.

Data collection was done individually in group as per availability of the participants and their convenience. Best endeavour was made to avoid external variables. The researcher was extremely co-operated by the parents and teachers because they helped her to get data with the participants.

Results

Mean, SD and correlation analyzed the obtained data. Findings were presented in five phases and they are given below:

Phase I : Frequency Distribution of Family Climate Scale

Obtained data were separated by extreme group strategy method and frequency distribution was made of those Ss who were selected for further studies. The frequency distribution is shown in Table 4.2.

Table 4.2: Frequency Distribution of Scores of Home Environment Scale

Class Intervals	*Frequency*
140-149	28
130-139	46
120-129	80
110-119	60
100-109	100
90-99	74
80-89	52
70-79	40
	480

Phase II: Area-wise Analysis of Family Climate Scale

In order to measure the interaction pattern of family climate scale an area-wise analysis of family climate scale was made. Mean values were computed and findings are shown in Table 4.3.

Table 3: Area-wise Analysis of Home Environment Scale

S.No.	*Name of the Areas*	*Urban*	*Rural*
1.	Attention and care	17.96	18.98
2.	Facilities	12.63	13.17
3.	Impartiality	5.20	6.90
4.	Parental Approval of Adolescent Activities	15.85	20.17
5.	Sharing of Ideas	8.55	11.90
6.	Trust	9.65	11.30
7.	Confidence	16.00	28.10
8.	Decision Making	13.40	23.22
9.	Parental Support and Encouragement	14.90	16.14
10.	Harmony among Family Members	16.17	20.15

A close perusal to table reveals that pattern shown by the Ss was not uniform. It was almost different at both cultural contexts. It was found that more favourable pattern of family climate was shared by the Ss of urban culture.

Phase III: Frequency Distribution of School Climate Supportiveness Scale

Similar to the HES data of school climate supportiveness scales were also the through frequency distribution and it is shown in Table 4.4. Table 4.4 shows that it is normally distributed everywhere.

Table 4.4: Frequency Distribution of Scores on School Climate Supportiveness Scale

Class Intervals	*Frequency*
200-209	3
190-199	3
180-189	5
170-179	8
160-169	8
150-159	12
140-149	22
130-139	23
120-129	26
110-119	29
100-109	35
90-99	14
80-89	12
70-79	14
60-69	6
50-59	10
40-49	10
	240

Phase IV: Areas-wise Distribution of School Climate Supportiveness Scale

Moreover, an area-wise analysis of school climate supportiveness scale was made and it is shown in Table 4.5.

Table 4.5: Area-wise Analysis of School Climate Supportiveness Scale

S.No.	*Name of the Area(s)*	*Rural*	*Urban*
1.	Physical Environment of school	53.86	61.75
2.	Teachers' Behaviour	30.99	34.71
3.	Teachers' Expectancy	45.07	51.20
4.	Peer group Behaviour	35.00	36.87
5.	Peer Expectancy	24.95	34.67

Table 4.5 shows that boys and girls were entirely different in rural and urban culture.

Phase V: Correlational Analysis of Data: Dimensional Analysis of Family Climate and School Climate

In order to get the clear profile to data scores were subjected to correlation and coefficients are presented in their correlation matrix and they are presented in Table 4.6.

Table 4.6: Co-relational Analysis of family climate and school climate

SCHOOL

S.No.	*Name of the Area(s)*	*1*	*2*	*3*	*4*	*5*
1.	Physical Environment of school		.79	.48	.49	.64
2.	Teachers' Behaviour			.39	.59	.67
3.	Teachers' Expectancy				.80	.47
4.	Peer group Behaviour					.64
5.	Peer Expectancy					—

FAMILY

S. No.	*Name of the Area(s)*	*1*	*2*	*3*	*4*	*5*	*6*	*7*	*8*	*9*	*10*
1.	Attention and care		.59	.49	.64	.85	.46	.36	.31	.74	.49
2.	Facilities			.68	.71	.45	.48	.33	.54	.66	.70
3.	Impartiality				.38	.68	.55	.59	.55	.60	.69
4.	Parental Approval of Adolescent Activities					.60	.76	.54	.49	.46	.60
5.	Sharing of Ideas						.68	.70	.49	.59	.60
6.	Trust							.79	.60	.68	.69
7.	Confidence								.43	.49	.58
8.	Decision Making									.89	.79
9.	Parental Support and Encouragement										.37
10.	Harmony among Family members										

Table 4.6 reveals a close relationship of dimensions analysis of home environment and school climate.

Findings are as follows:

1. Data was normally distributed.
2. Cultural difference was noticed.
3. Sex related discrepancy was visited.

4. Dimensions were closely related.
5. Inter-correlation was quite high.

Discussion

Obtained data were analyzed by means and correlation and they were discussed as every dimension of home and school climate. They are given below:

Home Environment

The total score of Home Environment Scale represented the quality of various interactions going on between the child and other members of family. A higher total score represented good home environment, while lower score represented lack of it. The dimensional analysis is given, hereunder.

Affection and Care

The first dimension of Home Environment referred to the 'Affection and Care' perceived by adolescents among members of their home. It was construed that when members of home express affection for each other and provide mutual care, the home experience becomes pleasing and satisfying. Satisfactory relationships among family members are very much likely to influence children's adjustment, attitude and behaviour and it is most conducive for better adjustment. Home with poorer degree of affection and care tended to facilitate maladjustment.

Facilities

In general, 'facilities' dimension of Home Environment refers to economic aspect. It is expected that in home which are better financially will provide the child an environment in which he will feel more adequate and self-sufficient. On the other hand, low economic status families will be deficient in some essential facilities.

Impartiality in Home

'Impartiality' represents unbiased of children by elders of home parents tend to like one or other child in their family and behave in a positive way towards him or her. Special consideration to such a child often takes the form of suppression in negligence of other children's genuine needs and demands. It is likely that these negligent children become poorly adjusted and start viewing their parents in negative way. In this connection, it is also every much likely that whatever may be the behaviours of parents, it is the perception of impartiality or partiality by children which is more significant in their adjustment or attitude formation.

Parental Approval

Approval of adolescents' various activities in home provide a measure of parental acceptance of the various demands of adolescents. In home where various activities of adolescents are accepted by their parents or rather encouraged by them, the adolescents feel more satisfied. This may lead towards better adjustment and attitude formation.

Sharing of Ideas

Home situation, in which several members have interaction with each other, demands exchange of ideas, conflict and trust. Decision making is a normal phenomenon in which these members are sometimes involved or others only few members of the family take decisions. Involvement of every member of family in decision making, through continuous interaction in the form of expressed ideas and trust becomes a prerequisite for healthy home environment.

Parental Support and Care

Parental support was an important factor and it laid its significance. It was thought that running of children should be based on parental support and encouragement on the basis of which children should be developed properly.

Harmony among Family Members

Harmony among various family members is another important aspect of home environment. Parents and their children interact with each other in relation to their roles and personality needs. Something, the quality of interactions going on in home is such that these interactions remain mutually satisfying. However, in some homes members remain in conflict with each other. These conflicts may have significant bearings on personality development and attitude towards authority of adolescents.

School Climate

School is the second major institution which provides opportunities to children for their growth and development. A child who comes to school brings with him his experiences obtained in his home. The home situation provides him opportunities to interact with a limited member of individuals. It also ascribes certain roles to him. In contrast, school is a large society where roles become more specific. In the place of parents, who guide children in their day to day behaviour in home, the teacher comes to play a significant part in the life of children. Peer group, study groups and co-curricular groups come into existence and the child becomes a member of one or more such groups within a larger society. It is very much likely that experiences gained and behaviour patterns developed in the settings of school have a profound influence on personality adjustment and attitude towards authority of the children.

There are two factors that may be considered as responsible for the perception of the school climate. They are (i) interest in the perceiving individual and (ii) in the specific features of his environment. Factors with special reference to the individual that influence perception of school climate are his value structure, personality and needs. An important environmental factor related to the perception of lack or support is the behaviour of teachers and peers. Teachers' expectancy and peer group acceptance have been found significant in determining the supportiveness of the perceived climate (Rosenthal, 1974; Zuckerman, 1979; Dweck and Reppucci, 1973; Weiner, 1979). Teachers' expectations are related positively to the motivation and achievement of the students' belongingness to deprive.

In this study, it was noted that Ss differed in school and home climates Roaming in the whirlpool of this study, the investigator thought that do variation in home and school climate produce variation in other activities like behavioural dysfunctions that may be due to emotional disturbance. In order to answer this question the investigator thought to launch Study Two. It is reported on proceeding pages.

REFERENCES

Biswas, A. and Aggarwal, J.C. (1971). *Encyclopaedic Dictionary and Directory of Education, Vol. 1*, Academic Pub., New Delhi.

Bloom, M. (1968). *Stability and Change in Human Characteristics*, John-Willy & Sons, New Delhi.

Dhaundiyal, V.R. (1993). *Emotionally Disturbed Adolescents Social Work Journal 15(1)*, 73-85.

Good, C.V. (1973). *Dictionary and Education*, IIIrd Ed., McGraw Hill Co., New York.

Murdock, G.P. (1949). *Social Structure*. McMillan Co., New York.

Platt, H. G.; Jurgenson and Chorost, S.B. (1962). Comparison of Child rearing attitude of mothers and father of emotionally disturbed adolescents, *Child Development*, 33, pp. 117-122.

Rosenthal, R. (1974). *On the Social Psychology of Self-fulfilling Prophecy: Further Evidence for Pymalion Effects and their Mediating Mechanisms*, New York: MSS Modular Publications.

Shah, C.K. (1982). *Personality Development in Children*, Mull Tech. Pub. Co., Bombay.

Shukla, A. and Mishra, S. (1993). *School climate supportiveness scale*, Unpublished Script. Deptt. of Psychology, CSM University, Kanpur.

Statt, L.H. (1974). *The Psychology of Human Development*, Halt, Rinehart and Winston, New York, p. 208.

Weiner, B. (1979). A theory motivation for some classroom experiences. *Journal of Educational Psychology, 71*, 3-25.

Wolman, B.B. (1977). *International Encyclopaedia of Psychiatry, Psychology, Psychoanalysis and Neurology,* Van Nostrand Reinhold Co., New York.

Zuckerman, M. (1979). Attribution of success and failures revisited, or the motivational bias in alive and well attribution theory. *Journal of Personality, 47*, 245-287.

5

Women Managers in Indian Organizations

H.L. Kaila

Introduction

Though women workforce has risen to a greater extent, the old attitudes of men still exist in organizations. For example: a woman was not introduced while sharing a stage with men when everyone else was. Another woman was asked repeatedly by his boss whether she can work in shifts even though she happened to be a qualified engineer holding senior manager position. A senior man in the organization denied concession in work timings to a pregnant lady who requested so. Do these instances indicate that men lack sensitivity on women specific issues?

Women in offices quite often have to travel along with men as part of their duties or stay together during conferences. Men would readily agree to travel with a woman whereas a woman would face several questions from various fronts. She herself is in dilemma sometimes, whether should she accept this? How the family would react to it? How would organization address such gender issues? Whether this is an issue for young women working in MNCs?

In a study on stress coping styles among German managers (Kirkcaldy, B.D. and Furnham, A.F. 1999), the abbreviated German version of Occupational Stress Indicator's Coping Scale was completed anonymously by over 160 managers. No difference in coping profiles of men and women was found, but different levels of management and educational status did influence preference for coping styles. More specifically, it was seen that at the most senior levels of management, delegation and maintaining stable relationships are considered the most useful forms of coping with stress.

Comparative study on managerial stress in Hong Kong and Taiwan: (Oi-ling, Luo Lu & Cary L. Cooper, 1999) investigated occupational stress in managers in Hong Kong and Taiwan using the Occupational Stress Indicator-2 (OSI-2). The results showed that there were gender differences in managerial stress in Hong Kong: female managers scored higher in sources of stress and quitting intention; but had lower job satisfaction, worse mental and physical well-being than male managers. These differences could not be found in Taiwanese managers, yet Taiwanese female managers did report more stress related to "managerial role" than their male counterparts.

Kaila H.L. (2002) studied 120 managers in metropolitan Mumbai and found that 80 per cent of them experienced the most common workplace stresses and challenges such as: meeting deadlines, working in a competitive industry, managing finances, exhausting working hours, and rotation work in addition to handling regular tasks (such as sales, marketing, training, research and development, and accounts of core clients).

A Malaysian survey on occupational stress among managers (Taap, A.M; Fontaine, R.; Chong Siong Choy, 2003) examined sources of stress among Malaysian managers working in multinational companies. A total of 440 managers participated in this survey. Data was collected through a questionnaire distributed to the managers in 34 multinational companies operating in Malaysia. It was found that workloads, working conditions and relationship at work were main concerns of the managers that lead to stress at the workplace. The results also indicated that certain demographic variables do influence the level of stress among managers.

Kasper, K.; Meyer, M. and Schmidt, A. (2005) conducted an explorative analysis on managers dealing with work-family conflict. The sample was drawn largely according to the principles of theoretical sampling; family-work constellations provided the basis of selection. Thirty problem-focused interviews were content analyzed. Results showed three distinct prototypes of dealing with work-family-tension: career as subject of social fascination, family as a factual task, the tradition of two worlds, double burden and the pressure of tasks. One outstanding result was that if both partners were professionally active, the family was increasingly dominated by merely functional requirements.

Armstrong-Stassen (2005) compared the reactions of executive-level and middle managers prior to a large-scale downsizing, during initial and final phases, and following the downsizing. Compared with executives, middle managers perceived greater job insecurity, were more likely to use escape coping, and reported lower job performance and higher levels of health symptoms. Over time, both executives and middle managers reported a decline in perceived threat of job loss but an increase in sense of powerlessness, a decrease in the use of control-oriented coping strategies, and reduced job performance in the initial phase of downsizing. Although less so, executive-level managers were also adversely affected by the downsizing, suggesting that this group should be included in stress management interventions.

The studies on managerial psychology recently as well as in the past depict that cross-culturally there are similarities and differences on managerial behaviours. Secondly, female managers report more stresses regardless of cultural background. Thirdly, the sources of managerial stress across cultures are similar. Moreover, the managerial researches so far have been based on quantitative methodologies. Hence, it is postulated that the use of qualitative and narrative methods on the study of managerial issues would broaden our understanding and provide us more depth in the field.

Method

A structured questionnaire using the following three open-ended questions was presented to individual managers in their respective organizations:

- What do you think was the greatest problem you faced in the past 12 months? Please describe below.
- Please explain in which ways did it affect you personally or professionally?
- Could you give a title or heading to this problem and how did you overcome this problem? Please explain.

The managers were asked to narrate their experiences. The women managers took time out of their really busy and hectic schedule to share their problems and issues in organizations. Though managerial problems and coping have been researched using quantitative research techniques, the depth of understanding on managerial issues is lacking. Hence, a narrative approach was attempted in this study in order to enrich the managerial research.

Sample

The sample consisted of 140 female managers between 26 to 55 years of age in 81 organizations (including private and public sector, and MNCs) from different parts of India such as Mumbai, Bangalore, and Hyderabad, ranging from banks to IT, pharmaceutical companies to call centres. Data were collected from varied work backgrounds, different age groups and different levels of management: upper, middle and lower working in various departments through in-depth personal interviews and e-mails in a few cases with the help of a structured questionnaire using open-ended questions.

Results and Discussion

The survey results have been presented under the following section:

Problems faced by women managers, the ways in which the problems affect the women managers, and the coping strategies used by women managers to overcome their problems

The first question asked to managers was: What do you think was the greatest problem you faced in the past twelve months? Please describe. The second question asked was: Please explain in which way did problems faced by you affect you personally or professionally? The third question asked to managers was: Could you give a title or a heading to the problem faced by you and how did you overcome the problem? Please describe. In this way, the manager herself titled the problem.

The women managers responded:

1. Time Crisis: The greatest problem I have faced during the last 12 months is Time Constraints to meet deadlines. At a managerial level, I am assigned with a lot of responsibilities and the expectation of the superiors from me is also high. Since I have a family to look after, it is even more difficult to attend to my work responsibilities. Many a times, it leads to an injustice on my part towards either the home responsibilities or work responsibilities.

My problem has affected me positively and negatively. In a negative manner it brought about a lot of work pressure as I was falling short of time and I could not spend appropriate time on the assignments given to me by my superiors. Secondly, I found it difficult to maintain a balance between my home and work responsibilities also. But in a positive manner because of my constant efforts as well as correct planning I have become "immune to stress".

I overcame the problem by planning and prioritizing the tasks based on urgency, discussion with my colleagues and collectively resolving issues leading to lesser burden of work. Since, I cannot take long holidays, I take short breaks of 20 minutes from my work and listen to soothing music. I also watch plays in the theatre with my family to keep me in good spirits.

2. Relocation Trauma: During the recent times, I faced the problem of relocation and shifting of archives because of the merger. Since we relocated from our old office to the current one, we had to physically shift more than 100 cartons of important documents and arrange it in the new location. Since there was very little time and less help, I had to manually fill the boxes and arrange them in the new location.

Manually shifting archives affected me personally and professionally. Personally, it caused physical discomfort and muscle pull due to manual shifting of archives. Professionally, it affected because being a qualified professional I did not find it a pleasing task to do the work of shifting files and cartons by myself.

I overcame the first problem of shifting by doing what was required, i.e., shifted all the cartons manually with colleagues' help and took proper medications for the muscle pull.

3. Time constraints to meet deadlines: The greatest problem I have faced is the time constraint to cope up with multiple activities. Since I am a family woman, I have to manage both the home as well as office. My responsibilities in office are also tremendous and I have to do multitasking but the time is so little that I sometimes have difficulty in completing my assignments on time.

The problem of coping with multiple activities in a limited time has affected me personally because I have to complete many assignments together I have to stay late in office which amounts to a lot of physical strain as well as neglect in my home responsibilities. I also tend to miss important events in my personal life. It affected me professionally as I find it difficult to finish projects on the given deadline because of the limited time available to me thus causing stress. It also leads to crashed expectation from my superiors as they expect a lot out of me. Therefore, I am constantly under pressure to prove myself in front of them.

I have managed to overcome my problem by prioritizing my work based on urgency of the tasks. I plan and organize my time so that multiple activities can lead to their goals. Sometimes, I take a day or two off after hectic work schedules and go to resorts. When I return from there, I feel recharged and like a new person altogether.

4. Glass Ceiling/Competition: The greatest problem, was related to my upgradation. Despite performing well year after year, I was not promoted to the higher cadre. I neglected a lot of areas of my life in the bid to get promoted but unfortunately I was never noticed when it came to promotion. Despite achieving all the goals on time, I saw that a higher number of males had risen to good posts and were the preferred candidates for promotion, resulting in humiliation.

The problem affected me very badly personally. I started neglecting my personal life in the bargain to do well so that at least in the next appraisal I could get promoted. Similarly, I endured a lot of mental trauma and physical strain as I used to work till long hours in office and remain tensed about my promotion. Communication with my family decreased. My self-esteem took a huge blow as I started doubting myself. Professionally, I did not let it affect my work; in fact I started working more so that I could do my best.

I have not completely got over the problem as I am still struggling to understand why there was a bias towards the males and why hardworking deserving women like me were left out. But off late I have stopped thinking about it anymore, as it does not lead me anywhere. I constantly take support or spend time with my friends by going out for movies or dinner. I am doing my best but do not harbour the hopes of promotion any more. Volunteering or buying things for my nieces and nephews also helps me divert my attention from core problems.

5. Job Insecurity/Uncertainty: During the recent times, I have faced the problem of insecurity and uncertainty in my job. This is due to the recent merger that took place between the two pharmaceutical companies. The merger changed the whole structure of our organization. Many posts were declared unnecessary leading to ouster of many employees from the organization. I was constantly living under the fear of being asked to leave from the organization. With many new colleagues joining in there was uncertainty in what I was supposed to do and whether I was required by the organization or not.

Personally I felt lost. I felt stressed as I was constantly thinking about my work. For a short while I began to avoid pleasurable events. Professionally, I was very unclear as to where my job was leading me. For a while, I was also contemplating to leave my current job and look for a new one. I was confused, as my role in the organization was not defined.

I have tried to overcome my problem with the support of my colleagues at work and seniors. Secondly, I started spending more time with my child and being with her itself was extremely de-stressing as for some time I would forget about my own problems. It has been nine months since the merger so I am now getting acquainted with the new structure and begun to understand my job responsibilities better. There have been constant talks with the Management and I being assured that my job is secure hence I have stopped worrying about that aspect also.

6. Clash with Superior: The problem I suffered recently is altercation with my boss. He wasn't particularly happy with the way one of our core team members was performing. But instead of reprimanding him, my boss started to blame all the core team members. Since I am the project leader of the team, I had a few altercations with my boss. I was aware of the performance deficiency of my teammate and the remaining team was compensating for that person. Instead of appreciating the good contacts and trust we were building with the customers/clients, he was getting upset about it. So in order to overcome this he started to harass mentally a few of us. He started to bad mouth about the team members against each other.

This affected my social as well as professional life. Since my manager could not find any faults with my work, he started criticizing me for my behaviour. This made me lose interest in my work and as a result, I was not able to give my 100 per cent to my job. It also increased my stress level and I was not able to concentrate on my social life.

This problem can be solved if my boss handles this situation in a more mature and intelligent manner. Instead of harassing us to gain an upper hand he can make use of the good connections and trust that we have built up to get more business. Secondly, he can speak to our team member about his performance deficiency and guide him to perform better. In this way not only will our organization benefit but also all the team members will feel secured by having a good boss around us. I haven't been able to overcome the problem but whenver I feel stressed out I go with my friends for a movie or have a good meal somewhere and then I feel better for some time.

7. Honesty is the best policy in case of Fraud: Due to bogus stamp papers distributed in the workplace and stolen National Savings Certificate issued through authorized vendors, my employees and I faced serious problems. We were accused of creating a fraud in the organization. The customers of my bank could not repay the amount within the stipulated period of time.

Though there was no mistake on our part but as employees we underwent serious problems. We were taken to court where enquiries were made. Professionally, it affected me because as a Manager I was under pressure to save the reputation of my organization. Secondly, it was my duty to support my subordinates and participate honestly in the enquiries made by legal authorities. Personally, I was under tremendous pressure and stress. I suffered from a mild heart attack because of the pressure I underwent. My family also underwent massive worries.

If people were honest and did not commit such a crime then we would not have undergone such stress. Being an honest person, I participated in all the enquiries made on the organization and me, as I had nothing to fear. I fully supported my subordinates and stood by them. I was constantly in discussion with the top management regarding this scam. We won the court case and the culprits were arrested. Thus, we all stuck together like one family at the time of crisis. During stressful times I would either read books so that I could divert my attention from problematic issues or involve myself in making painting and handicrafts to get away from the problems.

8. Un-cooperative Subordinates: The greatest problem I faced in the past 12 months was un-cooperative attitude of my workers due to the interference by the internal union. Some of my workers were a part of the internal union. For silly reasons they used to be instigated by their core members to suspend work at the drop of a hat.

The above problem affected me personally and professionally. Personally because I used to be under constant stress because I was unable to understand why the workers were behaving so erratically and why they were not working. Professionally, it affected me because our daily production was affected because they were suspending work. Secondly, my superiors were under the impression that I was unable to handle the workers under my department.

I called the workers under my department in groups of 5 and advised them about the losses incurred because of suspending the work for some silly reason. I asked them the reason for suspending work and 50 per cent said that they didn't know the reason and they were doing it because their fellow workers were doing it, 40 per cent said that they were doing it because their union head had asked them to do so. Whereas, the remaining 10 per cent were among the ones who were lazy and liked to drop work at the slightest reason. I looked into the matter with the help of our top management and as far as my workers were concerned I brought in an Industrial/Occupational Counsellor who gave them appropriate counselling regarding the disadvantages of being instigated by others to suspend work and generally made them aware of their contribution towards their organization so that they could work sincerely in the future. As far as my personal coping was concerned spending time with my baby was itself quite a stress buster and secondly since I am religious by nature, I would say my prayers and keep full faith in God.

9. Loss of Communication: The greatest problem I faced was loss of communication with colleagues in my prior organization. The merger brought about a whole lot of changes. One of them being shifting the heads of all departments to the Head Office. This relocation led to loss of communication with my colleagues because a lot of them were not at higher posts so they remained in the old office.

Loss of communication affected me personally by the way of setting in monotony and boredom. I was not in touch with many of my colleagues due to the merger so I was not aware of what was happening with them. In a way my social support system has broken down because with my job I rarely got the time to give them a call or keep in touch with them. In a professional way, less communication means I was not clearly aware of what was happening in different business areas because of the merger. Since, I was new in the current organization and not well acquainted with my new colleagues there was ambiguity on the professional front.

I haven't been able to overcome the second problem because I have completely lost touch with my old colleagues due to my hectic routine. I feel as if I have lost a backbone, as now I have no one to share my problems with. In the current organization there is still loss of communication as I am new here and not well acquainted with my new colleagues. So there is still ambiguity with respect to my job role also. In order to get away with tension I spend some time on my own "me time" so that I feel much better and relaxed.

10. Shift Work Problem: The greatest problem I face is working Night Shifts. Since I am in a call centre, night shifts are inevitable.

Working night shifts affected me personally and professionally. Personally it becomes very difficult to manage my home and work together because at home I have to attend to my 2 years old baby and responsibilities in office are equally pressurizing. I felt guilty since I do not get time to spend with my family. Night shifts disrupt the whole schedule due to which I encountered a lot of health problems such as fatigue, headache and a lot of stress. There is often a spillover of tensions from home to work and work to home. Professionally, my health problems decreased my productivity at work. Though I was unable to handle my team, my appraisal rating from my superiors took a blow.

I have been able to overcome the problem with the support of my family. When I am not around my husband takes care of our baby. Secondly, I spend some of my times with my friends who are not from call centres, which takes some load off. I am a member of an N.G.O. named 'Aakansha' and there is no other bigger pleasure than buying gifts for the needy children and seeing a smile on their face. I plan and organize my schedule during night shifts so that I can spend adequate time with my child too.

The above responses revealed that majority of the women managers faced the problem of meeting deadlines due to time constraints. Many women managers combine their full time paid work with parenthood or household responsibilities. They tend to remain the primary caretakers on the home turf in spite of being assigned with a job which requires long hours of physically and mentally demanding work. Other main problems included getting work done from subordinates, relocation problems as well as feelings of job insecurity and uncertainty. It was also found that women managers find internal politics between their colleagues/subordinates as well as altercations, lack of communication with colleagues/friends and clashes with their superiors extremely stressful. The "Glass ceiling effect" was also reported by one woman manager who said, "She felt that there was a bias against women who wanted to move up the ladder." Lastly, night shifts too posed a major hindrance for a woman manager who reported, "Night shifts are inevitable in call centres, but I feel guilty for not spending time with my family." According to a woman manager, "The glass-ceiling effect and not being able to handle one's subordinate are problems that are very gender specific. In many organizations, in spite of working so hard, many women still face discrimination."

Women managers reported that their problems affected them personally as well as professionally.

Women managers who faced the problems of meeting deadlines due to time constraints, working night shifts and insecurity and uncertainty regarding one's job reported that personally overwork was causing a strain on their families and relationships as it robbed them of time, energy and attention needed to maintain healthy relationships with partners and children. They also reported missing out on important social events such as weddings or outings with families. According to one female manager, "I have to complete many assignments together so I have to stay late in office which amounts neglect in my home responsibilities." Feelings of insecurity and uncertainty regarding one's job created a lot of anxiousness and stress in women managers because they were constantly bombarded with thoughts about their future in the organization. They also remained tensed, as they were unclear regarding their job function in the organization. Many of these women also reported a spillover of tensions about one's work to home and from home to work. This spillover resulted in conflicts between them and their spouses. Their problems are further compounded because they also tended to suffer from health problems due to long working hours or disruptions in shift hours. They complained of headaches, back pain, fatigue, weakness and other physical ailments. Their problems also brought along professional hazards for them in the form of dissatisfaction of superiors regarding their quality of work and low productivity in their performance in the organization.

Women managers who were concerned of interpersonal conflicts at work felt demotivated and stressed out seeing the conflicts between their colleagues. According to a woman manager, "it's a challenge to remain neutral and listen to both sides of the story." As far as clashes with bosses were concerned managers felt demotivated to work especially when the clash was a result of misunderstandings or feelings of insecurity harboured by the superiors. A woman manager reported, "Constant clash with my boss made me lose interest in my work and as a result I was not able to give my 100 per cent to my job."

Uncooperative subordinates posed a problem for women managers because the attitude of the subordinates gave an impression to their superiors that the manager was unable to handle the subordinates. This problem also affected the productivity of the organization as the subordinates used to suspend work. Women managers reported a lot of confusion as they were unable to understand the real reason behind their subordinates' erratic behaviours. They also reported being under constant work pressure as they felt a need to prove themselves in front of their superiors.

Women managers who faced the problem of discrimination in the workplace reported "feeling humiliated" and left out because of unfair appraisals. Decrease in their self-esteem was another apparent effect due to the discrimination in the workplace. They also reported of neglecting their family life in a bid to do well resulting in less communication with their family. Stress, feelings of anxiousness and work pressure were their chief problems.

Complaints of monotony, boredom and lack of social support were stated by women managers who reported the problem of communication. They also complained of feelings of ambiguity as they were unware of the ongoings in different bussiness areas due to restrictive communication. Health problems such as muscle pulls were the chief complaints of women managers who suffered from the problem of relocating from one office to another.

So far we saw the negative effects of problems faced by the women manager. But the results of this survey also revealed a welcome change. According to a few women managers, the stress, tension and anxiety caused to them because of work pressure and deadlines had made them "immune to stress" as a result of which they reported handling work pressure much better than before. This effect is called as eustress as it connotes a positive change in the behaviours with respect to handling of stressful situations.

Thus, it can be seen that the problems faced by women managers affected them personally and professionally and the effects of the problems they faced were positive as well as negative.

As far as coping with problems among women managers is concerned, it was seen that only a few managers were not able to overcome their problems. But overall, the responses towards coping with problems was positive.

Different individuals have different styles of coping with their problems. It was seen that many women managers worked actively towards eliminating their problems by meditating, going on holidays, taking short breaks and having appropriate medications. Other common coping strategies reported by women managers included, discussing problems with colleagues and seeking advise from superiors, spending time with friends by going for movies and holidays, planning and organizing one's schedule.

Many women managers were spiritually inclined as a result of which they participated in different kinds of religious activities to relax their minds such as singing *bhajans,* visiting temples or saying prayers. According to a woman manager, "whenever I face a problem I send a small prayer up there so that things go well with me." Other interesting ways of coping with problems included pampering oneself by going for shopping or having a good meal. Many women managers joined N.G.Os where they generously donated gifts. One such manager exclaimed, "There is no other pleasure than seeing a smile on children's face. It is very destressing." Many of them indulged in giving gifts to relatives and friends in order to feel better. But the unanimous votes went in the favour of spending time with one's family especially one's children. According to one manager, "It is extremely destressing to spend time with my child because for some time I forget that I have a problem." Other indulged in activities like painting or watching plays in a theatre to keep their minds off from work pressure.

Conclusion

When we observe International Women's Day on 8th March every year, we need to ponder over the gender issues in organizations. Male attitude is an issue to be addressed, attitudinal barriers from men trouble women. Though male dominance in organizations is changing a bit, still an issue remains to be addressed. Some suggestions can be considered to deal with these problems:

1. Successful women or women at higher positions should act as mentors to other women and make women friendly organizations.
2. Women' leadership training need to be emphasized so that they can tackle their issues more effectively.
3. The perspectives of international women's day need to go beyond gender and look at relationship building.
4. Include men in women's seminars and other programmes.
5. Gender sensitivity programmes at schools and organizations must be conducted on regular basis as a part of Human Resource Development.
6. Organizations need to develop women development cell for soft skills training and personality development programmes.
7. It is sexual harassment for some women and romance at work for others especially young people. These different sets of responses of women to the opposite gender need to be understood and addressed accordingly.
8. Essentially organizations have to take up work-family balance mechanisms such as pick-up facility, ATM machines, flextime, compressed week etc.
9. Women must come united, raise their voices on issues that haunt them, don't leave any single case of harassment unattended.
10. Introduce Employee Assistance Programme and counselling in organizations.
11. Psychosomatic ill-health of women working on computers is an issue to tackle. Yoga and health check-ups are necessary.
12. International Women's Day should be called as 'International Gender Day'.

Though men and women are socialized differently, women are more rigorously trained for family and social roles; whereas men remain weak in these roles or opposite gender related responsibilities. Do men need to be re-socialized at the organizations for becoming gender-friendly or gender-just people? MNCs today are becoming inclusive organizations and open to people's issues (both male and female employees as equal partners).

A few common solutions are suggested to make a woman's life easier in organizations such as compressed working week, creches at the workplace, employee counselling at workplaces, flexitime, compulsory periodical medical examinations, providing the facility of working from home, *yoga* for improved physical and mental health (Kaila, H.L., 2004; 2004a; 2005).

REFERENCES

Armstrong-Stassen, Marjorie (2005). Coping With Downsizing: A Comparison of Executive-Level and Middle Managers. *International Journal of Stress Management. 12(2),* 117-141.

Coleman. D., & lso-Ahola, S.E. (1993). Leisure and health: The role of social support and self-determination: *Journal of Leisure Research, 25,* 111-128.

Davidson, M.J. & Cooper, C.L. (1987). Female managers in Britain: A comparative review. *Human Resource Management, 26,* 217-242.

Duncan, M., & Messner, M. (1998). The media image of sport and gender. *Media Sport, 1(1),* 21-35.

Dworkin, S.L. & Wachs, F.L. (2000). *The morality/manhood paradox: Masculinity, sport, and the media.* London: Kogan Page.

Hunsaker, Philip L., and Michael W. Coombs. (1988). Mergers and acquisitions: Managing the emotional issues. *Personnel. 6(1),* 56-63.

Kaila, H.L. (2002). Stress Is A Way of Life for Mumbai Workers. *Psychology International,* Vol. 13, No. 3, Fall 2002.

Kaila, H.L. (2004). Indian Women Managers: Their Stresses, Health and Coping Behaviour—A Survey in Mumbai. *Journal of Health Management,* Vol. 6, No. 2, 147-161.

Kaila, H.L. (2004a). *Women of Mumbai towards New Millennium.* Mumbai: Himalaya Publishing House.

Kaila, H.L. (2005). *Women, Work and Family.* New Delhi: Rawat Publications.

Kasper, K., Meyer, M. and Schmidt, A. (2005). Managers dealing with work-family-conflict: An explorative analysis. *Journal of Managerial Psychology. 20(5)*, 440-461.

Kirkcaldy, B.D. and Furnham, A.F. (1999). Stress coping styles among German Managers. *Journal of Workplace Learning. 11(1)*, 22-26.

Oakeley, A. (1974). *The Sociology of Housework*. New York: Pantheon.

Oi-ling, S., Luo, L. and Cary, C. (1999). Managerial Stress in Taiwan: A comparative study. *Journal of Managerial Psychology. 14 (1)*, 6-25.

Taap, A.M., Fontaine, R., Chong Siong Choy (2003). Occupational Stress among managers: A Malaysian Survey. *Journal of Managerial Psychology. 18 (6)*, 622-628.

6

Understanding the Real Story of Women's World: *An Indian Scene*

Nishi Tripathi

Introduction

Traditionally, the role played by an Indian woman has had very little scope outside the confines of the household into which she was born or wedded into. The average Indian household does not believe or rather support the education of its female progeny. Right from childhood, the woman is taught not more than necessary to ensure the smooth running of her future home. Her education, apart from the regular schooling, revolves around the arts and crafts—sewing, singing, painting, sketching etc. Anything beyond this, the women is considered forward and bold, implying unsuitable for the tamed and domesticated role of homemaker that she is expected to do. Surrounded by this apathy, she is closeted by the expectations and latent demands that society impinges on her. Buckled by such beliefs and values, is it really a wonder that the Indian woman has not scaled the professional ladder as compared to her counterparts? From the Vedic ages, although the education of woman was advocated, her role was constricted to the mundane domestic chores. In effect, her domain of power was within the four walls labelled "home". This gave root to myopia that a woman cannot survive the "harsh" realities of the workplace. That she would be cowed by the male populace who lord the fields and that she will not measure up to the task delegated. The constant reinforcement of this pessimistic incline, right from the family to friends to society at large has taken its toll. The net result has been the unwillingness of the woman to step out of the house as a wage earner.

Another argument that stands in the way of a working Indian woman is the fallacious assumption that children cannot be raised in the absence of a mother. In keeping with the general opinion of the male dominated society it is drummed into the psyche of a woman that it is HER responsibility to raise the children. One forgets that the word parenting as well as parent is not a reference to the mother alone, rather it encompasses any individual who can and will assume the responsibility for a child. Instead of encouraging the decision, the working woman is fed with guilt for having "neglected" her family for the "selfish" perusal of her career. What they fail to appreciate is her balancing both her home and her official capacities, without compromising either, i.e., she does not shirk from her domestic chores, she will still come home to cook dinner for her loved ones. Rather than applauding her persistence and grit, she is emotionally attacked for abandoning her family.

At the outset it does seem that the woman is driven by her male counterparts, but is that the true picture? The Indian woman is forsaken by her counterparts from other generations as well! Very few mothers in law would accede to their daughters in law's professional aspirations, either as an entrepreneur or as an entity in an organization. Even a co-home-maker would express shock and disbelief at such a bold decision. When women themselves succumb to the dictates imposed by the conveniently labelled "values", what hope can there be for her acceptance into the corporate environs? Indeed, it seems as through the crossing of the corporate threshold by a woman amounts to a second marriage with new responsibilities and tasks and is looked upon unfavourably by the rest of the ilk.

From an organizational point of view, women are liabilities as they are more likely to take an evening off to spend time with the family than stay in to work late. Their commitment to familial ties prevents their being accepted into the throes of corporate boardrooms. The fact that they might get in the family way also increases apprehensions about the long holidays this would entail. However, the recruiters fail to take into consideration that women are treasure loyalty and dedication than men due to their emotional maturity, thus more likely to stay in the organization. This spurious reasoning for not employing women heightens the prejudice against her attempt to eke out a living. Yet another pestilence that dogged a woman's career climb was the infamous "glass ceiling" policy. Although women were recruited their career climb was stunted after a certain point of time. Preference was given to male colleagues as the organization could not bear the stigma of having a woman at the top.

Thus, women face discouragement not only from the home front but in some ways from the corporate one too. Surrounded by such a defeatist attitude, not many women dare to explore the horizons beyond the view from their haven and shelter. They mentally resign themselves to the fate of a lifetime married to the domestic clutter that is typical to households.

A grim tale: Pathetic Reality

Applying World (untampered) Sex Ratio of 1022 (1022 women per 1000 men), there are 36 million missing women according to Amartya Sen. While all ages sex ratio is slightly lower at 933 in 2001 census as against 935 in 1981 census, juvenile sex ratio (0-6 age group) has declined astonishingly from 971 to 927 for all-India.

Do not kill me: *Mujhe jeene do*

A recent television advertisement has had a terrific impact and shaken people's conscience, making aspirant baby killers feel guilty of the crime they intend to commit. This is Behaviour Change Communication (BCC) and it has the potential to usher in a revolution, writes Surekha Sule. A pregnant woman's abdominal sonography is underway. The doctor is listening to the baby's sounds and the husband too is right there. The doctor is perturbed by the sounds he hears and makes the to-be father listen to them. A tender voice is making an appeal, "Papa main aapki beti, mujhe mat maro." (Papa, I am your daughter, don't kill me.) The father is shaken, undergoes a change of heart and cancels the original plan of abortion after the sex determination test.

This recent TV ad has had a terrific impact and shaken people's conscience, making aspirant baby killers feel guilty of the crime they intend to commit. This is Behaviour Change Communication (BCC) and it has the potential to usher in a revolution in the patriarchic son-centric psyche of Indian society.

The Pre-natal Diagnostic Techniques (Regulation and Prevention of Misuse) Act (PNDT Act), which was passed in 1994, and concerted efforts of the Health Ministry as well as various social organisations may have had limited success in curbing the practice of female foeticide. However, they have definitely succeeded in creating all-around awareness about this issue. And now the time is ripe to go beyond just this.

Sufferings of Women in India: An Observation of Societal Attitude

In the following section of the chapter the focus is to pay attention on a societal problem involving women's social condition.

The recent disgraceful molestation incident of two Non-Resident Indian (NRI) young women by the rowdy mob on New Year's Day outside the J.W. Marriot hotel at Juhu, Mumbai, has shocked the nation. The incident terrifies most of us because it shows the fragility of the protection that society confers on its more vulnerable sections. It is as if the traditional mechanisms that society invents to keep order were no longer effective. In fact, it was an illustration of a range of assaults on women that takes place everyday of the year and in every part of the country. Crimes against women don't always make news. They hit the headlines only when they are particularly horrific, or when they affect women like us (that is urban, middle class women) or when they are captured on visual media. It is to be admitted that whether in Mumbai, Delhi, Kolkata, Bangalore, Chennai or wherever, nothing can be more disquieting than women being harassed, assaulted or molested by lecherous men. The men who molested the two hapless women outside the Juhu hotel are out on bail and are probably bragging about their exploit to awe-struck friends. It is a matter of grave concern and disgrace that men should behave in such a despicable manner and go after soft targets. It reveals the indifference and moral callousness of society to dignity and human rights of women, girls, minorities, *adivasis* and the poor and leads to introspection and a reality check. From this incident, it is apparent that if our laws were tough enough, men would think twice before pouncing on women. In this wondrous land of ours, society neither shames nor shuns those who violate the dignity of women.

The molestation of women in public places is perhaps one of the most serious unnoticed crimes in urban India. Women are groped in buses, felt-up in crowed spots like railway platforms, followed on lonely streets. Molestation is criminalised not just because it bodily violates the integrity of a woman, but also it is an affront to her dignity. The physical scars may heal over the time, but the scars on the psyche and the trauma caused by the assault may well alter the personality of the woman. It puts a question mark on what has long been established: that the right to life under Article 21 is not a right to mere vegetative existence, but to a life with dignity and a decent standard of living. Generally speaking, the incident at Juhu has brought to the fore the issue of safety of women in cities in general and in Mumbai in particular. According to the latest crime statistics, pertaining to 2006, released by the Home Ministry's National Crime Records Bureau (NCRB), there were 36,500 molestation cases in India. The most worrisome fact the report reflects is that a woman is molested in India every 26 minutes, but the rate may be higher because many of cases are not reported. Even in 2007, 835 cases of molestation were registered in Delhi, up from 713 cases in 2006. Last year, the Mumbai Police registered 356 cases of molestation, that is almost one a day and the railway police have a record of 1068 cases, almost three a day. When it comes to conviction rates of crimes against women, Maharashtra's record is worse than almost all other States. In case of molestation, only 11.5 per cent out of every 100 offenders chargesheeted and convicted in Maharashtra against the all-India average of 30.7 per cent. The only States with a lower conviction rate for molestation are Jammu & Kashmir with 11.2 per cent, Gujarat with 6.9 per cent and Karnataka with 6.2 per cent. There have been also at least a dozen cases of molestation of foreign tourists in the first couple of weeks of 2008.

Causes of Molestation

Rapid Urbanisation: As per the estimate, over 305 million Indians live in over 5000 towns and cities spread across the length and breadth of the country. They comprise 50 per cent of the country's total population, in sharp contrast to only 60 million who lived in urban areas in 1947. In numerical terms, India's urban population is second largest in the world after China, and is higher than the total urban population of all countries put together barring China, USA, and Russia. According to the 2006 NCRB figures, in India there is a population of more than a million in 35 cities. These cities are a melting pot of people coming from different parts and strata of the country. Here there is a mixed society which is largely dictated by a feudal mind-set. Besides, many people have acquired sudden wealth due to the rise in land prices in cities. In the absence of domestic and community life, neither binding social values nor stringent laws are there to be obeyed by the people. The deracinated people's sense of right and wrong behaviour is not determined by social norms and they have no sense of belonging or relating to the new environment. The youths of this section of society, guided by old feudal ideas, lose their control and seek to pounce on any woman.

Loss of Values: The root cause for the increasing number of molestation cases across the country is an all-pervasive meltdown of conservative values and the degradation of morality among the individuals in society. These start in the family and educational system. In the families, boys are not taught to respect girls and women. Young boys are groomed to be macho men. Similarly, in our educational system, there is no proper curriculum to teach children about values and morality which was prevalent from generation to generation in the past. In addition to this, today the hold of religion and tradition on sexual mores is slowly weakening in most parts of the country. It can be said that not installing proper values among the youths may be one of the reasons for the alarming increase in molestation cases in India.

Exposure of Children to Media: Another cause for the rising molestation crime against women can be attributed to the direct exposure of our children to the mass media. The advertisements, violent movies, porn magazines, and the internet have made sex sensational and titillating. For example, when children watch lewd movies they start looking at women as objects of sexual pleasure. Then they begin to lose respect for women. Promoting a culture of momentary enjoyment unfortunately comes at the cost of other's suffering.

Commodification of Women: It is a matter of fact that the market economy and commodification of women by slick advertising adds another dimension to the plight of women in our patriarchal society. Most advertisements, whether on television or in the print media, draw attention to the products they promote by featuring beautiful women. Their presence are purely ornamental and passive and serves only to attract the attention of men. The process which has been called commodification tends to portray women as commodities, inanimate objects that, unlike living beings, don't have feelings and can be treated any way by the person owning them. What is more important is the triggering devise that activates the conscious and sub-conscious urges borne out of patriarchal mind-sets and advertisement-induced perceptions into acts of rape and molestation.

Non-adherence to Guidelines: The reason for the growing incidence of molestation, of particularly women tourists, is that they are not abiding by the guidelines. They ignore the rules and regulations of the visiting country. In many of the cases, the incident takes place when the person involved doesn't have the knowledge of the system. Some of the foreign tourists also show tendencies to stay back even after the expiry of their visa. Women travellers, especially when travelling alone, often get unwanted attention and have been sexually harassed and assaulted.

Measures to Prevent Molestation

These incidents have triggered a host of ideas on the measures to prevent such occurrences and to ensure the safety and security of women. Some of these are as follows:

Strengthening Molestation Law: Worried over the sexual assaults on women tourists, which have the potential to damage the tourism industry as well as the country's image, the Central Government should make plans to bring about changes in Section 354 of the Indian Penal Code (IPC) in order to make punishment for molestation more stringent, especially for habitual offenders. The present definition is sexual assault with the intent of outraging the modesty of women. Many legal experts say the problem with the definition is that proving the intent of the guilty in a court of law becomes extremely difficult. Because in many cases, the punishment is not more than a few months if the person is found guilty. Thus, our law needs to be given more teeth to come down heavily on people who commit such crimes against women.

Security at Tourist Spots: There have been growing incidents of sex-related crimes against women tourists including foreigners who are visiting different parts of the country. Against this backdrop, the Centre should decide to review the safety and security situation and arrangements for tourists taken by the States at tourist destinations. Realising the gravity of the situation, the Centre should urge all States to put in place the 'tourist police' and post a trained, dedicated and disciplined watchdog force comprising ex-servicemen as 'tourist wardens' or 'tourist buddies' at prominent tourist destinations in the country with special police powers for providing adequate protection to women visitors from harassment and molestation by unscrupulous elements that has assumed alarming proportions. Currently, only ten States have such a mechanism in place.

Installing Values: The best way to root out such deviant behaviour is to work on the minds of children when they are in their formative years. Right from when they are young, boys need to be told that girls have a mind and personality of their own and are as entitled to dignity and freedom of choice as they are. Children have to be educated about how touching of certain parts of their body is abuse. This kind of sensitisation to the boy child to the other sex is the best way to ensure a safe world for women. Thus, the process of gender sensitisation has to begin early.

Helpline in Police Stations: Expressing concern over increasing incidents of sexual assault on women, the States should speed up the setting up of helpline in police stations for counselling the victims to reach a compromise and provide them with immediate relief. Also, all States should establish a Crime Against Women (CAW) cell by their Police Departments on the lines of Delhi to deal with women related crimes like rape, dowry deaths, molestation and eves teasing. Further, more women cops should be inducted as molestation victims feel more secure in their presence and talk freely about their problems.

Adherence to Travel Advisories: Alarmed by frequent cases of sexual harassment of female foreign tourists in India, foreign missions should issue travel advisories for them from time to time. Women should be asked to instinctively and unquestionably avoid the badly lit streets even if it means taking a longer route to their destination. They should not dress up in provocative clothes in public. Women should be advised not to go out in the middle of crowds of men. They should be advised to observe and respect local dress and customs, taboos and the cultural norms of the visiting country. Women should avoid walking at night in deserted areas, including city streets, village lanes and beaches. Such advice could also be extended to Indian women travelling within the country. The States should try to educate the visitors on safe conducts while they are there.

Sensitisation Programme: The importance of looking at our cities through a gender lens is that the police need to be committed to make the cities safer for women. They should work to create safe space and environment for women and girl child in the cities through a change in mind-set by launching mass education and social awareness and sensitisation programmes for the police and amongst the general public to improve their response towards women. The people need to be sensitised about the need for a more respectful attitude towards women in public places as the happy experience of the tourist is intricately linked to the economic well-being of the state. This can be made possible and also effective by the cooperation of the community and society with their sharp vigil and strong support and by the exhibition of awareness movies in road shows. Such sensitisation must take place cutting across all classes. If the cities are safe for women, they will be safe for everyone.

Societal Objective of Law: The protection of society and deterring the criminal is the avowed object of law and these can be achieved by imposing appropriate sentence on the offender. The socio-economic status, religion, race, caste and creed of the accused or the victim should not be relevant considerations in passing the sentence. It is the duty of every court to award proper sentence having regard to the nature of the offence and the manner in which it is executed or committed. That is because public abhorrence of the crime must find reflection through imposition of appropriate sentence by the court. There is also a need to provide free legal service to victims who invariably cannot pay fees to the private lawyer.

Control Over Media: A civilised society needs to ensure that the beast in the man is kept in check and not enticed. The starting point could be to ensure that the electronic media/films are not allowed to show images of women which reduce them to mere sex objects. For this, the government needs to change and amend the Indecent Representation of Women (Prohibition) Act, 1986 to deal effectively with the growing menace new and more advanced technologies being used, especially in the new media, to depict women as sexual commodities. Besides, a far more effective way would be for women themselves not to associate with any activity which demeans not only them, but also their gender as a whole. In addition to this, women should be submissive and modest, dress and behave in a particular manner and avoid certain professions and places.

Make Law Stricter for the Culprit: The state should make legal provisions aiming at dealing with persons who wilfully target women and harass them at public places. According to the recommendations of the National Commission for Women (NCW) "whoever with a sexual purpose or with the intention to insult women, utters any word, makes any sound or gesture, or exhibits any object or a part of the body with a intention of intruding upon a woman's privacy should be made punishable with the imprisonment and fine. Further, anyone by means of telecommunications device or by any other electronic form creates or solicits any comment, request, proposal, image or other communication which are obscene, lewd, lascivious or indecent would be taken into jurisdiction." Also, those who are witness to such incidents whether in public places, offices or elsewhere and don't intervene to help the victim should be made a party to the offence and liable for prosecution.

Conclusion

The harassment of women tourists, be it domestic or foreign, is a national problem. The protection of them in public places is an issue that has many ramifications, including the future of India. The fact is we in India simply don't know how to treat our women as human beings who have a right to dignity and safety. We love and take pride in welcoming outsiders with the Sanskrit word "Atithi Devo Bhavah", but the many cases of crimes against foreign nationals hardly inspire the tourist. This could eventually hurt the prospects of the tourist industry in India. It is very well for us to gloat over our economy's growth rate and dream of achieving a superpower status of India. But economic progress minus a secure law and order environment is not going to take us far. An unsafe India will hurt us deeply in both the social and economic spheres. No project of modernisation can be possible when one half of the population is unsafe. Therefore, the issue warrants a more nuanced understanding of the aspects involved. It requires a collaborative rather than a confrontationist approach.

Sexual violence apart from being a dehumanising act is also an unlawful intrusion of the right to privacy and sanctity of a female. It is a serious blow to her supreme honour and offends her self-esteem and dignity. It degrades and humiliates the victim and leaves behind a traumatic experience. Therefore, the courts are expected to try and decide cases of sexual crime against women with utmost sensitivity, sternly and severely. The trend to impose inadequate sentence would do more harm to the justice system and undermine public confidence in the efficacy of law. Society cannot for long endure such serious mob-molestation as happened in Mumbai and Delhi on the eve of the New Year. Thus, the demand for more stringent laws, better policing, more effective courts, and greater vigilance becomes most essential in the circumstances.

Success Story of Indian Women: Contribution in Film-making

The Indian film-making industry has for a long time been a male dominated domain. The women have at best contributed in the industry by way of acting, script-writing or singing for films. But the last two to three decades have seen women working behind the cameras, directing and producing films. And what is more several of them have won laurels for their films at national film festivals in India as well as at international film festivals abroad.

Aparna Sen is one such internationally acclaimed film director. She made her debut in films in 1961 in Satyajit Ray's film *Two Daughters.* Since then she has acted in several films made by noted film directors, such as Mrinal Sen, James Ivory and Satyajit Ray himself. Aparna's first directorial venture was *36 Chowringhee Lane* in 1981. It won the Grand Prix at the Manila International Film Festival in 1982 and the National Award for Best Direction and Best Cinematography in India.

Sai Paranjpe, the eminent film-maker is also a writer and a Marathi playwright. Her films, *Sparsh, Chudian* and *Papiha* won wide popularity for production and story presentation. She has also made two films for children: *Jadu ka Shankh* and *Sikander.* They were shown at the 10th International Children Film Festival held in Hyderabad in 1997. Her first film *Sparsh* won top awards in India, thus establishing her as a film-maker with a sparkling sense of humour and an original bent of mind. Since then she has directed over half a dozen films and each has broken new grounds. Sai's Marathi play *Jaswani* has been translated into several Indian languages.

Mira Nair made several movies, including *Salaam Bombay,* and *And My Own Country,* among others. All her films received wide acclaim. As a film producer, Mira Nair came into limelight with her debut film *Salaam Bombay,* based on the life of the Mumbai street children. This film was shown in the recent international film festival of India. She was highly acclaimed for it and honoured at several film festivals for its superb presentation of a common theme. Inspired by her celluloid success, she launched her second film *Kama Sutra* based on the great Indian ascetic sage Vatsayayan's treatise *Kama Sutra.* A large number of women saw and praised this film, in spite of the social and family taboos.

Another film-maker Deepa Mehta has always been in the limelight because of the controversies her films generate. Her films *Fire, Earth 1947* and latest project *Water,* provoked a tremendous debate. Water was sought to be based on the sad plight of the widows living on the banks of the river Ganges in Varanasi. The film's shooting had to be given up because of vehement opposition from some religious groups. But Deepa is determined to make this movie soon. She began her career as a scriptwriter for children's films. Some of her films won awards at the Columbia International Film Festival. And she won generous praise for the film *Fire,* which depicts a lesbian relationship between two sisters-in-law in a middle class Indian home.

Prema Karanth is another well-known director who has consistently used cinema to explore the female psyche. Though she would not like to call herself a feminist, her films have always focused on the psychological problems that a woman faces in a man's world. Her film *Phaniyamma,* based on M.K. Indira's novel by the same name, won a national award for its sensitive documentation of a simple and straightforward woman's struggle in a male-dominated society. Her film *Bandh Jharoke* highlights an essential truth. The central theme of the film is that a woman is much more than a mother, a daughter, a sister, and a wife. She is an individual in her own right and there exists a life beyond traditional role-playing.

Pamela Rooks is yet another film-maker who got name and fame through her film *Miss Betty's Children*. This film got her recognition at the international level. The idea for *Miss Betty's Children* came from her own novel.

Noted producer-director Mahesh Bhatt's daughter, Pooja Bhatt got the Nargis Dutt award for her latest film *Zakhm,* dealing with social and religious strife, communal tensions, violence and disharmony in contemporary times. The film has a message of love and peace conveyed in a sensitive way. Pooja began her production career with *Tamanna* three years ago, and this has become her first love. *Tamanna* is Pooja's first feature film and it tells the story of an unfortunate girl born of an illicit relationship between a man and a woman. The woman is afraid of social stigma and throws her newly born baby girl into a garbage bin. The character of the girl is played by Pooja herself. The girl is nurtured by a eunuch.

Sehjo Singh is a documentary film-maker who became famous through her various films. She has been awarded the Silver Lotus at the National Film Festival on three separate occasions. An independent film-maker, Sehjo is also a member of the jury for the national awards (non-feature films) in India. She has been a member of an international jury in Switzerland. She has made many movies on social issues such as *The Women Betrayed, Who is Afraid of Little Child?, Dreams of Ghasi Bai,* and *KoI Tales,* among others.

Sumitra Bhave is a social scientist-turned-film-maker. Her film *Doghi* won the National Award for the best film on social issues in 1996. Her film *Chakori* got 11 State and three national awards. She has also made films like *Bai, Pani Mukti, Samvad, Sahyog, Chakori, Sarshi* and *Lahoo.* Both *Pani* and *Bai* have received national awards. Her films have been screened abroad at many festivals.

Basically a doctor by profession, Dr. Santhawana Bardoloi has made several films on women's issues. Her film *Adajya* was appreciated at the 29th international film festival in Delhi and received the Silver Peacock award.

Mitra Sen is yet another women film-maker who has won numerous awards for her documentary entitled *Bridging the Gap* including the Best Documentary at the Montreal student film festival. Mitra began her career in the Canadian film industry. Her latest film for children *Just A Little Red Dot* is an inspiring story based on a true incident that occurred in a Scarborough School in May 1994. From a precious gift of Red dots unfolded a unique sequence of events that created an invaluable learning opportunity for the students. The film was appreciated at the children's film festival held in Hyderabad.

Keeping in line with the information revolution many women have been opting for courses in film-making, script-writing and other aspects of direction and production. An important thing to be noted is that most of the films and documentaries being made by Indian women film-makers are on socially relevant themes which strike an instant chord with the audience. All in all, Indian women film-makers are doing their best to show their talent and ability to entertain and educate the masses.

Conclusion

Behaviour Change Communication (BCC) techniques are extensively used in HIV/AIDS campaigns worldover. BCC uses a combination of techniques, designed to encourage and facilitate a voluntary adaptation of the behaviour that is being promoted. It includes market and social research, advocacy, social marketing communication, monitoring and evaluation. Mass media, community outreach and interpersonal communication are integral components of strategic planning for BCC. During market and social research, the psychographics of the target are studied to identify the necessary triggers that stimulate behaviour change. The research begins with the individual, advances into the community and investigates societal factors such as demographics of the target population, economic and other factors that shape a society's basic values. It also explores the benefits of preventive measures and credibility and accessibility of potential sources of prevention messages. From the information collected, the target is encouraged to adopt the behaviour being promoted.

7

Developmental Analysis of Deprivational Experiences in Rural and Urban Kumauni Women

Aradhana Shukla and *Ruchi Kakkar*

Deprivation is defined as lack or insufficiency of basic needs, which can be emerged in infancy and continues along time or ceased when a person finds himself/herself gratified. Truly speaking, it regards the behaviour and this fact is established widely by Indian (Agrawal, 1996; Bora, 1998; Pandey, 2001; Shukla, 2003) as well as from western front (Bronfrenbrennr, 1974; Weight *et al.*, 1978).

In this context, it can also be said that when a person is surrounded by experiential enrichment and the level of experiential deprivation is very low he can think about his self-esteem and enhance his personal identity. Contrary to it when a person cannot avail minimum requirements to meet the life demands how can he think about his self-esteem? In addition, gender issue is also very important in this regard. Moreover, women in our society are still treated as second grade nationals. So, they cannot think about their self-esteem. In this study, an attempt has been made to find out the pattern of experimental deprivation and self-esteem in rural and urban Kumauni women in development perspective.

The self is not an innate identity because man is not born with sense of self. It develops gradually in lifetime when he recognizes his body parts, names, and feelings, *i.e.*, the self-structure, which provides him a sense of self-identity. This takes him to the things outside of him and self-identity that provides the individual a sense of adjustment and sets some goals in terms of extent of his awareness. It is our awareness of the self that makes existence meaningful, providing continuity between past, present and future, lastly, it is after the development of the sense of self-identity that the man evaluates himself in the positive or negative terms. (Srivastava, 1996; Pandey, 2002).

Thus, Self plays a part in development is explicated more fully in recent approaches to this issue. Theodore Sarbin (1986) proposed that mechanism as a root metaphor in psychology be replaced by narrative. Sarbin draws on both literary and psychological material to demonstrate the fundamental role of narrative in our making sense of the world, especially when this activity is sensitive to context. And as Kenneth and Mary Gargen propose, it is regarding the construction of self in a social context that the use of narrative has much to offer (Gargen & Gargen, 1988). Here, stories seem to enable others to share one's point of view. A recent writer in this field states, "when we understand someone, we understand his or her stories" (Keen, 1986).

The sense of self that follows from this is simply a reflection of one's own theories about others. However, rather than attempting to predict one's behaviour. One's attempts to create information about oneself that will fulfil one's self-theory. In discovering a match between self-theory and information about one-self, one gains self-esteem. The notion of self as autonomous creator of theories that predict other's behaviour and make sense of one's own identity would seem to be a pure example of a paradigmatic understanding of identity. Thus, despite the constructivist assumptions of implicit personality theory, the process it posits as the logic of identity formation are unsympathetic to the narrative mode in practice.

The objectives and hypotheses of the study were as follows:

(1) The first objective of the study was to find out the impact of chronological age on self-esteem and

experimental deprivation of Kumauni women. It was hypothesized that increase in age would accentuate self-esteem and experiential deprivation. In this study, it was aimed to ascertain the pattern of self-structure of Kumauni women. Does it not change with due course of time or its structure develops to with incearse image? On the basis of these notions this study was planned in developmental perspective.

(2) The second objective of the study was to find out the impact of residential setting of the self-esteem and experiential deprivation among Kumauni women. It was hypothesized that urban women was high in self-esteem and low in deprivation as compared to their rural counterparts

(3) The third objective of the study was to find out the relationship between experiential deprivation and self-esteem. It was hypothesized that increase in deprivation would lower the self-esteem.

Method

In order to find out the pattern of experiential deprivation and self-esteem in Kumauni women this study was planned in the frame of 2×2 factorial design. Developmental pattern and residential setting were the independent variables and experiential deprivation and self-esteem were self-used as dependent variables.

Sample

The sample was consisted of one hundred Kumauni women in the age range of 19-45 years. They hailed from the urban and rural segments of Almora. They were arranged according to the requirement of 2×2 between model factorial design with 2 levels of age (19-25 and 35-45 years) and two levels of residential setting (Urban and Rural) The schematic presentation of experimental design is given in Table 7.1.

Table 7.1: Schematic presentation of experimental design

A			
A1		A2	
B		B	
B1	B2	B1	B2
25	25	25	25

Legends:
A—Chronological age
A1—15-25 Years
A2—35-45 Years
B—Residential Setting
B1—Urban
B2—Rural.

Measures

The measures used here are as follows:

The Experiential Deprivation Scale

The scale (Shukla, 1995) of experiential deprivation is a revised version of Shukla (1982). This scale consisted of 49 five-point items and deals with four major domains of life where deprivation can be manifested or at least fell. They are, housing condition and home environment, parental and peer group relation, motivation, emotional and scholastic experiences. Low score indicates low level of experiential deprivation and high score *vice versa.* The split of all reliability of this scale +0.70 and test retest reliability is +0.82. This measure is successfully used in other studies of cognitive and personality development. (Arya, 1999).

Measure of self-esteem

The self-image scale prepared by Shukla and Mishra (1993) was used and it was aimed to measure self-image and self-identity. In this measure there are 40 items in Yes - No form, *i.e.* 20 for self-image and 20 for self-identity. One score was given for yes and two score was given for no answer in some items. Item 2, 5, 6, 8 and 9 for self-image and item 1, 2, 3, 4, 10, 13, 14, 17, 18 and 19 for self-identity. High score is the indicator of low self-image and low score *vice versa.*

Procedure

At first, the investigator contacted the Kumauni women hailing from Almora-urban and Almora-rural and established rapport properly. Then experiential deprivation scale was administered on them followed by an informal observation of their homes. After this, the self-concept scale was administered on them. Data collection was made individually. Best attempts were made to avoid external distractions.

Results

Obtained data was analyzed by 2 way analysis of variance and interpreted in terms of chronological age and residential setting as effectors of experiential deprivation and self-esteem. Separate analysis was made for experiential deprivation and self-esteem. Moreover, co-relation coefficients were also computed between experiential deprivation and self-esteem scores. Thus, analysis was made in three subsequent sections and it will be reported likewise.

(I) Impact of Chronological Age and Residential Setting on Experiential Deprivation

Summary of analysis of variance showing the effect of chronological age residential setting on experiential deprivation is reported in Table 7.2.

Table 7.2: Summary table showing the effect of chronological age and residential setting on experimential deprivation

Sources of variation	*Ss*	*df*	*ms*	*f*
A (Chrcnological age)	4.48	1	4.48	4.19*
B (Residential Setting)	10.40	1	10.40	9.72**
AB	11.44	1		10.69**
Error (Between)	102.72	96	1.07	
		99		

* P < .05

** P < .01

It is apparent that the main effect of chronological age was significantly (F1, 96 = 4.19 P < .05) showing the fact that young ladies were less deprived (× 126.04) rather than old ladies (×=135.38). The next main effect of residential setting was insignificant (F1, 96 = 9.72 P < .05) and it revealed that though the rural population was higher in experiential deprivation (× = 118.38) than their urban counterparts (× = 143.0) yet the magnitude was not able to yield its significance. The 2-way interaction of chronological age and residential setting was significant (F1, 96 = 10.69 P < .01) and it is reported in Fig. 7.1. Fig. 7.1 revealed that a sharp and fine interaction was shared by these variables.

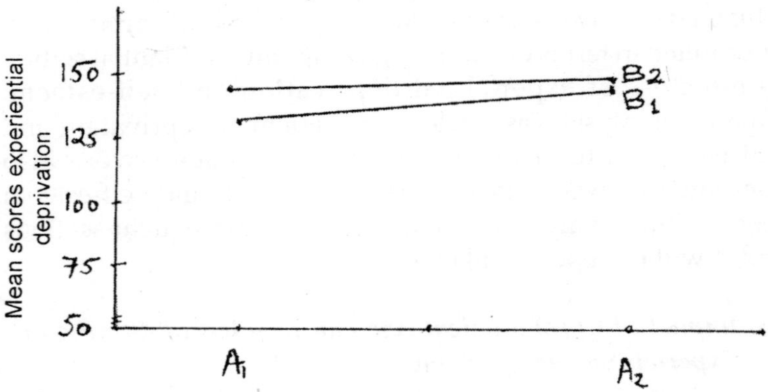

Fig. 7.1: Effect of chronological age and residential settings on experiential deprivation

Legends:

A—Chronological age	B—Residential Setting
A1—15-25 Years	B1—Urban
A2—35-45 Years	B2—Rural.

(II) Impact of Chronological Age and Residential Setting on Self-Esteem

As earlier findings of this sub-section were also analyzed by 2-way analysis of variance and summary table which shows impact of chronological and residential setting on self-esteem (Table 7.3).

Table 7.3: Summary table showing the effect of chronological age and residential setting on self-esteem

Sources of variation	*Ss*	*df*	*ms*	*f*
A (Chronological age)	16.78	1	16.78	8.79**
B (Residential Setting)	23.14	1	23.14	2.21^{NS}
AB	25.09	1	25.09	13.14**
Error (Between)	183.36	96	1.91	
		99		

** P < .01
NS—Non-significant.

Table 7.3 clearly reveals that the main effect of chronological age was significant (F1 <99=8.79<0.05) and it indicated that self-esteem in young ones was relatively less than old ones. Also, the main effect of residential setting was significant (F1, 96=12.12P<0.01) and it showed that rural Ss were less in self-esteem (×=71.62) than urban Ss (×=53.52) .The chronological age × residential setting was further significant (F1, 96=13.14 P<0.01) and it is presented in Fig. 7.2. Fig. 7.2 presents a fine interaction between age and residential setting in relation to self-esteem.

(III) Relation Between Experiential Deprivation and Self-Esteem

The third part of the result was related with the relationship of deprivation domain with self-esteem. For this purpose correlation coefficient were computed and they are presented in Table 7.4.

Table 7.4: Relationship of Deprivational Domains with Self-esteem

Deprivational Domain	*A*		*B*	
	A1	*A2*	*B1*	*B2*
Housing condition and Home environment	-.42	-.54	-.38	-.62
Parental and peer group relations	-.59	-.52	-.39	-.32
Motivational emotional and Socio-cultural experience scholastic experience	-.53	-.49	-.56	-.64

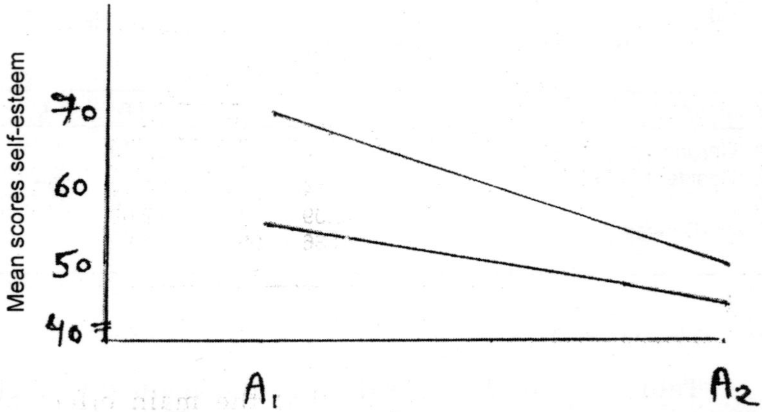

Fig. 7.2: Effect of chronological age and residential setting on self-esteem.

Legends:

A—Chronological age	B—Residential Setting
A1—15-25 Years	B1—Urban
A2—35-45 Years	B2—Rural

Table 7.4 shows that a common trend was visited everywhere. It was the fact that increase in deprivational score retarded self-esteem. Findings, in sum, are as follows:

1. Rural Ss were relatively higher in experiential deprivation than urban Ss.
2. The magnitude of self-esteem was relatively higher in low deprived Ss.
3. A fine interaction was noticed when data were manipulated for residential setting and chronological age for experiential deprivation and self-esteem respectively.
4. Significant negative correlation were found for experiential deprivation retards self-esteem.

Discussion

Obtained findings were analyzed by 2-way analysis of variance and correlation coefficients and interpreted in terms of experiential deprivation and self-esteem as effected by chronological age and residential setting. Prior to start this investigation, some hypotheses were formulated which were accompanied by pertinent objectives. A theoretical base will be given to their findings based on these hypotheses.

(I) Increase in age would accentuate self-esteem and experimental deprivation

Our first hypothesis was related with development of self-esteem and experimental deprivation. It was found that our hypothesis was confirmed stating the notion that older Ss were higher in self-esteem and experimental deprivation. Our first step to be discussed is the development pattern of experimental deprivation. Several researches (Sinha, 1976; Tripathi, 1980; Shukla, 1982) have pointed out that deprivation accentuates with age. With increase in age, a person accumulates more experiences. They may be pleasant or painful. In the case of painful experiences, it can be said that it is very difficult to forget these experiences. In addition, it is the tendency of some persons that they cannot be satisfied in any situation. They always feel themselves as lagged or deprived. This tendency increases with age. Moreover, with increase in age a person becomes more matured and meets with external surrounding. At the time, he/she starts to compare himself/herself with the other members who were enriched in their life conditions and feeling of deprivation emerges in him/her. It is the fact that our subjects were hailed from Almora city and remote areas so, it is very natural that rural and other could develop a feeling of deprivation themselves.

The next point of discussion was based on the developmental structure of self-esteem. It was hypothesized that with increase in age Ss would be higher in self-esteem. Our findings confirmed our assumption and it was resulted that other. Ss were higher in self-esteem than younger Ss. In a common parlance self-esteem is the capability of a person to know about himself, his good characteristics, show it according to the demand of time and procure it. It is a motivational force which appears in a person when he/she finds himself/herself gratified with psychological needs and needs for shelter and love and belonging. To fulfil these needs, a person cannot think about self-esteem. Moreover, it can also be said that till the time person has developed himself/herself in such a way that he/she needs self-identity and self-esteem to organize, develop and cultivate their traits. It was found that the pattern of self-esteem was not so high as it should be. It may be due to the fact that we selected only female Ss for study. Still in our society women are treated as second grade nationals. They are committed to believe that they should live in control of father, brother, husband and sons. Therefore, they cannot search there identity. As it is true that feelings of self-respect, higher education, job and marriage on ground, on the basis which a women can develop her self-esteem and it does not hyphen in young age. Therefore, we can say that our young Ss were rather low in their self-esteem as compared to their old counterparts.

(II) *Urban Ss would be low in experiential deprivation in self-esteem*

Our second hypotheses was related with the impact of residential setting of experiential deprivation and self-esteem. It was assumed that rural Ss would be low in self-esteem and higher in experiential deprivation. Our findings confirmed the hypothesis.

It is true that environmental impoverishment causes the behaviour detrimentally and blackens the competence. Our rural Ss were hailed from the interiors of Almora where nobody can think modern civilization. As a result, feeling of deprivation is an ever persisting phenomenon for them. Further, it can also be said that these rural people are full of behavioural blockage and inferiority that develops a feeling of deprivation in them. Moreover, our rural Ss were females and they are earning members by grass cutting, weaving etc. They are uneducated so they cannot think apart to uplift their career. So they are considered as highly deprived than their urban counterparts who possess all amenities and luxuries around them. Ou. findings are in close consonance with Shukla and Najhoon (1992). Shukla and Karnataka (1995) have mentioned that increase in environmental impoverishment causes deprivation.

In such condition when a female is highly deprived of experiences and she does not think apart to meet with her everyday demands how she can think about self-enhancement. The traditional system of women torture have blocked her self-esteem identity so she is rather deprived. Self-esteem was found higher in urban ladies who have been satisfied by physical, social and affectional needs. They are educated and they are in high class jobs. So they are less deprived and they cannot tolerate to be labelled by the society. On the basis of these findings, it can be said that deprivational experiences were more pronounced in old and rural ladies while self-esteem was quite higher in old and urban females.

Remedy of Experiential Deprivation : How can the level of deprivation be minimized?

It is established that deprivation is felt factor, which can be reduced when concerned needs are fulfilled. Some components of experiential deprivation can be reduced in proper way. So, some intervention strategies can be employed to raise the socio-cognitive state of mind. They are as follows:

1. Every society has its own values, thinking and living norms and values in which its children are reared and developed. They have potential values for their society and culture. If they are transferred to other socio-cultural set-up, they can loose their self-confidence and develop a feeling of inferiority and in spite of the available facilities development they may deteriorate. So, community based programmes can be launched and attempts should be done to develop them in their own environment.
2. **Providing Supportive Family and Scholastic Environment:** The deprived people generate environment either familial or scholastic. In this regard parents should be trained properly so that they could provide proper training to their children. In addition, there is a need to make an improvement in scholastic

environment. The most important thing is that the teachers should treat all students equally and their concern should be based on the academic talent of students in spite of their socio-economic status.

3. **Need of Tangible Rewards:** It has been mentioned in several studies (Shukla, 1995; Bora, 1998) that variation in reward condition causes variation in behaviour. While no reward condition can make any significant change in performance tangible reward facilitates it. If in impoverished environment deprived children are tangibly rewarded, it is very sure that they will reduce their deprivational standard and want to learn more.
4. **Improvement in Linguistic Skills:** In impoverished environment people mostly concentrate on verb-related and restricted code (Bernstein, 1959, 1970) because they cannot concentrate on symbolic thought. In addition people in too highly deprived class use absurd language in common parlance so there is a need to improve their linguistic network and modify their cognitive structure.
5. **Compulsory Education:** "Education for all" is needed to raise the mental faculty of underprivileged society so that a commonly approved intellectual climate is managed. It can be said that by implementing these suggestions, magnitude of deprivation can be reduced. But internal satisfaction, self-awareness, knowledge about own limits, will to win and realistic attitudes are the important factors through which deprivation can be reduced or at least minimized in addition, spiritual exercise is also warranted to minimize deprivational experiences.

REFERENCES

Agarwal, N. (1996). Causal Attribution in young children: A test of Weiner's model. *Unpublished Ph.D. Thesis,* Kumaun University, Nainital.

Arya, M. (1999). A study of grade and sex in Kumauni students as effector of approval motivation and mastery motivation. *Unpublished Master's thesis*. Deptt. of Psychology. Kumaun University, Nainital.

Bernstein, B. (1959). A public language: Some sociological implications of a linguistic form. *British Journal of Sociology. 10*, 311-27.

Bernstein, B. (1970). Socio-linguistic approach to socialization with some references to educability. In F.W. Williams (ed.) *Language and Poverty: Perception on the theme*. Chicago Markham.

Bora, D.S. (1998). Developmental Impact of the degree of experiential deprivation and of Reward in cognitive Processes of children, *Unpublished Ph.D. thesis*, Kumaun University, Nainital.

Bronfenbrenner, V. (1974). Environmental and Human Ecology: A Reorientation to theory and Research on Socialization. Invited address. *American Psychological Association*, New Orleans (a).

Gergen, K.J. & M.M. Gergen (1988). Narrative and Self as Relationship: in L. Berkowitz (ed.), *Advances in Experimental Social Psychology*. New York: Academic Press.

Harre, R.D. (1985). *Motives and Mechanisms: An introduction to the Psychology of Action*. London: Methuen.

Keen, E. (1986). Paranoia and Cataclysmic Narratives: in T.R. Sarbin (ed.). *Narrative Psychology : The Storied Nature of Human Conduct*. New York:

Misra, G. & Tripathi, L.B. (1980). *Psychological consequences of prolonged deprivation*. Agra National.

Pandey, S. (2001). Metacognition and Achievement motivation in tribal and non-tribal male and female students. *Unpublilished Ph.D. thesis* Kumaun University, Nainital.

Sarbin, T.R. (1986). Narratology as a Root Metaphor in Psychology, in T.R. Sarbin (ed.), *Narrative Psychology: The Storied Nature of Human Conduct*, New York: Prager.

Shukla, A. (1982). Development of representational competence in children. *Unpublished Ph.D. thesis*. Deptt. of Psychology, Gorakhpur University, Gorakhpur published by National Psychological Corporation, Agra in 1988.

Shukla, A. (1982). Experiential deprivation scale. *Unpublished script*, Deptt. of Psychology, Gorakhpur University.

Shukla, A. & Najhoon S.K. (1992). Environmental deprivation and development of mastery motivation in children *Paper presented in P.P.N. College, Kanpur at the 1st Biennial Conference of Community Psychology*.

Shukla, A. & Mishra, S. (1993). The self-image scale. *Unpublished script*, Deptt. of Psychology, Kumaun University, Nainital.

Shukla, A. & Najhoon, S.K. (1995). Effects of scholastic variation and metocognitive competence on the concept of speed in children, *Psycholingua*, 17-20.

Shukla, A. (1995). Impact of Environmental Deprivation and Motivation feedback on some behavioural process: developmental study, *Paper presented at the 1st Biennial Conference of PLAI, Ferozabad.*

Shukla, A. & Karnataka, S. (1995). Impact of grade on academic motivation and academic stress: A study of rejected children, *Paper presented at PLAI, Ferozabad.*

Shukla, A. (2003). About experiential deprivation. *Indian Journal of Psychological Issues, 11, 2,* 93-100.

Srivastava, P. (1996). Developmental impact of Experiential Deprivation and Perceived parental attitude of subjects on their Cognitive, Motivational and Personality functioning. *Unpublished Ph.D. thesis,* Deptt. of Psychology, Kumaun University, Nainital.

Sinha, D. (1976). Social disadvantage and development of certain perception skills. Paper presented at IPA International Seminar on Psychology of cognition held at Delhi University, and in *Asian Journal of Psychology,* 1977, *52,* 115-132.

Weight, D.W., Golringer, M.F. & Kneene, JK.SA. (1978). Cultural Deprivation, Operational Deprivation in terms of Language Development. *American Journal of Orthopsychiatry,* 72-86.

Wenger, D.M. & R.R. Vallacher (1981). *Implicit Psychology*: Oxford: Oxford University Press.

8

Psychosocial Determinants of Health of Women in India

Anubhuti Dubey

> *"Women's health is a mixture of physical, emotional, social, cultural and spiritual well-being"*
>
> **—Paquette and Raine (2004)**

The last two decades have been marked by a rapid growth in the women's health movement around the world. India is one of the few countries in the world where women and men have nearly the same life expectancy at birth but Indian women have high mortality rates, particularly during childhood and in their reproductive years. The general health of women is determined by cultural, socio-political and economic factors as well as the biological factors and both sets are equally important in determining the health status of women. The health of Indian women is intrinsically linked to their status in society and is controlled and governed by various social norms and practices. There is a wide variation in cultures, religions, and levels of development amongst the 27 states and 7 union territories of India. It is not surprising that women's health also varies greatly from state to state. Women are a heterogeneous group whose experiences may vary with ethnicity and race, marital status, parental status, education, income, occupation, sexual orientation, labour force participation, and geographic location (e.g., rural *vs.* urban). Therefore, health needs (e.g., services and education), barriers to obtaining services, styles of coping, or bases for well-being may vary among cultural and socio-economic groups. In India, there are systematic problems with women's health. Women in low income and developing countries have shorter life expectancies due to inequality in access and quality of health services (World Health Organization, 2002; Tinker, 2000). Women's health is a very complex issue and determined by a host of social and economic factors besides the biological influences. Women's health status is related to the level of female education, the status of women in society, equal access to income activities or credit, and control over these resources.

Health of women is a serious issue, which is influenced by a host of socio-cultural and economic issues. Women in India face much serious health concerns. As a result of decreases in maternal mortality and infectious diseases, women's life expectancy has increased rapidly; however, there are a large number of chronic conditions that negatively affect the quality of life of women today: urinary tract infection, menstrual cycle disorders, hypertension, diabetes, osteoporosis, arthritis, eating disorders, substance abuse, and mental depression. The importance of good health and education to a woman's well-being—and that of her family and society—cannot be overstated. Without reproductive health and freedom, women cannot fully exercise their fundamental human rights, such as those relating to education and employment. Yet around the world, the right to health, and especially reproductive and sexual health, is far from a reality for many women. According to the World Bank, a full one-third of the illness among women ages 15-44 in developing countries is related to pregnancy, childbirth, abortion, reproductive tract infections, and human immuno-deficiency virus and acquired immune deficiency syndrome (HIV/AIDS).

This particular piece of work focuses on some key issues and tries to understand the psychocultural determinants in these health problems besides the physiological one: Reproductive Health and reproductive self-determination, Nutritional Status, Unequal treatment of Boys and Girls, HIV/AIDS.

Reproductive health and reproductive self-determination

Reproductive health is determined not only by the quality and availability of health care, but also by socio-economic development levels, lifestyles and women's position in society. In fact, the International Federation of Gynecology and Obstetrics asserts that improvements in women's health require state action to correct injustices to women. In World Report on Women's Health (1994), the Federation states that women's health is often compromised not by lack of medical knowledge, but by infringements on women's human rights. An estimated 1,600 women die everyday from complications caused by pregnancy and childbirth, 99 per cent in developing countries. About 70,000 women die every year from unsafe abortions, and many more infections and other consequences. Cancer of cervix, the most common form of cancer, linked to multiple births and sexually transmitted human papilloma virus in Indian region. The socio-cultural beliefs see reproduction as wholly the responsibility of women. She bears the responsibility of pregnancy, childbirth, contraception, family planning, infertility investigations, and sometimes undiagnosed sexually transmitted diseases, as lethal as AIDS. Indian society does not understand that reproduction and reproductive health is a dual commitment. The early marriage of girls is a religious and social imperative. To improve the reproductive health status of the women, it is very much essential to target the menfolk in reproductive health intervention programmes.

Reproductive health significantly influences the overall health of the individual and of the society. From the economic point of view also much attention had been paid on reproductive health. The ability of all people, especially women, to achieve reproductive health is an integral part of their reproductive rights. In 1994, at the International Conference on Population and Development (ICPD) in Cairo, 165 nations endorsed the following definition of reproductive health: *Reproductive health is a state of complete physical, mental and social well-being and not merely the absence of disease or infirmity, in all matters relating to the reproductive system and to its functions and processes.* Reproductive health therefore implies that people are able to have a satisfying and safe sex life and that they have the capability to reproduce and the freedom to decide if, when and how often to do so. Implicit in this last condition is the right of men and women to be informed and to have access to safe, effective, affordable and acceptable methods of family planning of their choice, as well as, other methods of their choice for regulation of fertility which are not against the law, and the right of access to appropriate health-care services that will enable women to go safely through pregnancy and childbirth and provide couples with the best chance of having a healthy infant. It implies further that people are able to regulate their fertility without risk of their health and they are safe in having sex (Mishra, 2006). Women's reproductive health has created controversies in many traditional juridical systems because of its relation to human sexuality and morals (Cook, 1993). Reproductive health rather than a biological process is deeply influenced by economic and cultural conditions and that affect people at more than one level (Parasher, 2005). Being married or being mother is important defining identities of women in Indian culture. Therefore, it is difficult to visualize how women in this cultural and social context will adapt risk reducing and health seeking behaviours as part of their life (Chatterjee and Hosain, 2006). India has a high maternal mortality ratio. The high levels of maternal mortality are especially distressing because the majority of these deaths could be prevented if women had adequate health services (either proper prenatal care or referral to appropriate health care facilities) (Jejeebhoy and Rao, 1995). The causes of maternal mortality often have their roots in the poor nutrition or inadequate health care provided to the woman long before the 1st pregnancy. Early and frequent pregnancies and heavy physical labour are among the many factors that contribute to maternal death. To combat the traditional negligence, a new viewpoint is emerging which views women's reproductive health as a condition in which childbearing occurs in a state of physical, mental, and social well-being. It implies that women have the capacity to reproduce, regulate their fertility, and enjoy sexual relations. However, when it comes to reality it was found that both in India and Pakistan; women knew about male condoms but few had used them; their overall feeling was that partner cooperation was simply not feasible (*Progress in Reproductive Health Research*, 1997).

Violence and Reproductive Health: Violence not only causes physical injury, it also undermines the social, economic, psychological, spiritual and emotional well-being of the victim, the perpetrator and the society as a whole is so deeply embedded in tradition that millions of women consider violence as destined in their life. Domestic violence is a major contributor to the ill-health of women. It has serious consequences on women's mental and physical health, including their reproductive and sexual health. Around the world, gender-based violence is a profound human rights abuse and health problem for women. Gender violence can occur throughout a woman's lifecycle. Gender violence touches all social classes and types of people in almost every country of the world. Gender-based violence include sex-selective abortion, battering during pregnancy, coerced pregnancy through rape, female infanticide, differential food and medical care for girls, child marriage, genital mutilation, child prostitution, dating and courtship violence, psychological abuse, marital rape, sexual harassment, trafficking in women, dowry abuse and murder, and abuse of elderly women, pornography, population control, war and state violence, exploitation of refugees, political violence, and reduction in state services which increases the stress and workload for women etc. Much of the violence against women occurs in the context of sexuality and reproduction. The health consequences of violence often occur in the context of reproductive health and seriously contribute to the burden of disease in women and young people (Dr. Hiroshi Nakajima, Director General of the World Health Organization).

At first, many forms of verbal and psychological abuse seem harmless, but gradually and subtly they expand and grow in a menace over a period of time. With the passage of time, the victims adapt to abusive behaviour, the verbal or psychological tactics can gain strong 'foothold' in victims' mind, making it difficult for them to recognize the severity of the abuse over time (Fact sheet, 2005). The physical health consequences of domestic violence are obscure, indirect and emerge over the long-term. WHO (2001) report refuted the fact that women who subjected to violent attacks during childhood were bothered by menstrual problems and irritable bowel syndrome in later life. The physical and mental health outcomes have social and emotional squeals for the individual, the family, the community and the society at large. Women's physical injuries, psychological trauma and mental troubles disrupt their educational and career paths leading to poverty and economic dependence. Family life also shattered which have significant impact on children, including poverty (if divorce or separation occurs) and a loss of faith and trust in the institution of the family. These squeals not only affect the quality of life of individuals and communities, but also have long-term effects on social order and cohesion (WHO, 2001).

There is enough evidence to support that higher reproductive morbidity is seen among women experiencing domestic violence. Stephenson, Koening, and Ahmed (2006) conducted a study in North India have shown elevated odds ratio of gynecological symptoms, while comparing women with husbands reporting no domestic violence and women who experienced physical and sexual violence. It may be attributed to the fact that abusive men were more likely to engage in extra marital sex and acquire STDs, thereby placing their wives at risk of acquiring STDs. There was also lesser condom use reported among such men. Married women are rarely in a position of empowerment to force menfolk to practice protected sex. These make women more susceptible to HIV infection, and the fear of violent male reactions, physical and psychological, prevents many women from trying to find out more about it, discourages them from getting tested and stops them from getting treatment. Martin *et al.* (1999) also found that in Uttar Pradesh unplanned pregnancies are significantly more common among wives of abusive men. Besides this, research has shown that battered women are subject to twice the risk of miscarriage and four times the risk of having a baby that is below average weight. In some places, violence also accounts for a sizeable portion of maternal deaths (WHO, 2001). Reproductive health care that incorporates domestic violence support services is needed to meet the special needs of abused women. Unwanted pregnancies terminated by unsafe abortions also have negative consequences for women's health. Reducing fertility is an important element in improving the overall health of Indian women. Violence is a serious health issue for Indian women, it is difficult to say how widespread it is.

Psychological trauma of abortion: In the reproductive years of many women there comes a decision to go for abortion for several reasons ranging from medical to social one. Although abortion is completely an intense personal and threatening experience, it carries serious and significant consequences for women. The choice of abortion confronts moral reasoning, beliefs, personal identity, family structure and functions, role conflicts in relationships and one's belief in the future. The millions of women and men whose lives have been touched by abortion are often confronted by a lifetime of unasked, unspoken, and typically unanswered questions. Women's reactions after abortion span from feelings of relief to acts of suicide, empowerment to victimization, elation to grief, denial, avoidance, and repression. In reality, abortion is not as psychologically safe as the public has been led to believe. Researchers had suggested that some women experience serious psychological problems after abortion. When the victim is already devalued (a woman, a child), she may find that the most traumatic events of her life take place outside the realm of socially validated reality. In this respect, many women are traumatized not only by their abortion experiences but also by an unsympathetic society. Those women who dare to violate the social silence surrounding abortion find their psychological and emotional experiences are denied, discredited, or simply ignored. They are in fact blamed for their post-abortion problems; they are re-victimized. In India, where the son preference is enormous especially in the northern states many women had been forced into unwanted abortions by husbands, in-laws and significant others for unsafe abortion of female foetus. The pressure for abortion is done by the people whom she loves, respect and relies for support and help, this creates a sense of betrayal. These woman who are repeatedly been a victim of domineering abuse, such an unwanted abortion may be perceived as the ultimate violation in a life characterized by abuse. There are not many studies on the psychological trauma experienced by these helpless and powerless Indian women. However, the Western studies had showed that women who suffer from post-abortion trauma may lose their basic beliefs regarding safety, trust, self-worth, meaning in life, pleasure, and their relationships with others. They may feel unable to forgive themselves and feel the need to punish themselves or others for their experience. Many feel guilty about surviving their abortion and may believe that they deserve to be punished by God. In a study of post-abortion patients only 8 weeks after their abortion, researchers found that 44 per cent complained of nervous disorders, 36 per cent had experienced sleep disturbances, 31 per cent had regrets about their decision, and 11 per cent had been prescribed psychotropic medicine by their family doctor (Ashton, 1980). Thirty to fifty per cent of women who face abortion report experiencing sexual dysfunctions, of both short and long duration, beginning immediately after their abortions. These problems may include one or more of the following: loss of pleasure from intercourse, increased pain, an aversion to sex and/or males in general, or the development of a promiscuous lifestyle (Belsey, *et al.*, 1977).

Nutritional status: The physiological make up of women call for additional nutritional supplements. From the beginning of menstruation cycles to childbirth and until the menopause, are iron depleting physiological processes. Gender disparities in nutrition are evident from infancy to adulthood. In fact, gender has been the most statistically significant determinant of malnutrition among young children and malnutrition is a frequent direct or underlying cause of death among girls below age 5. Young children, pregnant and lactating women are nutritionally the most vulnerable groups, especially in the developing region of the world. The cultural practices deprive women in many ways and add to their poor nutritional status. Across the country, it is customary in many homes that women should eat at last and eat the leftover when the menfolk have had their food (Dube, 1988). Research has shown that numerous pregnancies and closely spaced births erode a mother's nutritional status, which can negatively affect the pregnancy outcome (e.g., premature births, low birth-weight babies) and also increase the health risk for mothers (Jejeebhoy and Rao, 1995). Nutritional deprivation has two major consequences for women: they never reach their full growth potential and anemia. Besides posing risks during pregnancy, anemia increases women's susceptibility to diseases such as tuberculosis and reduces the energy women have available for daily activities such as household chores, childcare, and agricultural labour.

Unequal treatment of girls and boys: Attitude towards health and general well-being of girls is very pathetic. Cultural norms which establish preference for boys or men's dominance in decision-making severely hinder female access to proper nutrition or health care. The effect of tropical diseases in women reflects their disempowered status. The role of female gender is submissive and little involvement in household decision making and little control over household resources. Particularly in the northern states of India the son preference is evident by looking at the male-female ratio in states like Haryana, Punjab, Madhya Pradesh, Rajasthan etc. Numerous ethnographic studies had witnessed that son preference shapes the practices of feeding, medical care and love and warmth in families in North India (Miller, 1997). Giving extra helpings of food and savouries to boys is a common practice in North India, however, in South India such differentials are not as much pronounced as in North India. When it comes to medical care, it is seen to be delayed and less expensive for girls (Khan, *et al.*, 1987). Barua and Kurz (2001) conducted a study in Maharastra and reported that married adolescent girls neither have decision making power nor have influence in the matters of seeking health care for their problems. The culture of silence also prevails when it comes to sexual health problems, leads the problems untreated and become severe. A primary way that parents discriminate against their girl children is through neglect during illness when sick, little girls are not taken to the doctor as frequently as are their brothers. Women's socialization to tolerate suffering and their reluctance to be examined by male personnel are additional constraints in their getting adequate health care.

HIV/AIDS: Around the world, women are seen as having an increased risk for contraction of sexually transmitted diseases. The large majority of women who acquire Human Immuno-Deficiency Virus (HIV) and other sexually transmitted diseases (STDs) are in their childbearing years and the gender-related inequalities which affect women are their lack of power to successfully control many aspects of sexual relations. India has been acknowledged as the epicentre of HIV/AIDS pandemic, with over five million people living with HIV/AIDS aged between 15-49 years. In a study carried out in Mumbai and Bangalore, Bharat, Aggleton and Tyrer (2001) found that the HIV/AIDS patients experienced discrimination, stigmatization and denial in a variety of context as healthcare, home and community, workplace, schools etc. They also observed discrimination as *"gendered phenomenon."* The gendered discrimination was most prominent in marital households. It is clear that the son had given the disease to the daughter-in-law, yet it is the woman who is most likely to be subjected to the discrimination like refusal to shelter, denial of property and access to children, and also access to treatment and unwillingness to spend money on daughter-in-law's treatment. Bharat (1996) stated such discrimination as *"shared fate, gendered experiences."* Young women are several more times likely to get infected than young men, due to both physiological and cultural reasons. Worldwide about half of the HIV infections are among youth ages 15-24. Women's lack of power to negotiate successfully concerning sexual relations and their lack of access to a means of preventing STDs under their own control are factors in their vulnerability.

Socio-economic Disparities and Health: The socio-economic status (SES) plays a significant role in health. Dr. Len Syme, Emeritus Professor of Epidemiology at the University of California, Berkeley, in a meeting of health researchers was asked 'what he would want to know if he had to predict a person's health status' and his response was that he would need just one piece of information: the most powerful predictor of health status was SES, Health improves as SES improves at all levels. *Socio-economic status encompasses education, income and occupation.* Michael McGinnis and his colleagues identified five factors that are known to affect health and have estimated the magnitude of the impact of each on premature mortality. SES affects four of the five factors: behaviour, which accounts for about 40 per cent of premature mortality; social circumstances, which account for about 15 per cent; deficiencies in medical care, about 10 per cent; and environmental exposures, about 5 per cent. In terms of medical care deficiencies, the less educated experience a poorer quality of care. From the perspective of social circumstances and the social environment, education can provide access to many things. These include higher occupational status, a greater sense of control over your life and increased social support—all of which may affect a person's interactions with the health care system and choices they make. Women in less well-off socio-economic groups have consistently been shown to be at the greatest disadvantage with regard to many aspects of health. Within households the division of resources and living standards may not always be equal, so portraying the household as an income-sharing unit may mask significant inequalities between household members. Women's true socio-economic status thus may not be accurately identified using their husband/partner's occupation, making it difficult to gain an authentic picture of inequalities in any society (Conlon, 1999). The knowledge of family planning is almost universal but only 36 per cent of married women aged 13 to 49 currently use modern contraception. Illiteracy is correlated to high fertility as women with no education have 4.0 children compared to 2.2 for women with a high school education. India's maternal mortality ratio is—453 deaths per 1,00,000 births in 1993—which researchers attribute to the lack of access to health care (*The World Bank,* 1995).

The cost-benefit ratios for educational interventions may change substantially when health effects are factored in. It is also important to think about education at all levels—from early childhood through adulthood. Highest reward-to-cost ratio if a serious investment is made in the education of mothers. In most parts of the developing world, this would mean educating young women. Education may cause changes in intellectual flexibility, leading to better skills in using and evaluating information. Education may improve people's abilities to manage their own health—to comply with medical advice and to change behaviours that are bad for them. Education may also help individuals feel more confident about using the health care system. Wealth and recent family income were the indicators that were most strongly associated with subsequent mortality. A study was conducted to understand the inequalities in health in 22 European countries and the findings showed that in almost all countries, the rates of death and poorer self-assessments of health were substantially higher in groups of lower socio-economic status, but the magnitude of the inequalities between groups of higher and lower socio-economic status was much larger in some countries than in others. These inequalities might be reduced by improving educational opportunities, income distribution, health related behaviour, or access to health care (Makenbach, *et al.,* 2008). Better educated women experience lower level of morbidity, mortality and have fewer children (Ross & Mirowsky, 1999). The lack of financial resources has a detrimental effect on nutrition, access to health care, and other preventive behaviours. The health education linkage is also dependent upon the development status of the region where the women is living. In India, there is a great inter-regional diversity. The Indian states differ not only in cultural practices but also in socio-economic development. The womenfolk of southern states like Kerala, Tamil Nadu and Andhra Pradesh enjoy higher education and autonomy. However, the northern states' women are subjected to traditional conservatism, comparatively less education and less likely to work outside.

Access to Health Care: Access to health care underlies five key elements: geographic or physical, economic, administrative, cognitive and psychosocial accessibility. Hence, access does not connote only proximity to health centre or availability of transportation but refers to dimensions of psychosocial access. In India, caste and class advantage play it out and also there is an urban bias in country's health care infrastructure (Mishra, 2006). Health care centres are disproportionately concentrated in urban areas, neglecting the needs of huge rural population. The weakening of public health care systems had given rise to privatization and it is usually the urban and elite who gets timely and competent care. Apart from such dimensions of access, women's access to health care is 'mediated by gendered experiences' (Mishra, 2004). Health care systems are frequently tuned to treat patients on the basis of their biological constructions, utterly ignoring their social construction, thereby perpetuating health inequities (Sen *et al.*, 2002). In fact, the leading contributor to high maternal mortality ratios in India is lack of access to health care (*The World Bank*, 1996). The quality of health care women usually receive is unsatisfactory at almost all levels.

Initiating Women Empowerment for Health: Nearly half of illiterate women received no care compared to just 13 per cent of literate women. Women in rural areas were much less likely to receive prenatal care than women in urban areas (42% and 18% respectively). Most women who did not receive health care during pregnancy said they did not because they thought it was unnecessary (IIPS, 1995). Thus, there is a definite need to educate women about the importance of health care for ensuring healthy pregnancies and safe childbirth. Medical research shows that early age at first birth and high numbers of total pregnancies take their toll on a woman's health. Severe anemia accounts for 20 per cent of all maternal deaths in India (*The World Bank*, 1996). Severe anemia also increases the chance of dying from a haemorrhage during labour. Decision making and goal setting are essential lifelong skills needed to health enhancing behaviours. These skills make it possible for individual knowledge into healthy lifestyles, thus improving quality of life. Women's self-worth is also an important area which should be taken into consideration for initiating women empowerment for health. Women are subjected to numerous inequalities within family and in society right from infancy which shapes their self-worth. The unequal and demeaning treatment leads to general feeling of low self-worth.

Suggestions: There is an urgent need to sensitize the health care providers to the health needs of women, especially the poor, illiterate and less informed clients and also encourage behavioural changes. The health service providers' polite and sensitive behaviour will simultaneously create an opportunity to raise awareness among womenfolk and the community in general regarding appropriate health seeking behaviour and the timely use of health services. Health is influenced by a variety of factors that co-exist within society. The ability to analyze, evaluate and interpret the influence of culture, media and technology on health is important in a rapidly changing world. The health literate, responsible and productive citizen draws upon the contributions of these factors to strengthen individual, family and community health. Fact Sheet: Domestic violence: Older women can be victims too. Health plans now offer a range of health and wellness activities, including traditional worksite health fairs, screenings and educational seminars; access to behaviour modification programmes, such as weight management and smoking cessation; and online tools, including health risk assessments. Gender-planned health services are planned on the basis that women and men play different roles in society and have different medical needs. The feminist movement has provided a broad charter of rights for women, reflecting women's needs, but these have yet to be translated into operational programme (Raikes, Shoo & Brabin, 1992). To change social norms discriminating against women will require changing male attitudes. Health programmes can also change the attitudes of men towards women, including attitudes that are detrimental to women's health such as the belief that women are weak and that good women are quiet, subservient, and bear many children. Men should be knowledgeable about health services for women, because men are a source of information and financial support for women. Reproductive health strategies for men have been sidelined by the concern of feminists that women gain the right to control their fertility decisions. But FP groups do offer men information and education in an effort to increase men's responsibility for contraception (Raikes, Shoo & Brabin, 1992). It is important that research address the physiologic, psychosocial, and economic factors that together affect women's health status.

REFERENCES

Ashton (1980). The Psychosocial Outcome of Induced Abortion, *British Journal of Ob & Gyn., 87*: 1115-1122.

Bang, R.A., Bang, A.T., Baitule, M., Choudhary,Y., Sarmukaddam, S., Tale, O. (1989). High prevalence of gynecological diseases in rural Indian Women. *The Lancet* (January 14), pp. 85-88.

Bang, R.A., Bang, A.T., Reddy, M.H., Deshmukh, M.D., Baitule, S.B., Filippi, V. (2004). Maternal morbidity during labour and puerperium in rural homes and the need for medical attention: A prospective observational study in Gadchiroli, India.

British Journal of Obstetrics and Gynaecology, 111, 231-238.

Basu, A., and Kurz, K. (2001). Reproductive health seeking by married adolescent girls in Maharashtra, India. *Reproductive Health Matters, 1:7*, 52-62.

Belsey, *et al.* (1977). Predictive Factors in Emotional Response to Abortion: King's Termination Study - IV, Social *Science and Medicine, 11*: 71-82.

Bharat, S. (1996). *Facing the challenge: Household and community response to HIV/AIDS in Mumbai, India.* Mumbai: Tata Institute of Social Sciences (TISS).

Bharat, S., Aggleton, P., and Tyrer, P. (2001). *India: HIV and AIDS related discrimination, stigmatization and denial.* Geneva: UNAIDS. (UNAIDS Best practice collection: Key material).

Cook, R.J. (1993). Human rights, maternal mortality and reproductive health. *Profamilia, Jun, 9(21)*: 43-68.

Mackenbach, J.P., Stirbu, I., Roskam, A.J., Schaap, M.M., Menvielle, G., Leinsalu, M., Kunst, A.E. & European Union working group on socio-economic inequalities in health (2008). Socio-economic inequalities in health in 22 European countries. *New England Journal of Medicine, 5:358*(23), 2468-81.

Martin, S.L., Kilgallen, B., Tsui, A.O., Maitra, K., Singh, K.K., Kupper, L.L. (1999). Sexual behaviours and Reproductive health outcomes: Associations with wife abuse in India. *JAMA, 282*:1967-72.

National centre on elder abuse. Washington DC: 2005.

Pahl, J. (1990). Household spending, personal spending, and the control of money in marriage. *Sociology*. 24:119-138.

Paquette, M.C. & Raine, K. (2004). Socio-cultural context of women's body image. *Social Science and Medicine, 59,* 1047-1058.

Progress in Reproductive Health Research (1997). Attributes of contraceptive methods, No. 43, Part. 2.

Raikes, A., Soo, R., & Brabin, L. (1992). Gender-planned health services. *Ann trop Med Parasitol,* Aug, 86 suppl, *1*: 19-23.

Sen, G., George, A., & Ostlin, P. (2002). *Engendering International Health.* Massachusetts Institute of Technology Press, Cambridge, pp. 1-33.

Stephenson R., Koening M.A. and Ahmed S. (2006). Domestic violence and symptoms of gynecological morbidity among women in North India. *Int Fam Plan Perspect;* 32:201-8.

Tinker, A. (2000). Women's health: The unfinished agenda. *International Journal of Gynecology & Obstetrics, 70,* 149-158.

Volger, C. and Pahl J. (1994). Money, power and inequality within marriage. *The Sociological Review.;* 42:263-288.

World Health Organization (2001). *Domestic violence: A priority public health issue in Western Pacific Region.* Western Pacific Regional Office.

World Health Organization (2002). *Reducing Risks, Promoting Healthy Life.* World Health Report. Geneva.

9

Marketing and Rural Women

Gyanmudra and *V. Suresh Babu*

Entrepreneurship is the process of innovation that reallocates resources to new opportunities, often creating new opportunities, through unusual combinations of resources and the skill of risk-taking entrepreneurs. Entrepreneurship is the result of inspired strategy to exploit change. The changes generally are in terms of industrial changes, market changes, demographic changes and social and cultural changes. These changes opened doors for entrepreneurs to find new opportunities. Those who recognize and pursue potential profitable opportunities to conceptualize the venture strategy will prosper and grow and will be rewarded in terms of wealth and personal satisfaction.

A crucial requirement in the process of new venture creation is a match between the opportunity, the propensity to enterprise, and the ability to enterprise. Problems in business are important only as they relate to opportunities. A particular enterprise cannot, thus, be fully understood except in terms of its particular opportunities and how well they are exploited.

The contribution of women entrepreneurs to economic activity and employment has increased over time. Women entrepreneurs and their businesses are a rapidly growing segment of the business population. Women entrepreneurs are prominent not only in industries where they were traditionally active, but also in less traditional sectors (e.g. manufacturing, construction, and transportation). Women entrepreneurs have created a variety of new ventures and contributed to the development of a range of services and products.

The creative and entrepreneurial potential of women is a latent source of economic growth and new jobs and should be encouraged. Research has shown that women face a number of difficulties in establishing and maintaining businesses. Although most of these difficulties are common to both genders, in many cases they tend to be more significant for female entrepreneurs. This is due to factors such as a poor business environment, the choice of business types and sectors, information gaps, lack of contacts and access to networking, gender discrimination and stereotypes, weak and inflexible supply of childcare facilities, difficulties in reconciling business and family obligations or differences in the way women and men approach entrepreneurship.

Women's empowerment is a global issue and discussions on women's rights are at the forefront of many formal and informal campaigns worldwide. This is because women have been regarded as the nuclei of a nation and the builder and molder of its destiny. The position and status of women in any society is an index of its civilization. The concept of empowerment received momentum after the Bangladesh experiments of the 1980s led by Prof. Muhammad Yunus, founder of the Grameen Bank, got worldwide acclamation. Following the example, various countries including India, introduced empowerment models as a strategy for women empowerment. As a result, various women-led organizations were formed with the common focus of poverty reduction and empowerment of women.

The empowerment of women through entrepreneurship would lead to benefits not only to the individual women but also for the family and community as a whole. Empowering women is not just for meeting their economic needs but also more holistic social development. Rural women are more vulnerable in comparison to urban women, because the urban women have wide scope of activities around them to explore but rural women do not get enough opportunity to make use of their economic potential. Entrepreneurial skill and marketing talents are to be given to these women, through proper training programmes.

Given the rapid growth of entrepreneurship among women in recent years, it is important to understand the social, psychological and economic factors influencing the success of women-owned small business.

Stagnating rural areas deserve special attention. Rural women in India face formidable barriers created by their family status, socio-economic hardship and male dominance over women inside and outside the family. Equally important are ethnic and cultural, traditions, which go beyond gender issues. Indigenous women suffer both as the weaker sex and by the members of their communities. Religion, spirituality and faith occupy an important place in the lives and thinking of rural women.

Literature on demographic profile of women entrepreneurs and factors or problems affecting enterprises owned by women is quite inadequate, and limited. Socio-psychological factors which have significant association with entrepreneurial success has not been studied much. With this background, the present study has been designed to carry out. Selected individual women entrepreneurs from different economic and different sectors will be analysed.

Entrepreneur has been defined in the traditional literature as a person who undertakes business and bears associated risk, innovative ability, high need achievement, religious belief, socially good and economic background, business community (Tiwari J., 1998).

Muthayya and Loganathan (1990) made an attempt to assess the personality of the different categories of respondents in order to identify whether they have the requisite personality dispositions to undertake activities which are independent and self-sustaining thereby contributing to their enterpreneurship. Misra (1995) examined the functioning of rural leadership by identifying the interactive relationship between leaders' personal characteristics, strategies adopted by them and different situation by employing the in-depth probing method. Husain and Khan (2001) focused on the motivational factors of rural development personnel. Motivational factors included individual and work values and individual needs. Kumari (2000) has drawn the parameters of empowerment including: building up a positive self-image and self-confidence, developing the ability to think critically.

Locus of control and need of achievement was studied to analyse the psychosocial variables to the psycho-entrepreneurial disposition of women entrepreneurs (Ganesan, 2003; Ganesan, 2005). Chawdhary and Prakash (1997) have found entrepreneurial motivation amongst youth an important factor of psychosocial and economic development of community and country. Thakur, 2000; Ganeshan, 2003; Preetha and Parthsarathy, 1999; Nirmala O'cruz, 2003, Case study method (Devi and Thangamutha, 1997).

The structural change in rural areas that began in the 1960s and has escalated since has also inspired social psychologists. Social psychological research in the field has been concerned with small-scale entrepreneurship; policy questions related to it in rural development.

Attention has been focused, for example, to the construction of entrepreneurial identity and the experience of personal control as social psychological prerequisites for entrepreneurial agency and framing processes in the interactions and communications that are aimed towards rural development. It is difficult to theorise, in general terms, the phenomenon of entrepreneurship.

Classification of women entrepreneurs can be based on education, training, type of activity, investment etc.:

1. The first group consists of women with educational and professional qualification who takes the initiative and manages the business as well as man do. Women entrepreneurs who have the basic managerial training and educational qualification go for the medium and large scale units.
2. The second group consists of those women entrepreneurs who do not have education or any

formal training in management but have developed practical skills required for the small scale sector choose that product with which they are familiar. For example, garments, dolls, handicraft items etc.

3. The third category can be family business and investment—very small investment like vegetable vending as well.

Entrepreneurial activities are considered an important source of technological innovation and economic growth. Women are entering into entrepreneurship even while facing socio-cultural, economic, technical, financial and managerial difficulties. Women entrepreneurship movement can gain momentum by providing encouragement, appropriate awareness, training, environment and support. This would definitely enhance their socio-economic status of women.

Women entrepreneurs are divided into *three* categories:

1. The first group consists of women with educational and professional qualification who takes the initiative and manages the business as well as man do. Women entrepreneurs who have the basic managerial training and educational qualification go for the medium and large scale units.
2. The second group consists of those women entrepreneurs who do not have education or any formal training in management but have developed practical skills required for the small scale sector choose that product with which they are familiar. For example, garments, dolls, handicraft items etc.
3. The third group of women entrepreneurs works in cities and slums to help women with lower means of livelihood. They need Government support in marketing as well as in getting finance at concessional rates.

The growth of women entrepreneurship is haunted by a number of difficulties, snags and problems. They face stiff competition from male entrepreneurs. More or less majority of women entrepreneurs face similar kind of problem.

Therefore, it is important to understand the behavioural research on psychosocial and its potential influence on entrepreneurship.

Objectives

- To analyse development strategies for promotion of entrepreneurship among rural women and to examine the prcblems in their effective implementation.
- To study psychosocial-economic status of rural women entrepreneurs.

Methodology

Data and Measures

The study is to investigate the development of entrepreneurship among rural women through both Governmental and Non-Governrnental, have driven financial sustainability and integrated community development in India.

At the District and Block level, using the questionnaire schedule from a representative sample of individual women was conducted. Case study was done on successful entrepreneurs.

Study Area

The study was undertaken in the State of Gujarat (which was selected based on their performance report in SGSY programme published in the Annual Report 2005-06 published by Ministry of Rural Development, Government of India, New Delhi.

The present study was carried out in the district of Surat from Gujarat State primary data collection. 44 individual women entrepreneurs from Gujarat State, were taken as individual case study.

There was a discussion with the employees of different departments, i.e., Agriculture Department, Social Welfare department and others, in order to get the supportive data. There was an in-depth interview with Government officials at various levels to get qualitative insights.

Study findings

The study was conducted in the interior regions of Surat district. The study blocks of Surat are Palsana, Vyara, Songadh, Uchchhal, Valod, Mandvi, Mahuva and Choryasi. All the blocks comprised of tribal population, were in the Literacy rate comparatively low with the state average (69.1%). In the study

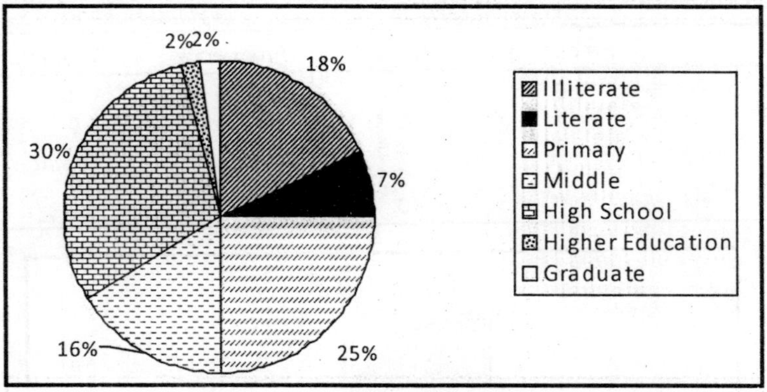

Fig. 9.1: Literacy status.

area, the major share of the population fall in the category of literate (30%) followed with primary education 25 per cent and the middle school (16%). However, among the surveyed population, the illiterate category occupies 18 per cent. The National Programme of Nutritional Support to Primary Education (School Meal Programme) gave a boost to Universalisation of Elementary Education (UEE) in terms of increasing enrolment, retention and attendance in primary classes by supplementing nutritional requirements of children attending primary schools. This is one of the ambitious programmes launched by the State Government that has envisaged the provision of nutritious and wholesome cooked meal of 100 gms of foodgrains per school day, free of cost, to all chiidren in dasses I-V. This scheme is one of the factors which have influenced the higher literacy and primary education in rural areas of Gujarat State.

It is evident from Table 9.1, the landholding among the respondents is very negligible. Maximum landholding is only one acre in case of dry land while three acres in case of wetlands. Most of the respondents were either artisan labourers or agriculture labourers.

Table 9.1: Landholdings in the study area

	Wetland Holding		*Dryland Holding*	
Acres	*Frequency*	*Per cent*	*Frequency*	*Per cent*
1	0	0	2	4.5
2	1	2.3	0	0
3	2	4.5	0	0
4	1	2.3	0	0
7	0	0	1	2.3

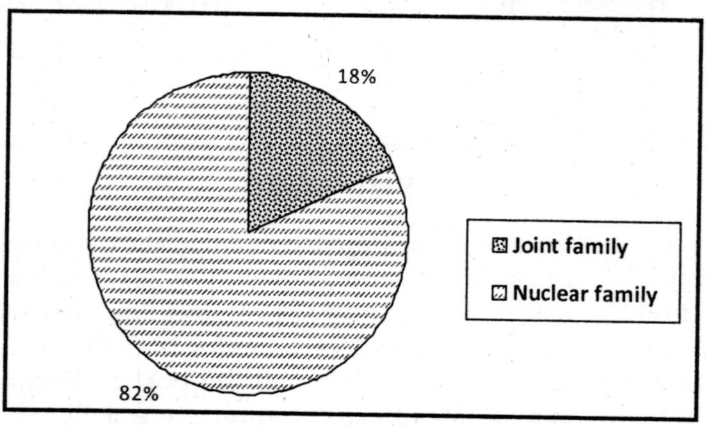

Fig. 9.2 : Type of Family.

In the study area, about 82 per cent of the households are nuclear families. This may be due to tradition in the tribal habitat. Once, a pair gets into the wedlock, they get separated from their parents. The reason may be to reduce the burden on the bread earner of the family and to bestow the family responsibilities to the newly married couple.

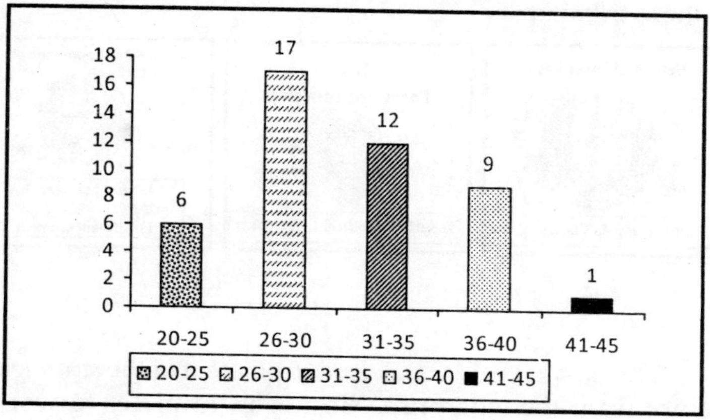

Fig. 9.3: Age-wise distribution of households.

From Fig. 9.3, it is also noticed that the maximum number of households are in the age group of 25-30 years followed by 31-35 years of age group.

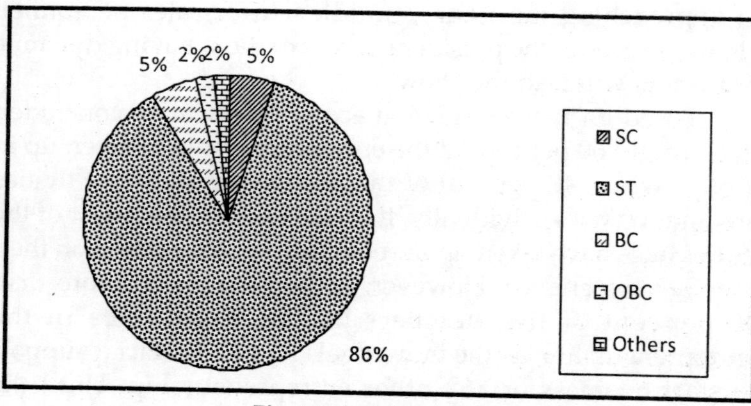

Fig. 9.4: Social category.

In the study areas, it was found that 86 per cent of the households fall in the category of Scheduled Tribes while, the other categories viz., Scheduled and Backward Castes are in 5 per cent. The domination of the Scheduled Tribes may be due to the location factor (tribal area). Due to certain industries like JK Paper Mills in Songadh and business centres established in Vyara has forced some of the social categories to establish in these tribal areas.

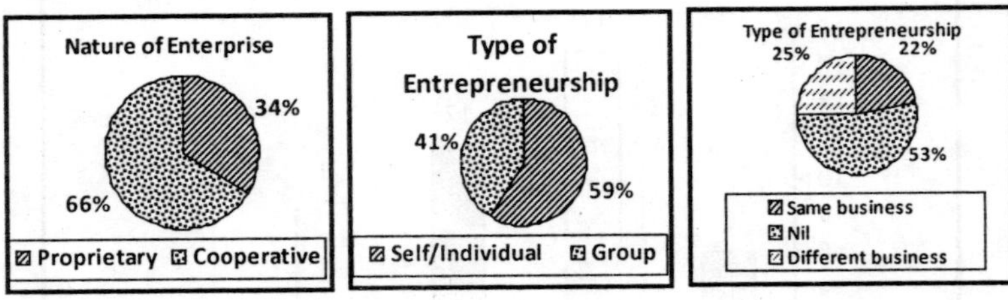

Fig. 9.5

The data reveals that nearly 66 per cent of the *swarojgaries* do not want the enterprise. Most of them prefer to work in groups as they find it convenient for the functioning. Apart from convenience, they also find that there is sharing of responsibility and guidance from the other members because it could build their self-confidence in the activity. Most of them are either literates or with primary education, find it difficult in approaching the trades, middlemen or sales personnel. Hence, in group, the president or few of them having dynamic characters will lead the show.

Based on the information acquired, it can be concluded that around 60 per cent of the entrepreneurship is taken up in groups while, 40 per cent of the income generating activities are undertaken individually. It is also noticed that most of the individuals have taken up the entrepreneurship based on their previous experience. However, among the group more than 50 per cent of the members had no experience in the entrepreneurship; as the individuals had no financial support to start business or any other entrepreneurship. Until the *Sampooran Grameen Swarojgar Yojana* (SGSY) came into existence in 1999, the bank never entertained the individuals to take up entrepreneurship without collaterals or mortgage.

From Table 9.2, it is noticed that approximately 64 per cent of the respondents had a business experience of 1 to 4 years while, only 11 per cent of the respondents fall in the category of 5-8 years business experience. It is also evident from the table, a mere 2.3 per cent of respondents are in the category of 13-16 years of business experience.

Table 9.2: Business experience

Years	*Frequency*	*Per cent*
1-4	28	63.6
5-8	5	11.4
9-12	0	0
13-16	1	2.3
Total	34	77.3

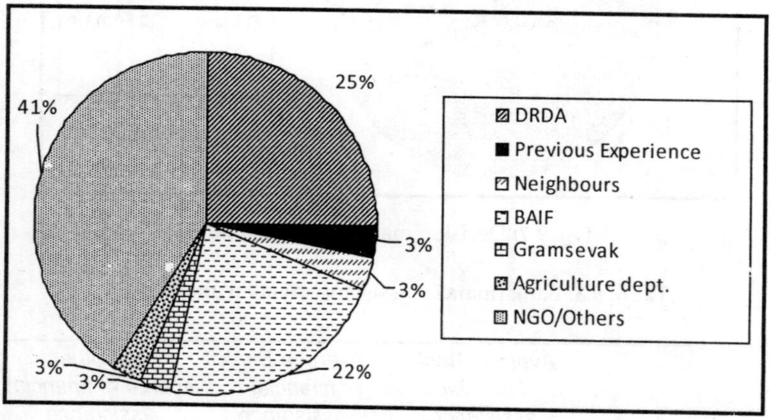

Fig. 9.6: Technology Provided by

From the date collected, it is learnt that nearly 88 per cent of the dissemination of technology takes place either by the existing local NGOs (41%), DRDA (25%) or BAIF (22%). Transfer of technology is very minimal through other sources like agriculture department, *gramsevak*, neighbours and previous experiences. This indicates that the majority of the entrepreneurs obtained the technology from the NGOs who act the grassroots level rural functionary.

In most of the tribal villages, decision making in the family matters lay with the male member or the head of the family. However, after entrepreneurship, the decision making power was also provided to few of the female members of the family, as they hold the major share of the total family earning. Before entrepreneurship, majority of the households were functioning based on the male decisions. However, we could find in some of the families decisions were taken collectively, involving all the members to share their opinions.

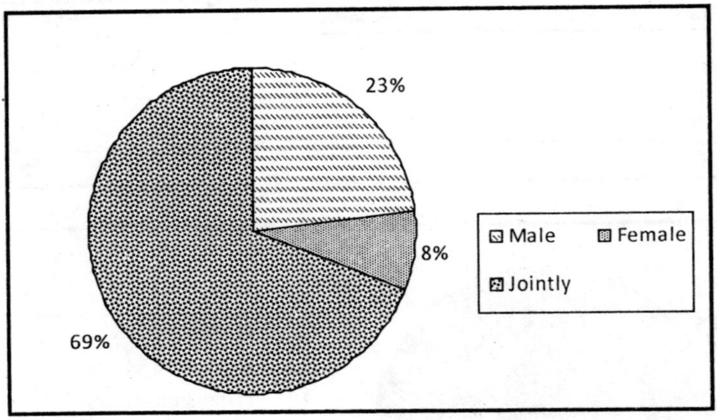

Fig. 9.7: Decision making in the Family.

Table 9.3: Bank financial assistance availed and repaid

	Average Bank financial assistance amount availed	*Average Bank financial assistance amount repaid*	*Any other source of financial assistance amount availed (Average)*
Valid	44	44	44
Mean	11613.64	5704.55	25345.45

The banks provided loan for the *swarojgaries* under SGSY programme. On an average each *swarojgary* has obtained financial assistanace of Rs. 11,613. Out of which, on an average nearly about Rs. 5,704 has been repaid. However, there are certain cases; wherein an entrepreneur had financial support apart from the DRDA funds. The NGO has obtained an external fund and provided a financial assistance to the entrepreneur. The average amount assisted under such financial assistance

Table 9.4: Credit mobilization Statement for the Year 2006-07
(Oct . 2006 Ending)

Sl. No.	*Taluk*	*No. of BPL*	*Credit mobilization*			*Expenditure*			*%*	*No. of Bene.*	*Per Family Invest-ment*
			Credit	*Subsidy*	*Total*	*Credit*	*Subsidy*	*Total*			
1	*2*	*3*	*4*	*5*	*6*	*7*	*8*	*9*	*10*	*11*	*12*
1.	Bardoli	13864	25.51	6.30	31.81	1.39	0.81	2.20	6.92	13	0.17
2.	Choryasi	16610	23.71	5.70	29.41	9.80	3.82	13.62	46.31	53	0.26
3.	Kamrej	9716	25.51	6.30	31.81	0.27	0.27	0.54	1.70	2	0.27
4.	Mahuva	17355	33.88	9.09	42.97	13.95	5.70	19.65	45.73	66	0.30
5.	Mandvi	16966	60.61	18.00	78.61	31.58	10.40	41.98	53.40	148	0.28
6.	Mangrol	17407	30.91	8.10	39.01	5.40	2.60	8.00	20.51	40	0.20
7.	Nizar	15495	30.91	8.10	39.01	4.52	2.68	7.20	18.46	4	1.80
8.	Olpad	13181	23.08	5.49	28.57	5.47	2.00	7.47	26.15	26	0.29
9.	Palsana	9716	24.88	6.09	30.97	1.21	0.72	1.93	6.23	9	0.21
10.	Songadh	21475	60.88	18.09	78.97	31.83	14.55	46.38	58.73	0	0.00
11.	Uchhal	14861	33.88	9.09	42.97	11.48	6.16	17.64	41.05	69	0.26
12.	Umarpada	12355	30.91	8.10	39.01	17.42	6.05	23.47	60.16	52	0.45
13.	Valod	7878	30.31	7.90	38.21	4.68	1.95	6.63	17.35	0	0.00
14.	Vyara	25331	60.88	18.09	78.97	35.78	14.64	50.42	63.85	0	0.00
		212210	**495.86**	**134.44**	**630.30**	**174.78**	**72.35**	**247.13**	**39.21**	**482**	**0.51**

is Rs. 25,345. Some of the Commercialised and Grameen banks operating in this region are Bank of Baroda, State Bank of Saurashtra, UCO, Surat Bharuch Grameena Bank, Bank of India, Central Bank of India, Syndicate Bank, Union Bank of India, GTDC, Surat District Cooperative Bank, Grameen Bank SBGB and Dena Bank. Totally 18 group and 271 individual application on which loan amount of Rs. 70.57 lakh and 134.26 lakh has been disbursed with subsidy amount of Rs. 19.41 lakh and 39.99 lakh has been released, respectively, from commercialized banks. However, 20 groups and 343 individual applications on which loan amount of Rs. 76.17 lakh and 170.96 lakh has been disbursed with subsidy amount of Rs. 21.06 lakh and 51.29 lakh has been released, respectively, from grameena banks for the year 2005-06.

On credit mobilization, totally 482 *swarojgaries* got benefited and the credit ratio is about 2.42 while, Rs. 0.51 lakh were invested per family as on October, 2006. (Table 9.4)

Mode of marketing: The respondents have adopted various means of marketing strategies based on the sources available to market their produce. In most of the cases, the products are sold through the NGO to the GRIMCO. Few of the groups got benefited through the *gram haats* organised by the DRDA and market linkages with handicraft corporations, GRIMCO, etc. Rest of the groups are disposing their products in the weekly markets, door to door delivery etc.

Table 9.5: Mode of Marketing

	Frequency	*Percent*
Door to door	1	2.3
Weekly market	5	11.4
DRDA sale counter	2	4.5
District level	1	2.3
Distribution network	9	20.5
Other means	25	56.7
All the above means	1	2.3
Total	**44**	**100.0**

In this study, the research team made an impact assessment of the entrepreneurship. The study findings reveal that the individual income prior assistance was Rs. 460 and after assistance is Rs. 1706 per month. In case of total income of an individual is Rs. 1130 per month prior to assistance and Rs. 2384 per month after assistance. As the standard deviation is very high, it indicates that the variation from respondent to respondent is also very high, hence the standard error is also high.

Table 9.6: One-Sample "t" test

Average self-income (per month)	*N*	*Mean*	*Std. Deviation*	*Std. Error Mean*	*Average Total income*	*N*	*Mean*	*Std. Deviation*	*Std. Error Mean*
Prior to assistance	44	459.89	458.27	69.09	Prior to assistance	44	1128.89	841.96	126.93
After the assistance	44	1706.50	1750.29	265.22	After the assistance	44	2384.68	1847.21	278.48

It is evident from Table 9.6 that there is an incremental income of Rs. 138 in the family income whereas the total annual incremental income is Rs. 1985. This is basically due to additional income of Rs. 500 to Rs. 1,200 noticed from the income generation activity or the women entrepreneurship.

Table 9.7: Family income before and after entrepreneurship

	Family income before entrepreneurship (Average)	*Family income after entrepreneurship (Average)*	*Total annual income before entrepreneurship*	*Total annual income after entrepreneurship*
Valid	44	44	44	44
Mean	734.77	873.07	1478.89	3463.64

The group has undergone various types of training under the SGSY or the NGO provided training. The type of training provided to the entreprenuers are general awareness, basic orientation, skill development, technical support and book-keeping. Among the various trainings provided, DRDA has given equal importance to all the types of trainings in order to make the *swarojgarie*: full-fledged in taking up an activity. However, the NGOs have laid emphasis on trainings such as skill development, technical support and book-keeping. The NGO was more conscious in skill development and book-keeping.

Table 9.8: Nature/type of training provided (No. of persons)

Type of training	*BAIF*	*PANCH*	*DRDA*	*Agri. Dept.*	*Trust/ Others*	*Animal Husbandry*
General awareness training	1	1	11			
Basic orientation training	5		9		1	
Skill development training	11	2	9	1	10	1
Technical support training	4	1	10	1	8	
Book-keeping training	14	2	12		2	

Achievements

The DRDA are interested to provide the SGSY scheme benefit to women entrepreneurs rather than the men groups or the mixed groups. This is basically due to following findings of the study, viz., 97.7 per cent of the respondents' income has enhanced, 91 per cent livelihood pattern has improved, 96 per cent have achieved food security, 73 per cent have achieved diversification of occupation, migration of the family has reduced in 68 per cent respondents and the access to wage employment is achieved by 96 per cent of the respondents. The women group has not only achieved betterment in their life and family but they are also more sincere in repayment of loan amount. Once, they earn some money they are judiciously utilizing the earning in diversifying their products and extending their production targets along with quality standards. (Table 9.9)

Table 9.9: Perception about Achievements

Description of item	*Percentage*	
	Yes	*No*
Achievement enhanced in income	97.7	2.3
Achievement in better livelihood pattern	90.9	2.3
Achievement of food security	95.5	4.5
Achievement of diversification in occupation	72.7	27.3
Achievement of decrease in migration	68.2	11.4
Achievement of access to wage employment	95.5	2.3

The psychological traits were also assessed in the study area. Most of the respondents were falling under the category of medium class in respect of achievement motivation (77%), stress (50%), leadership (55%), need for the power (64%), task motivation (73%), decision making (66%) and risk taking (41%). These indicators clearly indicate that the women entrepreneurs are not at all feeling the stress of managing the enterprise and the family simultaneously. Further, few respondents are even ready to take high amount of risk (25%), power (30%) and leadership (39%). With such attitudes they are not only changing their lifestyle but also bringing vast changes in their children in terms of education, outlook, social involvement, etc.

Table 9.10: Psychological Traits

Details	*Less*	*Medium*	*High*
Achievement motivation	0	34 (77.3)	8 (18.2)
Stress	16 (36.4)	22 (50.0)	0
Leadership	3 (6.8)	24 (54.5)	17 (38.6)
Need for power	3 (6.8)	28 (63.6)	13 (29.5)
Task motivation	1 (2.3)	32 (72.7)	11 (25.0)
Decision making	0	29 (65.9)	15 (34.1)
Risk taking	68 (33.2)	79 (41.4)	56 (25.4)

Based on the observation, the study team tried to analyze the risk taking capability of the respondents. Interestingly, it was noticed that among the total respondents, 68 of them were ready to take-up extreme risk followed by the moderately risk taking respondents of 60 number. Among the left out categories, not at all risky category was highest with 41 respondents, followed by in between moderately and extremely risky (19 nos.) and in between not at all and moderately risky (15 nos.). Risk taking attitude is considered to be one of the important indicators which represent the risk taking ability of the respondents. This also indicates that the respondents are not only anticipating the income generation for the subsistence livelihood but also trying their best to compete with high standard of living class. To achieve their life, objectives and upcoming in their lives they are ready to take extreme risks for their well-being in the society.

Table 9.11: Caste-wise income prior and after the assistance

Social Category	*N*	*Total income per month (Rs.)*	
		Prior assistance	*After assistance*
SC	2	1300.00	2700.00
ST	38	1118.00	2377.00
BC	2	1050.00	2687.00
OBC	1	500.00	550.00
Total	43	1129.00	2385.00

From Table 9.11, it is evident that the overall impact of monthly income, as such is comparatively on the higher side after assistance (Rs. 2,385) as compared to the prior to assistance monthly income (Rs. 1,129). There is nearly 47 per cent increase in the monthly income of the respondents. However, among the social categories, the incremental income is in the order of BC (155%), ST (113%), OBC (110%) and SC (108%). It is clearly noticed that BC performance in terms of monthly income is comparatively on higher side as compared to the other categories in the study area.

Table 9.12: Income details of different business category before and after Assistance

Business Category	*N*	*Total income per month (Rs.)*	
		Prior assistance	*After assistance*
Nil	27	1202.00	2547.00
Same Business	8	1069.00	2081.00
Different business	9	797.00	1539.00
Total	44	3068.00	6167.00

Table 9.12 clearly indicates that there is a significant difference in all the social categories. Overall income per month prior to assistance was only Rs. 3068 as compared to Rs. 6,167 after assistance. Individually, in almost all the categories, the rise of income after assistance is above 50 per cent as compared with the prior to assistance income. The groups which had no business experience have done comparatively better than the other two business experiences group. The study area is located in remote areas which are dominated by tribal population, who had literally no financial assistance to start their own entrepreneurship, till SGSY came into existence. However, the groups with no experience have achieved better results with all their sincerity and DRDA officials' efforts.

Although rural areas and individual entrepreneurs face unique hardships, they also have unique resources designed to encourage and support their growth. While rural communities may continue to lag behind in terms of national scores, employment rates and earnings, continued entrepreneurial enthusiasm and the formation of more resources can only work to strengthen these regions.

Environment conducive to entrepreneurship

Behind each of the success stories of rural entrepreneurship, there is usually some sort of institutional support. Besides individual or group entrepreneurial initiative, the enabling environment supporting these initiatives is of utmost importance.

The creation of such an environment starts already at the national level with the foundation policies for macro-economic stability and for well-defined property rights as well as international orientation. Protection of the domestic economy hinders instead of fosters entrepreneurship. National agricultural policies such as price subsidies to guarantee minimum farm incomes and the keeping of land in production when overproduction already exists are definitely counter-productive to entrepreneurship.

Financing Difficulties

Credit is available for women through a plethora of schemes but there are still bottlenecks and gaps. The multiplicity of schemes is not adequately listed nor is there networking among agencies. As a result, clients approaching one institution are not made aware of the best option for their requirements. A closely integrated data bank into which all concerned agencies are plugged is a real need.

Training in Skills

Appropriate training is still the key to a successful programme to develop entrepreneurship among women. There are funds available from several sources; finding effective trainers is the greater problem. NGOs like RUDSET in Karnataka have succeeded in achieving reasonably high success levels, but others including governmental bodies have still not reached these levels. Continuous monitoring and improvement of training programmes should eventually spread the cult of entrepreneurship among young women.

The findings from Gujarat clearly shows that training with respect to number of days, types of training, skill development etc. have been imparted, which comes out from their work whereas in Uttar Pradesh no such training has been given. No such interest has been shown by government or NGOs.

Confidence in Marketing

A major area of difficulty for women entrepreneurs is marketing. Several initiatives have been put in place to remedy this defect. At the initial stages women prefer to be locked into programmes which ensure almost total marketing support, since they seldom have the time or the confidence to seek out and develop markets. Even when they are otherwise in control of an enterprise, they often depend on males of the family in this area. Marketing means mobility and confidence in dealing with the external world, both of which women have been discouraged from developing by social conditioning.

Strategies adopted for enterprise promotion

The policies and programmes targeted specifically to the development of entrepreneurship do not differ much with respect to location. From the perspective of the process of entrepreneurship, whether the location is urban, semi-rural or rural is not important in itself. For example, the needs of would be entrepreneur or an existing small business do not differ much from those in an urban area. To realise their entrepreneurial ideas or to grow and sustain in business, they all need access to capital, labour, markets and good management skills. What differs is the availability of markets for other inputs.

Involvement of the People's Organisations in all aspects of planning:

- Preference to woman-headed families, women entrepreneurs, the landless, other poor families and traditional artisans.
- Strengthen traditional artisans by providing them better tools and equipment, training and exposure. Assist them in establishing and strengthening backward and forward linkages.
- Assess the local market situation in terms of potential income from different forms of enterprises. This

provides a practical basis for shortlisting the potential enterprises.

- Facilitate the process of selection of enterprises by first-generation entrepreneurs and create awareness among them about feasibility factors, market demand and profitability.
- Recommend selection of potential enterprises from those with a low gestation period and those involving minimal risk, because the participants belong to the poorest stratum.
- There should be an appropriate contribution by the entrepreneur family in the enterprise.

These are the reasons why rural entrepreneurship is more likely to flourish in those rural areas where the two approaches to rural development, the 'bottom up' and the 'top down', complement each other. Developing entrepreneurs require a much more complex approach to rural development than is many times the case in practice. It requires not only the development of local entrepreneurial capabilities but also a coherent regional/local strategy. Evidence shows that where this is the case, individual and social entrepreneurship play an important role in rural economic, social and community development. The top down approach gains effectiveness when it is tailored to the local environment that it intends to support. The second prerequisite for its success is that ownership of the initiative remains in the hands of members of the local community. The regional development agencies that fit both criteria can contribute much to rural development through entrepreneurship.

Conclusion

The transition to a market economy makes things worse. Saddled with numerous social responsibilities and constrained by lack of equality, women easily lose whatever advantages they had. The condition of rural women deserves special attention as many of them face specific problems related to the rural way of life, economic hardship, agricultural technology and local customs.

Socio-economic problems are especially affecting women who are the sole breadwinner in the family. They and their children are the likeliest victims of the widespread impoverishment. Poor education and training force them to agree to a mere pittance.

The economic transition has directly affected women's status in society. In the past, women's status in society and economy depended on rules defined by the state. Today, the influence of the state is waning. Social allocations will inevitably shrink and state interventions in any area will be on a much smaller scale. Women should be more active in defending their interests. They should abandon unrealistic and unreasonable expectations. Women should also be more active in their search for solutions to social, economic and political problems.

REFERENCES

Chawdhary and Prakash (1997). Entrepreneurial Motivation—Factors and Features, Center for Entrepreneurship and Small Business Management, Maharshi Dayanand Saraswati University, Ajmer.

Devi and Thangamutha (1997). A Case Study of Women Entrepreneurs in Trichyrappalli District, Bharathidasan University Trichirappalli.

Ganesan, S. (2003). *Status of Women Entrepreneurs in India,* Kanishka Publications, New Delhi.

Ganesan, R. (2005)."Psychosocial Disposition towards Emancipation of Women Entreprenuership - A Study on Women Entrepreneurs in Food Processing Enterprises", *1st International Biennial Conference, Centre for Entrepreneurship and Small Business Management,* Maharishi Dayanand Saraswathi University, Ajmer, Rajasthan, Sep. 9-11, 2005.

Husain, Akbar and Khan Mohd. Ilyas (2001). Motivational factors for rural development personnel. *Journal of Community Guidance and Research, 18(1),* 17-24.

Kumari, Souda (2000). Women's empowerment. *The Educational Review, 106(11),* 190-191.

Misra, Rajeshwar (1995). Personal characteristics and strategies as factors of rural leadership effectiveness. *Journal of Rural Development,* (Jan), *11(1),* 59-68.

Muthayya, B.C. and Loganathan, M. (1990). Psychosocial factors influencing Entrepreneurship in rural areas. *Journal of Rural Development*, Hyderabad Vol 9(1), pp. 237-281.

Nirmala D'cruz (2003). Constraints on Women Entrepreneurship Development in Kerala, Kerala Research Programme on Local Level Development, *Centre for Development Studies*, Thiruvananthapuram.

Preetha and Parthsarathy (1999). Entrepreneurship Development of Women at Micro-Level, *Centre for Adult, Continuing Education and Extension Institute for Entrepreneurship and Career Development.*

Tiwari, J. (1998). Indian Social Order of Emerging Values. *Indian Journal of Psychometry and Education, 29(1)*, 13-16.

Thakur (2000). "Explaining Entrepreneurial Success: A Conceptual Model", *Indian Institute of Management, Calcutta*, Kolkata.

Anonymous (2007). Gujarat: Destination of Choice. *Vibrant Gujarat Global Investors' Summit*, 12-13 January, 2007.

Anonymous (2006). *Socio-economic Review*, Gujarat State 2005-06.

www.ibef.org

www.gujaratindia.com

10

Religiosity and Well-being of Pregnant Women

Shobhna Joshi and *Shilpa Kumari*

Introduction

Psychologists have long been interested in the role that religion plays in the interpretation of response to life events and its manifestation in everyday psychological adjustment. Religion is a very important component of human lives and is a very significant social force in shaping human behaviour. It plays a tremendous role in directing, shaping and moulding social behaviour at both individual and group levels. It is closely related with the development and change of attitudes and beliefs, the arousal and reduction of anxiety and guilt, and the determination of cognitive and motivational processes. The personal, domestic and social life of the people is largely influenced by the philosophy of their own religion. Religion has existed in all human history and covers the world geographically. Since time immemorial, man has worshipped some unknown force. To this unknown force the title, "God" was given and to this God were attributed unexplainable happenings. Each religion codifies and expresses the cultural values of the society as a whole. The manner in which the individual adheres to religion has a tremendous effect on his personality, attitudes, behaviour and overall outlook on life.

A specific definition of religion and religiosity remains to be the subject of debate. For most, religion involves a social or institutional dimension. Webster's Dictionary defines religion as: "a set of beliefs concerning the cause, nature and purpose of the universe...usually involving devotional and ritual observances and often containing a moral code for conduct of human affairs; set of beliefs and practices generally agreed upon a number of persons". Similarly, Galloway (1956) has defined religiosity as "A power beyond himself whereby he seeks to satisfy emotional needs and gain stability of life and which he expresses in acts of worship and survive". The term religiosity is related to religious faith and practices. It is also manifested in moral and ethical duties (Shukla, 1990).

Religiosity (Dittes, 1975) in psychological literature has been considered as having three components. Theoretically, it refers to an individual's faith in God; emotionally, it refers to his dedications and devotions to God and God related rituals and practices and practically, it is reflected in his observance of the ethical-cum-moral duties as Divine commands (Bhusan, 1970). Now, it is hardly new that religion can have important influence on human health and behaviour as, religiosity has a great, therapeutic value for masses.

Religion and well-being

Given the prevalence and importance of religiosity in the population, it is reasonable to consider the impact of religiosity on well-being such that to clarify its positions in the existing literature.

Religious resource figure predominantly among the methods that call on when coping with life stress and illness (Cole & Pargament, 1997; Dein & Stygal, 1997; Koenig, 1997; Pargament, 1997; Pargament, Smith, Koenig, & Perez, 1998). Religion may (a) produce a sense of meaning, something worth living and dying for (Spilka, Shaver & Kirkpath, 1985); (b) stimulate hope (Scheier & Carver, 1987) and optimism (Seligman, 1991); (c) give religious people a sense of control by a beneficent God, which compensates for reduced personal control (Pargament, Echemendia, Johnson, Cook, McGath, Myers, 1987); (d) prescribe a healthier lifestyle that yields positive health and mental health outcomes; (e) set positive social norms that elicit approval, nurturance, and acceptance from others; (f) provide a social support network; or (g) give the person a sense of the supernatural that is certainly a psychological boost—but may also be a spiritual boost that cannot be measured phenomenological (Bergin & Payne, 1993).

Religious beliefs can shape a person's psychological perception of pain or disability. According to Koenig, Larson, and Larson (2001) when people become physically ill, they rely heavily on religious beliefs and practices to relieve stress, retain a sense of control and maintain hope and sense of meaning and purpose of life. It is suggested that religion acts as a social support system; reduces the sense of loss of control and helplessness; provides a cognitive framework that reduces suffering and enhances self-esteem; gives confidence that one, with the help of God, could influence the health condition and creates a mindset that enables the person to relax and allow the body to heal itself. Thus, the practice of religion has a significant effect on happiness and overall sense of personal well-being.

Well-being or wellness is often referred to as "wholeness of body, mind, and spirit in terms of health, prosperity and self-actualization" (Maslow, 1968). According to Fromm (1976) well-being is only possible to the degree to which one is open, responsive, sensitive, awake, and empty. Psychological well-being may be defined as the state of feeling healthy and happy, having satisfaction, relaxation, pleasure and peace of mind. It deals with people's feelings about everyday experiences in life activities. Such feelings may be negative mental states or psychological strains such as anxiety, depression, frustration, emotional exhaustion, unhappiness, dissatisfaction to a state which has been identified as positive mental health (Jahoda, 1958; Warr, 1978). Bradburn and Caslowitz (1965) have discussed a dimension variously called mental health, adjustment, happiness or psychological well-being and the individuals who can be meaningfully described as relatively high or low on such a dimension. According to Witmer and Sweeney (1992) psychological well-being includes majority of characteristics of the healthy person which includes a sense of worth, a sense of control, realistic beliefs, spontaneity and emotional responsiveness, intellectual stimulation, problem solving, creativity and a sense of humour.

Various researches have shown that psychological well-being is deeply related to the individual's religious beliefs. Religious beliefs means, how closely an individual's beliefs conform to the established doctrines of a religious body. David Seedhouse (1995) introspects that the term "well-being" as used in present-day health promotion literature is an extremely vague notion. Psychologists believe well-being is constructed out of three components: (1) Life-satisfaction, (2) Positive affect, and (3) low Negative affect. Myers and Diener (1995) define high subjective well-being as frequent positive affect, infrequent negative affect and a global sense of satisfaction with life. Thus, it can be concluded that judgments of well-being are irreducibly subjective and that the meaning and content of the term are seen to fluctuate, depending on who is using it and why it is being used (Krishna Mohan, 2001).

Based on the above discussion an operational definition of well-being may include the following: Firstly, it may be understood as a scientific sounding term for what people usually mean by happiness. Secondly, it refers to what people think and feel about themselves, i.e., the cognitive and affective conclusions they reach when they evaluate their existence. Thirdly, it involves the individual's entire condition, i.e., psychological, social, and spiritual aspects of one's existence, and fourthly, well-being is a relative state of affairs—relative to the situation as well as to the values of the particular culture one belongs to, such as the traditional "Indianness" of avoiding extreme and maintaining equilibrium, of having good health and practicing self-control, self-realization and dissolution of the self.

Several studies have demonstrated a positive relationship between religiosity and psychological well-being. In a meta-analysis, Witter, Stock, Okun, and Haring (1985), summarized 28 studies which provided a total of 56 results for relationship of religiosity to well-being. The effect sizes for these findings ranged from -.01 to +.58, with a 95 per cent confidence interval for the size of the relationship ranging from .14 to .25. Witter *et al.* concluded that religion was positively associated with subjective well-being. They also noted that the relationship tended to be stronger for older people. A study by Hadaway (1978) on religiosity concluded that religion is one potential resource in people's lives. Religious mindedness was found to be positively related to both mental well-being and personal competence. In another study, Hadaway and Roof (1978) found a measure of religious meaning (importance of faith to one's life) and two measures of religious belonging (church membership and attendance) to be positively related to worthwhileness of life. More recently Myers and Diener (1995) in their survey of related studies observe that links between religion and mental health are impressive and that culture and religiosity may provide better clues to understanding the nature of well-being.

A large epidemiological study conducted by University of California at Berkeley in 1971 also found that the religiously committed had much less psychological distress than the uncommitted. (Williams, Larson, Buckler, Heckman, & Pyle, 1991). Similarly, in a longitudinal study of 720 adults conducted by David Williams, shown that regular religious attendance led to much less psychological distress (Larson & Larson, 1991). In a systematic review by David Larson (1991) on studies of religious commitment and personal well-being suggested that the relationship is powerful and positive; overall, psychological functioning improved following a resumption of participation in religious worship for those who had stopped (D'Antonio, 1980). A systematic review of the literature uncovered 100 studies that statistically examined the relationship between religiousness and well-being. Of those studies, 79 (79%) reported at least one positive correlation between religious involvement and greater happiness, life satisfaction, morale, or positive affect. Of the remaining 21 studies, 13 found no association, 1 found a negative association, and 7 reported mixed or complex relationships (Koenig, McCullough & Larson, 2001).

Levin and Markides (1988) explored the connection between religious attendance and psychological well-being in a probability sample of 375 middle-aged and 375 older Mexican-American. Regression analyses of this largely Catholic population revealed that frequent church attendance was significantly related to greater life satisfaction for middle aged women ($p<.01$) and older women ($p<.05$).

Other studies of Canadian have also reported significant relationships between religious measures and well-being (Harvey, Barnes & Greenwood, 1987; Gee & Veevers, 1990; Jamal & Badawi, 1993; Krause, 1993; Frankl & Hewitt, 1994). Krause (1992) examined the relationship among stress, religiosity, and psychological well-being in a sample of 448 African-Americans over age 60 who participated in the American Changing Lives Survey. Structural equation modelling was used to analyze the data. Religiosity was assessed using measures of self-rated religiosity, personal religious activity, and church attendance. Outcomes included emotional support, personal control, self-esteem, and depressed affect, each assessed by two or three questions. Subjective religiosity was significantly related to emotional support ($\beta=.31$, $p<.01$) and to self-esteem ($\beta=.26$, $p<.05$), but not to personal control or to depressed affect. Krause concluded that subjective religiosity affects psychological well-being among elderly African-Americans primarily by bolstering feelings of self-worth. Krause (1993) also examined the relationship between religiousness and well-being next in a sample of 709 persons age 55 or older who participated in the World Values Survey (only data from United States and Canada were included in this report). Religious measures included organizational religiosity, subjective religiosity, and religious belief; Life satisfaction was measured by 3 items. Using structural equation modelling (LISREL), Krause found a positive relationship between a second-order religiosity factor and life satisfaction ($\beta=.16$, $p<.01$), as well as positive relationship between subjective religiosity and life satisfaction ($\beta=.26$, $p<.05$). It shows that there is a strong relationship between religiosity and different components of well-being.

Religious belief and practice play an important role in the lives of millions of people worldwide. Research relating stress to religion indicated that religious and non-religious people tend to experience equal amounts of stress but religion may help people deal better with negative life events and their attendant stress (Schafer & King, 1990). A study by Maton (1989) also supports the view that high level of stress individuals are likely to benefit from perceived spiritual support and is consistent with the stress and coping model based on religion proposed by Pargament. Individuals with strong religious faith have been found to report higher levels of life satisfaction, greater personal happiness, and fewer negative psychological consequences of traumatic life events (Ellison, Gey, & Glass, 1991).

Religious beliefs and practices are consistently related to greater life satisfaction, happiness, positive affect, morale, and other indicators of well-being. Koenig, McCullough & Larson (2001) found 101 studies that examined the relationship between level of religious involvement and depression, eight of which were clinical trials. Of the 93 cross-sectional or prospective studies, 60 (65%) reported a significant positive relationship between a measure of religious involvement and lower rates of depression or depressive symptoms; 13 studies reported no association; four reported greater depression among the more religious; and 16 studies reported mixed findings (positive associations with some religious variables and negative associations between with others). Of the 22 prospective cohort studies that examined the relationship between religion and depression, 15 (68%) found that greater religious involvement predicted lower rates of depression over time. Finally, eight clinical trials have examined the effects of religious intervention on speed of recovery from depression. Five of these eight studies showed that depressed patients receiving interventions recovered significantly faster than subjects in comparison or control groups. Thus, there is growing consensus in the literature that the religiously active are less likely to become depressed and less likely to stay depressed. Other studies also demonstrate that religious beliefs and practice help to prevent the onset of depression and help to faster recovery from depression among patients who suffer from it (Koenig, *et al.*, 2001). Religious beliefs also enhance mental health through coping and happiness. The cognitive psychological model considers religion as the coping mechanism used in cognitive structuring of life. In Beck's cognitive model of depression, decisive factors are hopelessness, pessimistic expectations about one's self, the environment and the future (Beck, 1967). An important feature of religion is that tries to mobilize or restore hope, which is likely to counteract hopelessness. In their stress-vulnerability model, Brown and Harris argue that loss events produce hopelessness impairing self-esteem, which further leads to generalization of hopelessness and development of depression (Brown, Harris, 1978). Religion prevents pessimistic attribution and may influence stress-vulnerability equilibrium by decreasing hopelessness.

Chatters (2000) states that, Religious doctrines may support positive views of human nature and the self that engender attitudes and emotional states that are associated with better physical and mental health outcomes. Beliefs in the intrinsic value and uniqueness of each individual may promote feelings of self-esteem. Religious injunctions may shape interpersonal behaviours and attitudes towards others in a way that emphasize a variety of positive and pro-social goals, i.e., interpersonal warmth and friendliness, love, compassion, harmony, tolerance, and forgiveness that reduces the likelihood of noxious and stressful interpersonal interactions.

A number of well-conducted clinical and epidemiological studies have shown that religiosity under some circumstances helps in preventing depression (Koenig, Larson, & Larson, 2001). Religiosity can provide hope to people in despair. It plays an important role in daily life; people have been reported as being able to experience deep peace even in the midst of mental distress (Underwood & Teresi, 2002). It enables people to step outside the mental distress and experience comfort and calm especially, in the midst of crisis, particular kinds of religiosity can prove to be a powerful resource which can be a real buffer against excessive mental distress and despair (Pargament, 1997). In a longitudinal study conducted in the University of

Michigan, revealed that regular religious attendance led to much less psychological distress (Larson & Larson, 1991).

William, Larson, Buckler, Heckman, and Pyle (1991), also demonstrated that the religiosity committed had much less psychological distress than the uncommitted. Similarly, Religion also appears to reduce the incidence of depression among those with medical problems. A study by Wright, Frost, & Wisecaever (1993), found those who attended religious services regularly were less depressed and less distressed by life events than those who did not. Younger people tend to experience fewer of the anxieties of growing up if they are religious. In a study, both male and female Texas highschoolers found that religious beliefs gave meaning to their lives and reduced the incidence of depression and anxiety among them (Fagan, 1996).

Religion and spirituality framework can provide with a sense of their ultimate destinations in life. In a study, Emmons (1999) has suggested that a number of mechanisms that link spiritual strivings are empowering and can provide stability, support and direction in critical times and people can hold on to a sense of ultimate purpose and meaning even in the midst of disturbing life-events (Baumister, 1991).

Religion is a frequently cited mechanism for dealing with problems in life. It seems to become especially important once an illness, particularly a life-threatening one, is diagnosed in a person. Those who use religious means of coping seem to cope more effectively with their illness than those who do not use means of coping (Plante & Sherman, 2001).

Studies of religious coping show little change over time in patients with a treatable disease and an increased religious coping in patients with a terminal disease (Plante & Sherman, 2001; Fehler & Maly, 1999). Another study of 100 hospitalized patients about to undergo cardiac surgery also identified religious practice as an important tool for coping with the stress of impending surgery. The researchers found that 96 per cent of the patients used prayers as a coping mechanism. When asked how helpful they found prayer to be, 70 per cent of those patients indicated that prayer was "extremely helpful".

Emmons argues that religiosity is an aspect of adaptive functioning that raises the possibility for reaching goals. It impacts the ways of how people view the world, solve problems and it includes the capability of forgiveness, gratitude, compassion and wisdom. According to this, truly religious persons could be more efficacious in adapting to trauma and they find meaning in suffering more easily (Emmons, 1999).

Studies on the relationship between religion and mental health of women have yielded mixed results. Shaver, Lenaurer and Sadd (1980) showed high religiosity was associated with improved mental health and physical health. Spilka, Hood and Gorsuch (1985) concluded that while religion may be responsible for suppressing mental disorder and free socialization, psychopathology and religion are not positively related. Religion helps in dealing with stress and maintaining self-esteem and self-identity. It is also true that a number of problems of women in their socialization leading to sex-typing. Higher incidence of depression and poor sense of adequacy in them may be traced to such differential socialization in which religion plays an important role.

Mechanisms linking religiosity and well-being

Although there is no direct empirical research, showing the relationship between religiosity and well-being but, the literature indicates three main ways in which religion impacts health: (1) religion provides framework to cope with and reduce stress of difficult life situations, (2) religion provides an outlet for social support, and (3) religion promotes healthier living habits.

Ellison developed a model of the ways through which religious involvement enables the receipt of social support: (1) regular religious fellowship provides access to constant and like-minded individuals that provide both emotional and tangible support during a stressful life event or chronic stress, and (2) when faced with a stressful life event active religious fellowship enables individuals to ascribe a meaning to the event within a larger context that offers greater meaning, and therefore individuals experience the event less negatively. This model implies that active religious participation can be a source of support, which in turn may help to buffer the effects of stress and promote well-being (Ellison & George, 1994).

The impact of religion on psychical and mental health may also be understood in the frame of new advances in psycho-immunodoctrinological research. Psychic, immune and endocrinological statuses have to be in balance to maintain homeostasis and prevent disease. Both emotions and religious feelings may influence immunoendocrinological function (Lissoni, Cangemi, Pirato, Roselli, Rovelli, Brivio, *et al.*, 2001). Social support can function as a stress buffer, reducing plasma level of cortisol elicited by stressors, be a predictor of longer survival among cancer patients, lower risk for cardiovascular disease and enhance rehabilitation after stroke (Spiegel, 1996; Strike, Steptoe, 2004; Bhogal, Teasell, Foley, Speechley, 2003). Higher levels of stress and depression are associated with release of hormones, such as cortisol that impairs immune function, and we can hypothesize that religion commitment improves stress control and even has an immunomodulatory role (Lissoni, *et al.*, 2001).

Religion and pregnancy

The literature on spirituality in nursing, medicine, and other disciplines has grown dramatically in the past twenty years (Berry, Bass, Fowler, & Allen, 2002; Flannelly, Flannelly, & Weaver, 2002; Greasley, Chiu, & Gartland, 2001; Mills, 2002; Newshan, 1998; Postwhite, Ceronsky, Kreitzer, Nickelson, Drew, Mackey *et al.*, 1996; Smucker, 1998; Tuck, McCain, & Elswick, 2001) but the research on the meaning that spirituality or religiosity may have for pregnant women remains limited.

Health and prosperity are meant for everyone but it is not with the case of Indian women. Women have continued to occupy a subservient and passive role in the patriarchal structure of the Indian society. Research shows that socially constructed differences between women and men in roles and responsibilities status and power and interact with biological differences contribute to differences in nature of mental health problems. Within the Indian context, since the 1960s several studies have shown that mental illness is more common among women. They often suppress their need for autonomy and neglect their health. The cause of most of the mental health problem lies in the family and society which put heavy demands on women that are sometimes incongruent with their own beliefs and attitudes. In the traditional Indian society, a girl is subjected to different kinds of socialization practices as compared to boy. She is consciously or unconsciously subjected to an environment where she has to behave in responsible, caring and submissive manner (Miller, 1984). Underlying factors of mental health demonstrate that depression and anxiety are more common in women. Women also experience considerable emotional distress and stress associated with reproductive health condition and problems.

Psychological well-being is intrinsically important, conferring a subjective sense of emotional well-being on the individual woman and extrinsically important, representing a significant resource to the broader society in which she lives and works. It is vital, therefore, the woman's health in general and women's well-being in particular are examined within a social model which gives an account of the physical and psychological well-being of common life stressors and events that are disproportionately experienced by woman. The different levels of susceptibility and exposure to various kinds of health risks that women face compared with men will be inevitably set limits on those opportunities for exercising control over the determinants of their psychological well-being.

Childbirth represents a major pain experience that accompanies the normal physiologic process of giving birth. Birth is also a profound psychological experience. Childbirth may be viewed as a list of womanhood, a test of personal competence, a peak experience, and the first act of motherhood. The origin of the word "birth" is from the Old Norse word burdinr or behr, which seems to imply "to bear" or "to endure". Women interviewed about their memories of pain experiences throughout their lives report that the pain of childbirth was the most memorable pain they had experienced (Niven & Brodie, 1995). Childbirth pain is a unique and complex sensory and affective experience that differs from acute or chronic pain of disease, trauma, or surgical or medical procedure (Niven & Murphy, Black, 2000; Sittner, Hudson, Grossman & Gaston-Johannson, 1998; Waldenstrom, 1996; Yerby, 1996). Birth is characterized by pain but also by the most positive of life-events-(creating) a new life" (Niven & Gijsbers, 1996, p. 131).

Pregnancy is a biological process invested with great social meaning and surrounded by values, customs and laws in all human societies. The personal meaning of childbearing are influenced by pervasive social values, religious belief system, governmental policies, economic and educational factors and family or reference group traditions. Pregnancy has been viewed variously as a period of psychological stress, a normative crisis, or a developmental phase. Pregnancy is perceived as a period of happiness in anticipation of motherhood. However, depressive, anxiety, stress and distress symptoms are prevalent during pregnancy (Beck, 2001; Copper, Murray, Hooper, West, 1996; Herberg, Wachlbeck, 1999). The studies of Bluestone and McGahee (1902) on normal pregnant women indicate that there is more anxiety during the period of pregnancy than before. Many studies have indicated the depression and anxiety during pregnancy affect neonatal outcome especially preterm birth and low birth weights have been associated with antenatal stress or anxiety (Copper, Goldenberg, Das, Elder, Swain & Norman, 1996).

Anxiety during pregnancy had its association with adverse birth outcomes have been examined in a few studies, some of which found an association (Gorsuch, 1974; Molfese, Bricker, Manion; 1987; Brooke, Anderson, & Bland, 1989) while others did not (Pagel, Smilktein, Regen, 1990; Peacock, Bland, Anderson, 1995; Wadhwa, Sanderman, Porto, 1993; Norbeck, Anderson, 1989). One study found that pregnancy related anxiety was associated with shorter gestations. High anxiety levels during pregnancy have been associated with lower Apgar scores at 5 min. after birth (Crandon, 1979; Schmitz &

Reif, 1994). A cohort study carried out by Teixeira *et al.* (1999) found an association between score of the STAI (Spielberg, Gorsuch, and Lushene, 1970) in pregnancy and higher mean uterine artery resistance index ($r=0.31, p<0.002; r=0.28, p<0.005$) respectively. This study suggests a mechanism by which the psychological state of the mother may affect fetal development, and may explain epidemiological associations between maternal anxiety and low birth weight.

A few studies examining depression and pregnancy outcome have shown an association (Orr & Miller, 1995; Steer, Scholl, & Hediger, 1992) while others have not (Perkin, Bland, Peacock, 1993; Peacock, Bland, Anderson, 1995). Depression during pregnancy has particularly been associated with Low Birth Weight (Zimmer-Gembeck & Helfand, 1996; Paalberg, Vingerhoets, Paaschier, Heinen, VanGeijn, 1999). Attention has focused on increased risks of spontaneous preterm delivery, Low Birth Weight, operative delivery (caesarean section and instrumental vaginal delivery), and admission to a neonatal intensive care unit among offspring of women with antenatal depression (Orr, James, & Blackmore Prince, 2002; Chung, Lau, & Yip, 2001; Hoffman & Hatch, 2000). Not only depression tend to shorten pregnancy but major life events, if they are perceived as stressful, tend to shorten it as well (Sjostrom, Thelin, Valentin, 1999; Dole, Savitz & Hertz-Picciotto, 2003). A study involving women with depressive symptoms late in pregnancy showed that these women had a 3.97 risk of delivering a Low Birth Weight, a 3.39 risk for having a preterm delivery, and 3.02 risks for intra-uterine growth rate (Steer, Scholl, Hediger, Fischer, 1992).

Birbring (1959, 1961) has described pregnancy, as a period of crisis involving profound psychological as well as somatic changes. A number of studies (Entwise & Doering, 1981 ; Leifer, 1977; Osofsky 1980; Shereshefsky & Yarrow, 1973) have clarified the normative psychological adjustment to pregnancy, the difficulties that may contribute to emotional disturbance during pregnancy and the process of adjustment to anticipation motherhood. Chertok (1969), Heinstein, (1967), and McDonald (1968) found that psychological factors influence pregnancy and long-term implications of psychological difficulty during pregnancy and following the childhood.

The belief that a mother's psychological status may affect her fetus has been common in every society, since ancient times. It was confirmed that psychological factors such as maternal psychological stress and distress have been associated with both birth weight and gestational age for example, low birth weight, prematurity and intra-uterine growth retardation (Rondo *et al.*, 2003). It was found that LBW and preterm delivery are associated with distress in 20-26 weeks gestation and in the 30-36 weeks gestation, respectively, even after controlling for other risk factors. Maternal psychological stress and distress have been associated with Low Birth Weight, Prematurity and Intra-Uterine Growth Retardation (Rondo *et al.*, 2003). Hedegaar Henriksens, Sabroe, & Secher (1993) carried out a research evaluating the importance of psychological distress in pregnancy (estimated by the GHQ questionnaire) on preterm labour, and found a dose-response relationship between distress assessed in the 30th week of pregnancy and risk of preterm delivery. Copper *et al.* (1996) also reported that women with a gestation age between the 25th and 29th weeks of pregnancy, who perceived their lives as being stressful, are at increased risk for spontaneous preterm birth and low birth weight.

Two reviews of the literature on stress and birth outcomes have concluded that life-events stress is most consistently corrected with prenatal events, particularly with preterm delivery or gestational age, rather than with complications during delivery (Levin & Defrank, 1998; Lederman, 1995). A large study from Denmark, evaluating the influence of psychosocial factors on intra-uterine growth retardation and preterm delivery shows that psychosocial stressors and duration of schooling appeared to influence preterm delivery (Nodensoft *et al.*, 1996). Pritchard and Teo (1994) studied the relationship between persistent stressful aspects of daily life and birth outcomes in 393 women from Scotland and revealed that psychosocial difficulty in the household role represents a risk factor for preterm birth and low birth weight.

A review covering the last 10 years of research on stress, social support and pregnancy outcome, concluded that acute life stressors have direct effects on birth outcome, whereas strong partner or family support as a promoter of fetal growth can almost equal certainly be ruled in (Hoffman & Hatch, 1996). Thus, it can be concluded that many studies show that preterm deliveries have often been preceded by stress situations (Austin & Leader, 2000).

Caplan (1960), described pregnancy as a crisis for women and suggested that the women's emotional state, which varies at different stages during pregnancy, depends on her capacity to adjust and physiological changes and that her reaction to sexual aspects of the reproductive process influence her emotional state and mental health during pregnancy. Pregnancy can be time to complete the miraculous nature of the experience and to deepen or renew spiritual connectedness (Goddard, 1995; Hall, 2001; Jesse & Reed, 2004; Louden, 1995). Some believe that there is no event more spiritually connected to our humanness than birth; new life enters to the world and the infant takes the first breath, translated as spirit in Latin and Hebrew (Ayers-Gould, 2000; Baumiller, 2002; Golberg, 1998). However, western societies have become more removed from their historical and cultural context with our emphasis on the physical aspects of birth, advances in technology, and medical innovation, the miracle of pregnancy and birth can be lost (Association of Radical Midwives, 2003; Ayers-Gould, 2000).

Najman, Williams, Keeping, Morrison & Anderson (1998) (n=6,566) were one of the first to report the relationship or religiosity to maternal and infant health. They found that religious sect members, defined as Mormon, Seventh Day Adventist, or Jehovah's witness, exhibited significantly fewer health-risk behaviours in pregnancy, such as use of alcohol, rugs or tobacco and other unhealthily lifestyle choices and practices. Their infants weighted significantly more and had a later gestational age at birth than infants of mainstream Catholics and Protestants.

A number of studies have been linked to spiritual coping. A study conducted by Jada G. Hamilton, Marci Lobel (2008) determined how women cope with stress across pregnancy and explored the association of coping with maternal characteristics, stress perceptions, dispositions and social support. Factor analysis of the revised prenatal coping inventory revealed three distinct types of coping: planning, preparation, avoidance and spiritual-positive coping. Spiritual coping was used most frequently during pregnancy, avoidant coping was used least often. Greater religiosity and optimism were the strongest predictors of spiritual coping.

Elizabeth Jesse and Pamela G. Reed (2004) conducted a study on sample of pregnant Appalachian women to determine the relationships of spirituality and psychological well-being to health risk behaviours and found that higher levels of spirituality and lower level of stress are associated with decreased health risk behaviours among pregnant women from Appalachia. Increasing spiritual resources and deceasing stress during pregnancy offer the potential to improve heath promotion efforts in pregnancy.

The findings obtained by Najman, Williams, Keeping, Morrison, & Anderson (1988) also suggest that there is a continuing impact of religious beliefs and practices on health related behaviours and the consequent health of pregnant women.

An analysis by Jesse and Reed (2004) reported that higher levels of spirituality (spiritual perspective and religiosity) were correlated with greater satisfaction with social support, higher levels of self-esteem, and decreased levels of smoking in Appalachian women. Magana and Clark (1995), who reviewed the literature on the relationship of religiosity and spirituality to birth outcomes in Mexican-American women, postulated that Mexican-American women experience less perinatal mortality and higher birth weights, despite lower socio-economic status and less prenatal care, because of the strong influence of spirituality and religiosity in Latino culture. Morgan's (1966) qualitative study (N=33) examined the cultural context of prenatal care for African-American women in urban and rural environment. An aspect of their findings was that women expressed the importance of spirituality as a way to feel a sense of balance.

Callister, Semenic, & Foster (1999) phenomenological study of Canadian Jewish (N=30) American Mormon (N=30) pregnant women evaluated women's childbirth experiences within religious and cultural context in which Jewish women described childbearing as an experience that created empowerment and as a way to fulfil their religious duties. Mormon women spoke of the connection between their spirituality and feelings of reverence, awe, purpose, and meaning of their birth experiences.

Emergent Themes

During the review of literature following emergent themes were revealed :—

(1) *Hope*: is a positive attitude that a person assumes in the face of difficulty. Without hope many people become depressed and are more prone to illness. Religion sustains a sense of meaning and provides hope during the traumatic and tough time.

(2) *Forgiveness*: A practice that is encouraged by many spiritual and religious traditions, forgiveness is a release of hostility and resentment from past hurts. The act of forgiveness can result in less anxiety and depression, better health outcomes, increased coping with stress and closeness to God and others (Worthington, 1997). Psychological research has consistently demonstrated that religious involvement is positively related to the disposition to forgive others. Rokeach (1973) found that people who reported greater church attendance, religiousness, and intrinsic as well as extrinsic motivation for religious involvement placed "forgiveness" as a higher priority in their personal value system than did people who scored lower on these religious indicators. Poloma and Gallup (1991) also found a positive relationship between

religious involvements and self-report of people's tendency to forgive those who have harmed them.

(3) *Guidance and support*: is the most common theme which emerged during the review. A study conducted by Elizabeth (2008) revealed that spirituality guided and supported them in one way or the other. Several studies have linked various dimensions of spiritual involvement with larger or more social networks and/or with perceived social and emotional support (e.g. Oman & Reed, 1998; Strawbridge *et al.*, 2001).

(4) *Creating a meaning life pattern*: This theme included the concepts of life transforming, and life satisfaction. In a study it was found that people living with a terminal illness challenged to face their own mortality, resulting in significant changes in behaviour. Individual with a history of long-term drug addiction recognized their self-destructive behaviour and sought out a new life direction. Religiosity and spirituality provides a way for healthy lifestyle, it promotes good and healthy practices. Several dimensions of religious involvement have been associated with well-established behavioural risk factors. Behaviourally strict denominations may discourage smoking and drinking of alcohol or encourage good health behaviours out of respect for the body as an instrument of God's service. Persons attending religious services more frequently have been found to engage in more exercise and less smoking and heavy drinking (Oman & Reed, 1998; Strawbridge, Shema, Cohen, & Kaplan, 2001).

(5) *Connectedness with God*: The essence of connectedness reflects a significant, shared meaningful personal relationship that one has with another person, a spiritual being, nature, or an aspect of one's inner self (Benner & Wrubel, 1989; Haase, Britt, Coward, Leidy, & Penn, 1992). It also involves both receiving and giving support. Connectedness is expressed in the concepts of activities, relationships, and altruism. Prayer and reading the religious texts were the two

frequently most cited sources for experiencing a relationship with God.

Conclusion

A general conclusion can be drawn from this chapter is that religiosity facilitates psychological well-being. However, there are several limitations inherent in this chapter. First, the nature of the relationship between religiosity and well-being may vary depending on which aspect or dimension of religiosity and which aspect of well-being is under consideration. It is generally agreed that both religiosity and psychological well-being are multidimensional constructs (e.g. Glock & Stark, 1965; Faulkner & De Jong, 1966; King, 1967; King & Hunt, 1975; Campbell, Converse, Roger, 1976). Consequently, it is quite possible that certain dimension of religiosity may be more relevant to certain types of well-being than are others. And generally, most of the studies have employed only one measure of religiosity as the independent variable. Since different dimensions of religiosity tend to be positively correlated, it is impossible to know from the above studies if the relationship they uncovered between a given measure of religiosity and well-being hold while controlling for other religiosity measures. Even the Hadaway and Roof (1978) study, which employed both belonging (church membership and attendance) and meaning (importance of faith) measures of religiosity, did not examine the effect of one measure while controlling for the effects of the measures.

Second, the literature on religion and mental health and physical health has increased dramatically in past few years but the literature on religion and pregnancy is rather very limited. At present times, an accurate need of assessment of women's psychological well-being is an essential element in effective health promotion, which remains hampered by inadequate sources of data. Women's mental health concerns extend beyond specific conditions or problems. They encompass the structure that govern the provision of health education, information and health care delivery, the processes that influence women's interaction with the health care system and the factors that determine whether the treatment they receive is gender sensitive. An overly biological, individual focus in research and theoretical models which often neglect to consider how women's low social status and material circumstances intersect with their family roles and their participation in paid employment in determining mental health outcomes.

REFERENCES

Anonymous: Webster's College Dictionary. (Random House Inc., New York, 1997).

Association of Radical Midwives (2003). *Midwives of the soul: The spirituality of birth.* Retrieved September 15, 2006, from http://www.radmid.demon.co.uk/spirituality.htm.

Austin, M. P. & Leader, L. (2000). Maternal stress and obstetric and infant outcomes: Epidemiological findings and neuroendocrine mechanisms. *Australian NZ Journal of Obstetrics and Gynecology, 40,* 331-337.

Ayers-Gould, J.N. (2000). Spirituality in birth: Creating sacred space within the medical model. *International Journal of Childbirth Education, 15,* 14-17.

Baumister, R.F. (1991). *Meanings of life.* New York: Guilford Press.

Baumiller, R.C. (2002). Spiritual development during a first pregnancy. *International Journal of Childbirth Education,* 17, 7.

Beck, A.T. (1967). *Depression: Clinical, experimental and theoretical aspects.* Harper & Row, New York.

Beck, C.T. (2001). Predictors of postpartum depression: an update. *Nursing Researchers, 50,* 275-285.

Beery, T.A., Bass, L.S., Fowler, C., & Allen, G. (2002). Spirituality in persons with heart failure. *Journal of Holistic Nursing, 20,* 5-25.

Benner, P., & Wrubel, J. (1989). *The primacy of caring.* Menlo Park, CA: Addison-Wesley.

Bergin, A.E. & Payne, I.R. (1993). "Proposed agenda for a spiritual strategy in personality and psychotherapy", in E.L. Worthington, Jr. (Ed.). *Psychotherapy and Religious Value,* (pp. 243-260). Grand Rapids, MI: Baker.

Bhusan, L.N. (1970). *Manual for religiosity scale.* National Psychological Corporation, Agra-2.

Bhogal, S.K., Teasell, R.W., Foley, N.C., & Speechley, R. (2003). *Top Stroke Rehabilitation, 10,* 107.

Bluestone, H. & McGahee, C.L. (1962). Reaction to extreme stress. *American Journal of Psychiatry, 119,* 393-396.

Bibring, G.L. (1959). Some considerations of the psychological processes in pregnancy. *Journal of Psychoanalytical Study of Child, 14,* 113-121.

Bibring, G.L. (1961). A study of psychological processes in pregnancy and the earlier mother-child relationship: (I) Some propositions and comments. (II) Methodological considerations. *Journal of Psychoanalytical Study of Child; 16,* 9-12.

Bradburn, N.M. & Caplowitz, D. (1965). *Report on happiness.* Chicago: Aldine.

Brooke, O.G., Anderson, H.R., & Bland, J.M. (1989). Effects on birth weight of smoking, alcohol, caffeine, socio-economic factors and psychosocial stress. *British Medical Journal, 298,* 795-801.

Brown, G.W., Harris, T.O. (1978). *Social origins of depression.* Tavistock, London.

Callister, L. C., Semenic, S., & Foster, J. C. (1999). Cultural and spiritual meaning of childbirth: Orthodox Jewish and Mormon Women. *Journal of Holistic Nursing, 17,* 280-295.

Camphell, A., Converse, P.E. & Rogers, W. (1976). *The quality of American life: Perceptions, evaluation and satisfactions.* New York: Russeli Sage Foundation.

Caplan, G. (1960). *Emotional implications of pregnancy and influences on family relationships in the healthy child: His physical, psychological and social development.* Cambridge, Harvard University Press. H.C. Stuart and D.C. Prugh, Eds. 72-82.

Chertok, L. (1969). *Motherhood and personality: Psychosomatic Aspects of childbirth,* Grahem D. London: Taristock Publications.

Chatters, L.M. (2000). Religion and health: Public health research and practice. *Annual Review of Public Health, 21,* 353-367.

Chung, T.K., Lau, T.K., Yip, A.S. (2001). Antepartum depressive symptomatology is associated with adverse obstetric and neonatal outcomes. *Psychosomatic Medicine, 63,* 830-834.

Cole, B.S. & Pargament, K.I. (1997). Spiritual surrender: A paradoxical path to control. In W.R. Miller (Ed.). *Integrating spirituality into treatment,* 179-198. American Psychological Association, Washington DC.

Cooper, R.L., Goldenberg, R.L., Das, A., Elden, A., Swain, M., Norman, G. (1996). The preterm prediction study: maternal stress is associated with spontaneous preterm birth at less than 35 weeks' gestation. *American Journal of Obstetrics & Gynecology, 175,* 1286-1292.

D'Antonio, W.V. (1980). The family and religion: Exploring a changing relationship. *Journal for the Scientific Study of Religion, 19,* 89-104.

Dein, S. & Stgyal, J. (1997). Does bring religious help nor hinder coping with chronic illness? A critical literature review. *Palliative Medicine, 11*, 291-298.

Dittes, J.E. (1975). Psychology of religion in G. Lindzey and E. Aronson (Eds.). *The Handbook of Social Psychology* (2nd edition) vol. 5. American Publishing Co., New York.

Dole, N., Savitz, D.A., Hertz-Picciotto, I. (2003). Maternal stress and preterm birth. *American Journal of Epidemiology, 157*, 14-24.

Ellison, C.G., Gey, D. A., & Glass, T.A. (1991). "Does religious commitment contribute to individual life satisfaction? *Social Forces, 68*, 100-123.

Ellison, C.G. & George, L.K. (1994). *Journal for the Scientific Study of Religion, 33*, 46-61.

Emmons, R.A. (1999). *The psychology of ultimate concerns: Motivation and spirituality in personality.* New York: Guilford Press.

Entwise, D.R. & Doering, S.G. (1981). *The First Birth: A Family Turning Point.* Baltimore: Johns Hopkins University Press.

Fagan (1996). "Rising illegitimacy: America's social catastrophe" and U.S. department of health human services, Report to Congress on out of neither wed-lock childbearing, September 1995, esp. chapter on "The consequences of non-marital childbearing for women, children and society" by Sarah McLanahan.

Faulkner, J.E. & DeJong, G.F. (1966). Religiosity in 5-D: An empirical analysis. *Social Forces, 45*, 246-254.

Fehler, S. & Maly, R.C. (1999). *Psycho-oncology, 8*, 408.

Flannelly, L.T., Flannelly, K.J., & Weaver, A.J. (2002). Religious and spiritual variables in three major oncology nursing journals: 1990-1999. *Oncology Nursing Forum Online, 29*, 679-685.

Frankel, B.G. & Hewitt, W.E. (1994). Religion and well-being among Canadian university students. *Journal for the Scientific Study of Religion, 33*, 62-73.

Fromm, E. (1976). *To have or to be.* New York: Harper and Row.

Galloway, G.G. (1956). *The philosophy of religion.* Edinburgh: T. & T. Clark.

Gee, E.M. & Veevers, J.E. (1990). Religious involvement and life satisfaction in Canada. *Sociological Analysis, 51*, 387-394.

Glock, C.Y. & Stark, R. (1965). *Religion and Society in Tension.* Chicago: Rand McNally.

Goddard, N.C. (1995). Spirituality as integrative energy: A philosophical analysis as requisite precursor to holistic nursing practice. *Journal of Advanced Nursing*, 22, 608-615.

Golberg, B. (1998). Connection: An exploration of spirituality in nursing care. *Journal of Advanced Nursing, 27*, 836-842.

Gorsuch, R.L. & Key, M.K. (1974). Abnormalities of pregnancy as a function of anxiety and life stress. *Psychosomatics Medicine, 36*, 352-362.

Greasley, P., Chiu, L.F., & Gartland, M. (2001). The concept of spiritual care in mental health nursing. *Journal of Advanced Nursing, 33,* 629-637.

Haase, J.E., Britt, T., Coward, D.D., Leidy, N.K., & Penn, P.E. (1992). Simultaneous concept analysis of spiritual perspective. Hope, acceptance and self-transcendence. Image. *The Journal of Nursing Scholarship, 24,* 141-147.

Hadaway, C.K. (1978). "Life satisfaction and religion: a reanalysis". *Social Forces, 57,* 636-643.

Hadaway, C.K. & Roof, W.C. (1978). "Religious commitment and quality of life in America". *Review of Religious Research, 19,* 173-190.

Hall, J. (2001). *Midwifery, mind and spirit: Emerging issues of care.* Oxford, UK: Books for Midwives.

Harvey, C.D.H., Barnes, G.E., & Greenwood, L. (1987).Correlates of morale among Canadian widowed persons. *Social Psychiatry, 22,* 65-72.

Heinstein, M.I. (1967). Expressed attitude and feelings of pregnant women and their relations to physical complications of pregnancy. *Merrill-Palmer Quarterly, 13 (3),* 217-236.

Hedegaard, M., Henriksen, T.B., Sabroe, S., & Secher, N.J. (1993). Psychological distress in pregnancy and preterm delivery. *British Medical Journal, 307,* 234-238.

Hertzerg, T. & Wahlbeck, K. (1999). The impact of pregnancy and puerperium on pain disorder: a review. *Journal of Psychosomatic Obstetrics and Gynecology, 20,* 59-64.

Hoffman, S. & Hatch, M.C. (2000). Depressive symptomatology during pregnancy: Evidence for an association with decreased fetal growth in pregnancies of lower social class women. *Health Psychology, 19,* 535-543.

Jahoda, M. (1958). *Current concepts of positive mental health.* New York: Basic Books.

Jamal, M. & Badawi, J. (1993). Job stress among Muslim immigrants in North America: Moderating effects of religiosity. *Stress Medicine, 9,* 145-151.

Jesse, D.E. & Reed, P.G. (2004). Effects of spirituality and psychosocial well-being on health risk behaviours in Appalachian pregnant women. *Journal of Obstetric, Gynaecologic and Neonatal Nursing, 33,* 739-747.

Jesse, D.E., Schoneboom, C., & Blanchard, A. (2007). The effect of faith or spirituality in pregnancy: a content analysis. *Journal of Holistic Nursing, 25,* 151-158.

King, M.B. (1967). "Measuring the religious variable: nine proposed dimensions." *Journal for the Scientific Study of Religion, 6,* 173-190.

King, M.B. & Hunt, R.A. (1975). Measuring the religious variable: National replication. *Journal for the Scientific Study of Religion, 14,* 13-22.

Koenig, H.G. (1997). Use of religion by patients with severe medical illness. *Mind/body Medicine, 2,* 31-36.

Koenig, H.G., Larson, D.B., & Larson, S.S. (2001). Religion and coping with serious medical illness. *Annals of Pharmacotherapy, 85,* 852-859.

Koenig, H.G., McCullough, M.E., & Larson, D.B. (2001). *Handbook of Religion and Health.* New York, Oxford University Press.

Krause, N. (1992). Stress, religiosity, and psychological well-being among older blacks. *Journal of Aging and Health, 4,* 412-439.

Krause, N. (1993). Measuring religiosity in later life. *Research on Aging, 15,* 170-197.

Larson and Larson (1991). "The forgotten factor in physical and mental health".

Larson, D.B. & Larson, S.S (1991). Does religious commitment make a clinical difference in health? *Second Opinion, 17,* 26-40.

Lederman R.P. (1995). Relationship of anxiety, stress, and psychosocial development to reproductive health. *Behavioural Medicine, 21,* 101-112.

Levin, J.S. & DeFrank, R.S. (1988). Maternal stress and pregnancy outcomes: a review of psychosocial literature. *Journal of Psychosomatics, Obstetrics and Gynecology, 9,* 13-16.

Levin, J.S., Markides, K.S. (1988). Religious attendance and psychological well-being in middle-aged and older Mexican-Americans. *Sociological Analysis, 49,* 66-72.

Lissoni, P., Cangemi, P., Pirato, D., Roselli, M.G., Rovelli, F., Brivio, F., Maligani, F., *et al.* (2001). *Neuroendocrinol. Lett., 22,* 175.

Louden, J. (1995). *The pregnant woman's comfort book.* San Francisco: Harper Collins.

Magana, A. & Clark, N.M. (1995). Examining a paradox: Does religiosity contribute to positive birth outcomes in Mexican-American populations? *Health Education Quarterly,* 22, 96-109.

Maslow, A. (1968). *Towards a psychology of being.* New York: Van Nostrand.

Maton, K.I. (1989). "The stress-buffering role of spiritual support: Cross-sectional and perspective investigations". *Journal for the Scientific Study of Religion, 28,* 310-323.

McDonald, R.L. (1968). The role of emotional factors in obstetrics complications: A Review. *Journal of Psychosomatic Medicine, 30,* 222-237.

Mellors, M.P., Erlen, J.A., Coontz, P.D., Lucke, K.T. (2001). Transcending the suffering of AIDS. *Journal of Community Health Nursing, 18,* 235-246.

Miller, J.G. (1984). Culture and the development of everyday explanations. *Journal of Personality and Social Psychology, 46,* 961-978.

Mills, P.J. (2002). Spirituality, religiousness, and health: From research to clinical practice. *Annals of Behavioural Medicine, 24,* 1-2.

Mohan, K.K. (2001). "Spirituality and well-being: an overview." Cornelissen, Matthijs (Ed.) *Consciousness and its transformation.*

Molfese, V.J., Bricker, M.C., & Manion, L.G. (1987). Anxiety, depression and stress in pregnancy: a multivariate model of intra-partum risks and pregnancy outcome. *Journal of Psychosomatics Obstetrics and Gynecology, 7,* 77-92.

Morgan, M. (1996). Prenatal care of African-American women in selected USA urban and rural cultural contexts. *Journal of Transcultural Nursing, 7,* 3-9.

Myers, D.G. & Diener, Ed.(1995). "Who is happy?" *Psychological Science, 6,* 10-19.

Najman, J.M., Williams, G.M., Keeping, J.D., Morrison, J., & Anderson, M.J. (1988). Religious values, practices and pregnancy outcomes: A comparison of the impact of sect and mainstream Christian affiliation. *Social Science Medicine, 26,* 401-407.

Newshan, G. (1998). Transcending the physical, spiritual aspects of pain in patients with HIV and/or cancer. *Journal of Advanced Nursing, 28,* 1236-1241.

Niven, C., & Brodie, E. (1995). Memory for labour pain: content and quality. *Pain, 64,* 387-392.

Niven, C.A. & Gijsbers, K. (1996). *The psychology of reproduction,* eds. Niven C.A. and Walker A., Butterworth Heinemann, Oxford 1996, 131-147.

Niven C.A., Murphy-Black, T. (2000). Memory for labour pain: a review of the literature. *Birth, 27,* 244-253.

Noebeck, J.S. & Anderson, N.J. (1989). Life stress, social support, and anxiety in mid- and late-pregnancy among low income women. *Research of Nursing Health, 12,* 281-287.

Nordentoft, M., Lou, H.C., Hansen, D., Nim, J., Pryds, O., Rubin, P., & Hemmingsen, R. (1996). Intrauterine growth retardation and premature delivery: the influence of maternal smoking and psychological factors. *American Journal of Public Health, 86,* 347-354.

Oman, D., & Reed, D. (1998). Religion mortality among the community-dwelling elderly. *American Journal of Public Health, 88,* 1469-1475.

Orr, S.T., James, S.A., Blackmore Prince, C. (2002). Maternal prenatal depressive symptoms and spontaneous preterm birth among African-American women in Baltimore, Maryland. *American Journal of Epidemiology, 156,* 797-802.

Osofsky, H.J. & Osofsky, J.D. (1980). *Normal adaptation to pregnancy and new parenthood.* In Parent-Infant relationships, Taylor, D.M. (ed.). New York; Grunc and Stratton, 25-48.

Paalberg, K.M., Vingerhoets, A.J.J.M., Paaschier, J., Dekker, G.A., Heinen, A.G., VanGeijn, H. P. (1999). Psychosocial predictors of low birth weight: A prospective study. *British Journal of Obstetrics and Gynecology, 106,* 834-841.

Pargament, K.I. (1997). *The Psychology of Religion and Coping: Theory, research, practice.* New York: Guilford Press.

Pargament, K.I., Echemendia, R.J., Johnson, S., Cook, P., McGath, C., Myers, J. & Brannick, M. (1987). "The conservative church: Psychosocial advantages and disadvantages". *American Journal of Community Psychology, 15,* 269-286.

Pagel, M.D., Smilkstein, G., Regen, H. (1990). Psychosocial influences on new born outcomes: a controlled prospective study. *Social Science Medicine, 30,* 597-604.

Pargament, K.I., Smith, B.W., Koenig, H.G., & Perez, L. (1998). Pattern of positive and negative religious coping with major life stressors. *Journal for the Scientific Study of Religion, 37,* 710-724.

Peacock, J.L., Bland, J.M., & Anderson, H.R. (1995). Preterm delivery: effects of socio-economic factors, psychological stress, smoking, alcohol, and caffeine. *British Medical Journal, 311,* 531-535.

Perkin, M.R., Bland, I.M. & Peacock, J.L. (1993). The effect of anxiety and depression during pregnancy on obstetric complications. *British Journal of Obstetrics & Gynaecology, 100,* 629-634.

Plante, T.G., Sherman, A.C. (2001). *Faith and Heal.* Guilford Press, New York.

Poloma, M.M., & Gallup, G.H. (1991). *Varieties of prayer.* Philadelphia: Trinity Press International.

Post-White, J., Ceronsky, C., Kreitzer, M., Nickelson, K., Drew, D., Mackey, K., *et al.* (1996). Hope, spirituality, sense of coherence, and quality of life in patient with cancer. *Oncology Nursing Forum, 23,* 1571-1579.

Pritchard, C.W., Teo, P.Y.K. (1994). Preterm birth, low birth weight and the stressfulness of the household role for pregnant women. *Social Science Medicine, 38,* 89-96.

Rini, C.K., Dunkel-Schetter, C., Wadhwa, P.D. (1999). Psychological adaptation and birth outcomes: the role of personal resources, stress, and socio-cultural context in pregnancy. *Health Psychology, 18,* 333-345.

Rokeach, M. (1973). *The nature of human values.* New York: Free Press.

Rondo, P.H.C., Ferreira, R.F., Nogueira, F., Ribeiro, M.C.N., Lobert, H., & Artes, R. (2003). Maternal psychological stress and distress as predictors of low birth weight, prematurity, and intrauterine growth retardation. *European Journal of Clinical Nutrition, 57,* 266-272.

Scheiner, M.P., & Carver, C.S. (1987). "Disposition optimism and physical well-being: The influence of generalized outcome expectancies on health". *Journal of Personality, 55,* 169-210.

Schafen, W.E. & King, M. (1990). Religiousness and stress among college students: A survey report. *Journal of College Student Development, 31,* 336-341.

Schmitz, K., Reif, L.A. (1994). Reducing prenatal risk and improving birth outcomes: The public health nursing role. *Public Health Nursing, 11,* 174-180.

Seedhouse, D. (1995). Well-being: Health promotions red herring. *Health Promotion International, 10,* 61-67.

Shereshefsky, P.M. & Yarrow, L.T. (1973). *Psychological aspects of a first pregnancy and early post-natal adaptation.* New York, Raven Press.

Shukla, A.P. (1990). Degree of religiosity as related to dependency and self-esteem in three religious committee: Hindu, Muslim, and Christian. *Indian Journal of Psychology, 65(1-4),* 1-7.

Smucker, C.J. (1998). Nursing, healing, and spirituality. *Complimentary therapies in Nursing and Midwifery, 4,* 95-97.

Sjostrom, K., Thelin, T., Valentin, L. (1999). Do pre-early, and mid-pregnancy life events influence gestation length? *Journal of Psychosomatic Obstetrics and Gynecology, 20,* 170-176.

Sittner, B., Hudson, D.B., Grossman C.C., Gaston-Johansson, F. (1998). Adolescents' perceptions of pain during labour. *Clinical Nursing Research, 7,* 82-93.

Spilka, B., Hood, R.W. Jr., Gorsuch, R.L. (1985). *The psychology of religion: An empirical approach.* Englewood Cliffs, NJ: Prentice Hall.

Spilka, B., Shaver, P., & Kirkpatric, L.A. (1985). A general attribution theory for the psychology of religion. *Journal for the Scientific Study of Religion, 24,* 1-20.

Spielberger, C.D., Gorsuch, R.I. & Lushene, R.E. (1970). *STAI Manual for the state-trait anxiety inventory.* Palo Alto, CA: Consulting Psychologist Press.

Spiegel, D. (1996). *British Journal of Psychiatry, 168,* 109.

Steer, R.A., Scholl, T.O., Hediger, M.L., Fischer, R.L. (1992). Self-reported depression and negative pregnancy outcomes. *Journal of Clinical Epidemiology, 45,* 1093-1099.

Strawbridge, W.J., Shema, S.I., Cohen. R.D., Kaplan, G.A. (2001). Religious attendance increases survival by improving and maintenance good health practices, mental health, and stable marriages. *Annals of Behavioural Medicine, 23,* 68-74.

Strike, P. C. & Steptoe, A. (2004). *Progressive Cardiovascular disease, 46,* 337.

Teixeira, J.M.A., Fisk, N.M., & Glover, V. (1999). Association between maternal anxiety in pregnancy and increased uterine artery resistance index: Cohort based study. *British Medical Journal, 318,* 153-157.

Tuck, I., McCain, N.L., & Elswick, R.K. (2001). Spirituality and psychosocial factors in persons living with HIV. *Journal of Advanced Nursing, 33,* 776-783.

Underwood, L.G. & Teresi, J. (2002). The daily spiritual experiences scale: development, theoretical description, reliability, exploratory factor analysis and preliminary construct validity using health related data. *Annals of Behavioural Medicine,* 22-23.

Wadhwa, P.D., Sanderman, C.A, & Porto, M. (1993). The association between prenatal stress and infant birth weight and gestational age at birth: a prospective investigation. *American Journal of Obstetrics & Gynecology, 169,* 858-865.

Warr, P.B. (1978). A study of psychological well-being. *British Journal of Psychology, 69,* 111-121.

Waldenstrom, U. (1996). The complexity of labour pain: experiences of 278 women. *Journal of Psychosomatic Obstetrics and Gynecology, 17,* 215-228.

William, R.W., Larson, D.B., Buckler, R.E., Heckman, R.C., & Pyle, C.M. (1991). Religion and psychological distress in a community sample. *Social Science Medicine, 32,* 1257-1262.

Witmer, M. & Sweeney (1992). A holistic model of wellness and prevention over the life span. *Journal of Counselling and Development, 71,* 140-148.

Witter, R.A., Stock, W.A, Okun, M.A. & Haring, M.J. (1985). Religion and subjective well-being in adulthood: a qualitative synthesis. *Review of Religious Research, 26,* 332-342.

Worthington, E.L. (Ed.). *Dimension of forgiveness: Psychological research and theological perspective.* Templeton Foundation Press; 1997.

Wright, L.S., Frost, C.J., & Wisecarver, S.J. (1993). Church attendance, meaningfulness of religion and depressive symptomatology among adolescents. *Journal of Youth and Adolescence.* 22, 559-568.

Zimmer-Gembeck, M.J. & Helfand, M. (1996). Low birth weight in a public prenatal care programme: Behavioural and psychosocial risk factors and psychosocial intervention. *Social Science Medicine, 43,* 187-197.

11

Telecommuting and Work-Family Conflict:

Issues and Challenges for Working Women

Urmila R. Srivastava and *Shamini Srivastava*

Introduction

There is an abundance of literature on the intersection of work and family (Barnett & Hyde, 2001; Edward & Rothbard, 2000; Frone, 2003; Grzywacz & Bass, 2003; Kinnunen, Feldt, Geurts, & Pulkkinen, 2006; Parasuraman & Greenhaus, 2002; Perrone, Stefania, Webb, & Blalock, 2006; Singh & Rai, 2004). More recently, however, research has begun to examine work and family roles simultaneously. This new focus is, a result of several demographic changes in work and family lives of workers such as the dramatic increase in the number of married women with young children joining the workforce and the increasing prevalence of employed adults who are part of dual-earner families, single-parent families, and families facing the demands of elder care (Burke & Greenglass, 1987; Hall & Richter, 1988; Matthews & Rodin, 1989; Zedeck & Mosier, 1990). On the job side, new requirements have brought an increased workload. Some of the factors which stimulate tension and even create a true conflict between requirements of professional life and responsibilities of family life are the following: downsizing, strategies of participation, professional lives characterized by more and more challenges, frequent changes of assignment, work and time schedules redesign, job insecurity and frequent relocations (Greenhaus & Beutell, 1985; Frone, Russel, & Copper, 1992). On the family side, the increase in the number of dual-career or single parent families, the special cases where particular care is to be given to members of the family (handicapped child, old parent), care to the youngest children, babysitting of the children outside the hours of school, unpredictable events (illness of the children, absence of a babysitter, etc.) are some of the factors, all of which complicate situation and augment difficulties of reconciliation of worker's and parent responsibilities (Beutell & Greenhaus, 1980; 1983; Frone, 2003; Frone, Russel, & Copper, 1992b; Jennifer & McGaugald, 2007; Voydanoff, 2004, 2005).

Most of the research have focused on the interface between work and family (Edward & Rothbard, 2000), by emphasizing the negative spillover between work and family domains, i.e., work-family conflict (Frone, 2003). Work-family conflict occurs when efforts to fulfil work role demands interfere with one's ability to fulfil family demands and *vice versa* (Greenhaus & Beutell, 1985). Because work-family conflict reflects the overall goodness of fit between work and family life, it has been conceptualized as an important source of stress that may influence an individual's well-being (Greenhaus, 1988; Greenhaus & Parasuraman, 1986; Voydanoff, 1987). In today's competitive environment, the workforce is becoming more diverse due to the social and structural changes in work and family domains; it is not surprising that workers are struggling to meet competing demands of their work and family lives (Barnett & Hyde, 2001; Edward & Rothbard, 2000; Grzywacz & Bass, 2003; Voydanoff, 1987).

The growing power, sophistication and portability of technology have made remote work a viable option in meeting the competing demands of work and family lives. Information technology has contributed to making work less geographically dependent (Ditlea, 1995; Dziak, 1993). The widespread availability of advanced technology in changing the way we think about "the office". Recent technological advances have enabled the large scale adoption of telecommuting and other forms of virtual work as organizations struggle to maintain their competitive edge (SHRM Foundation, 2001). One reason for growing popularity of telecommuting is its perceived ability to help individuals to balance competing demands of work and family (Duxbury, Higgins, & Thomas, 1992; Duxbury, Higgins & Neufeld, 1998; Hochschild, 1997; Hooks & Higgs 2002; Kraut, 1987; Rau & Hayland, 2002; Williams, 2000)

It is widely believed that technological innovation in microelectronics and telecommuting "could shift literally millions of jobs right back to the home, out of the factories and offices" (Toffler, 1981, p. 204).

Telecommuting originated with the idea that working away from conventional workplace, people can work in a variety of locations (e.g., home, neighbourhood office, at a client location) and communicating by the way of computer based technology (Nilles, 1994; Jasperson, Carte, Saunders, Butler, Croes, & Jhang, 2002). However, when this advanced technology related work has become rapidly important in recent years, we have not yet understood many of its implications for the employees and for the organization. Telework has been given more and more attention over recent years as a way to reduce urban pollution (Benchimol, 1984), as a new mode of work organization (Boivin, Rivard, & Aubert 1996), but also finally as a way of balancing work and family lives (Ashforth, 2001; Clark, 2000; Duxbury, Higgins and Neufeld 1998; Hylmö & Buzzanell, 2002; Richter and Meshulam 1993). Although researchers have provided a rich detailed literature independently on work-family conflict (Boyar & Mosley, 2007; Carlson, Kacmar, Wayne, & Grzywacz, 2006; Kinnunen *et al.*, 2006; Singh & Rai, 2004; Tiwari, 2003; Wayne, Grzywacz, Carlson, & Kacmar, 2007; Wayne, Musisca, & Flesson, 2004) and on telecommuting (Goodrich, 1990; Bailey & Foley, 1990; Barnes, 1994; Davis, 1994; DiMartino & Wirth, 1990), a substantial gap in literature still exists. First, only limited conceptual and empirical evidences exist to support the relationship between telecommuting and work-family conflict (Golden, 2003; Li & Sahni, 1991). Second: there is no consensus within the literature regarding the role of gender in the relationship between telecommuting and work-family conflict (Tremblay, 2003). Therefore, this review provides a broad picture of relationship between telecommuting and work-family conflict, with special reference to working women.

Therefore, by taking into consideration these two restrictions of existing theories and literature pertaining to telecommuting and work-family conflict, major objectives of this review is to examine one form of advanced technology enabled work, i.e., telecommuting and its link to work-family conflict with special emphasis on working women.

Therefore, the first section of this review involves description about work-family conflict, perhaps the most widely studied concept in the work-family literature. The next section focuses on telecommuting an important HR practice. Subsequent section focuses on the relationship between telecommuting and work-family conflict among working men and women with special emphasis on the challenges faced by the working women to balance their work and family domains. In the final section of this review, we have drawn some conclusions and implications on the basis of studies reviewed and recommended some suggestions about future research and practice.

Work-family conflict

Work-family conflict can be a source of occupational stress, especially in the modern age of electronic briefcase. It has been studied from role stress theory and defined as a form of inter-role conflict that occurs when demands of work and family are mutually incompatible in some respect for career oriented men (Boyar & Mosley, 2007; Frone, 2003; Frone, Yardley, & Markel, 1997; Goode, 1960; Greenhaus & Beutell, 1985; Higgins & Duxbury, 1992; Kinnunen, *et al.*, 2006).

Models of work-family conflict suggests that conflict arises when participation in one domain of life make it difficult to participate in another role and this conflict can have an important affect on the quality of both work and family lives (Greenhaus & Beutell, 1985, p. 77). This definition has also accepted and verified by many other researchers (Ahuja,

Kathrine, George, Kacmar, & Harrison, 2002; Allen, Herst, Bruck, & Sutton, 2000; Edward & Rothbard, 2000; Netemeyer, Boles, & McMurrian, 1996; O'Driscoll, Brough, & Kalliath, 2004; Rothbard, 2001; Frone, Russell, & Copper, 1992a, b, 1997; Voydanoff, 1988).

The phenomena of work-family conflict occurs when an individual attempts to balance his/her work and home demands that lead to loss of resources from either one domain or from both the domains (Grandy & Cropanzano, 1999; Hobfoll, 1989). In addition to this study Rothbard (2001), has reported that people have fixed amount of resources and fulfilment of multiple roles is likely to result in depletion of scarce resources and person ultimately in strain.

Several researchers have mentioned that conflict is a negative spillover, in which participation in one domain (e.g., work) has negative impact on participation in another domain (e.g., family), (Edward & Rothbard, 2000; Frone, 2003).

After reviewing previous studies pertaining to work-family conflict, Greenhaus and Beutell (1985) have conceptualized three different forms of work-family conflict, i.e., time-based, strain-based and behaviour-based conflict. Time-based conflict refers to time devoted to one role make it difficult to participate in another role. Strain-based conflict refers to the strain experienced in one domain intrudes into and interferes with participation in another domain. At last behaviour-based conflict means behaviour expectation in one domain make it difficult to participate in another domain (Carlson, Kacmar, & William, 2000; Fu & Shaffer, 2001; Major, Klein, & Ehrhart, 2002; O'Driscoll *et al.*, 2004).

In a very recent study, Steenbergen, Ellemers and Mooijaart (2007) have measured fourth type of conflict, namely psychological conflict (Greenhaus, 1988). It refers to being mentally distracted by or preoccupied with one role while physically present in other role (Cardenas, Major, & Bernas, 2004; Carlson & Frone, 2003). Carlson and Frone (2003) have defined psychological conflict as "the psychological preoccupation with one role, while performing another role that interferes with one's ability to become engaged in the last role" (p. 518).

Directions of influence of work-family conflict

Although much of the earlier researches have assumed that work-family conflict is a one-dimensional construct, but studies based on current thinking have revealed that it is bidirectional in nature and occurs in both the directions (work-to-family and family-to-work) (Carlson & Kacmar, 2000; Carlson & Frone, 2003; Frone, 2003; Fu & Shaffer, 2001; Greenhaus & Beutell, 1985). The existing evidences have revealed that most people experience greater work-to-family conflict in comparison to family-to-work conflict and these two directions of conflict are distinct constructs (Carlson *et al.*, 2000; Geurts, Sabine, Compier, Michiel, Roxburg, Susan, Houtman, & Irene, 2003; Kinnunen &, Mauno, 1998).

Work-to-family interference is characterized as when participation in work domain made it difficult by virtue to participate in family domain. On the other hand, when participation in family domain made it difficult by virtue to participate in work domain called family-to-work conflict. Existing evidences have shown that most people experience greater work-to-family conflict in comparison to family-to-work conflict and these two directions have positive reciprocal relationship with each other (Carlson & Kacmar, 2000; Carlson *et al.* 2000; Frone, 2003; Frone, Russell, & Copper, 1992a, 1992b; Frone, *et al.*, 1997, Greenhaus & Beutell, 1985; Kim & Ling, 2002; Netemeyer, *et al.*, 1996). Most of the researches have emphasized only on one direction of work-familly conflict, i.e., work-to-family interference and neglected another direction of work-family conflict, i.e., while measured bidirectional nature of work-family conflict (Frone, Russell, & Copper, 1992a, 1997; Greenhaus & Beutell, 1985). Due to this reason, antecedents and consequences of work-to-family conflict is reported three times greater than family-to-work conflict.

In summary, the behavioural research suggests that the combination of work and family roles create a series of conflicts. Work-family conflict occurs due to the mutual demands of work and family domains. In particular, work-family conflict is reflected in three different forms, i.e., time-based, strain-based and behaviour-based conflict. However, authors have also illustrated the fourth form of conflict, i.e., psychological conflict. These studies have conceptualized work-family conflict as a global and bidirectional in nature and occurs in both the directions, i.e., work-to-family conflict and family-to-work conflict.

The beginning of telework

The general term for doing work away from the office via telecommunication equipment is telework (Bureau of National Affairs, 1992; Callentine, 1995; U.S. Department of Transportation, 1993). Although telework was foreseen as early as in 1950, it did not become practical until the advent of personal computers and portable modems in early 1970s (U.S. Department of Transportation, 1993).

Telecommuting

Although, several popular press have been noticed the arrival of telecommuting (Hammonds, Furchgoot, Hamm, & Judge, 1997; Filipezak, 1992; Nilles, 1994; Tolbert & Simons, 1994; U. S. Department of Transportation, 1993). But little academic research has been examined the effect of telecommuting on employees and organizations. This lack of conceptual and empirical attention has shown that it requires more attention by the scholars and researchers.

It is only in the early 1990s telecommuting programme designed to accommodate the personal and/or family needs of employees. Some common rationale for telecommuting included: to enable a parent caring for an infant or toddler and to have an option of working from home (Ashforth, 2001; Clark, 2000; Duxbury, Higgins and Neufeld 1998; Gordon & Kelly, 1986; Hylmö & Buzzanell, 2002; Nilles, 1994; Richter and Meshulam, 1993).

Telecommuting is an alternative work arrangement in which employees perform tasks elsewhere that are normally done in a primary or central workplace, for at least some portion of their work schedule, using electronic media to interact with others inside and outside the organization (Bailey

& Kurland, 2002; Baruch, 2001; Feldman & Gainey, 1997). In telecommuting model (also known as work-at-home or work-home), some or all the jobs are moved away from the office to another fixed site, usually at the home and communicating by the way of computer-based technology. Telecommuter often maintains a traditional office and generally works from the home 1-3 days in a week (Nilles, 1994).

Definition of telecommuting acknowledges that telecommuting can be done by an individual as a part-time (alongside more conventional work arrangements) or full-time (exclusively working from home). Telecommuting usually does not refer to work that is conducted either very occasionally (e.g., person who works at home maybe once a month) or work done "on the road", such as training or sales. It is also important to make a distinction between telecommuting and flexible scheduling. Although many telecommuters work according to flexible schedules, some telecommuters are expected to work according to a fixed schedule (e.g., they need to be available 9 to 5, etc.) (Nilles, 1994; Jasperson, Carte, Saunders, Butler, Croes, & Chang, 2002).

Several researchers have reported that telecommuting has grown due to the demand of three constituencies: employees, organizations and society. First, employees' demands for more flexible work arrangements resulted from substantial change to the family structure and telecommuting is a viable option in meeting the demands for flexible work schedules (Schepp, 1990). Second, the organizations, because of demographic changes (including the dramatic rising in the number of women in the workforce and the increasing prevalence of dual-earner families, single-parent families, and families facing the demands of elder care) need to make accommodations to attract and retain employees. It is expected that the next generation of workers will be much smaller than the current workforce. Therefore, flexible work option would be required to recruit and retain high-quality employees for the fulfilment of the goal of the organization. At last, societal demands for environmental awareness is the third factor contributing to the demand of flexible work option (Igbaria & Guimaraes, 1999).

In a comprehensive review Oslon (1982) has reported three types of telecommuting locations: satellite work centres, neighbourhood work centres and home-based work centres. In satellite work centres, the employees work both outside of the home and away from the conventional workplace. They have selected that location which is convenient for the employee and/or customers. Neighbourhood work centres are the same as satellite work centres with one major difference in that neighbourhood work centres houses are more than one company employees. At last home-based work centres mean it exists when employees work at home on a regular basis.

Flexible work options are growing rapidly because of the numerous demands for alternatives to traditional work environments and advances in technology. Researchers have speculated that there has been an 85 per cent increase in the telecommuting since 1990 and this trend will be continued to grow (Fryxell, 1994). By the year 2000, it is estimated that 25 million will be telecommuters (Barnes, 1994), and by 2030 there will be over 90 million telecommuters in the U. S. alone (Wilkes, Frolick, & Urwiler, 1994).

Telecommuting is rising day by day due to its positive outcomes or clear benefits for organizations and their employees. A number of practitioner articles and company statistics have argued and demonstrated that at the organizational level, telecommuting reduces real estate costs (Apgar, 1998; AT&T, 1997; Dannhauser, 1999; Gajendran & Harrison, 2007). At the individual level as well, the benefits of telecommuting includes: improved work-life balance, heightened morale, and increased productivity (Apgar, 1998; Brownson, 2004; Gajendran & Harrison, 2007; Tergesen, 1998; Young, 1993).

Relationship between telecommuting in work-family conflict among working women

Since last decades extensive research have focused on work-family conflict (Ahuja, Kathrine, George, Kacmar, & Harrison, 2002; Boyar, Maertz, Pearson, & Kough, 2003; Edward & Rothbard, 2000; Frone, Russell, & Copper, 1992a, b, 1997;

Netemeyer *et al.* 1996; O'Driscoll *et al.*, 2004; Rothbard, 2001; Voydanoff, 1988; Voydanoff, 2004a, 2004b, 2005). In addition, telecommuting has also received due attention in recent years (Ashforth, 2001; Barnes, 1994; Clark, 2000; Davis, 1994; Jasperson, Carte, Saunders, Butler, Croes, & Jhang, 2002; Fryxell, 1994; Gardon & Kelly, 1986; Oslon, 1982; Wilkes, Frolick, & Urwiler, 1994). However, the relationship of these both constructs, i.e., work-family conflict and telecommuting has not been thoroughly explored (Golden, 2003; Li & Sahni, 1991). In other words, researchers have focused very little attention on the relationship between work-family conflict and telecommuting among working women Therefore, future research must examine the relationship between telecommuting and work-family conflict with special reference to working women.

In the past decades, the contemporary developing society is undergoing rapid social and structural changes, including population growth, inflation and economic pressures, breaking of joint family system, entering of a large number of women into the labour force, urbanization and industrialization. Traditionally, men have been the primary financial providers for their families, while women have been the primary caregivers (Rice, 1993). Even today men are primary financial providers of the family and likely to spend more time than women at paid work. Today's diverse workforce has now become increasingly populated with mothers (having young children), single parents and dual career couples (Boyar & Mosley, 2007; Greenhaus & Beutell, 1985; Steenbergen, *et al.*, 2007; Frone, 2003). On the one hand, women have assumed increased financial responsibilities for their families. At the same time, women (full time workers) continue to spend more time on child care and household works than do men (Schwartz & Scott, 2000). Many women accept part-time jobs in order to accommodate both family and their work responsibilities (Reskin & Padavic, 1994). While other women need flexible work arrangements in the condition of full-time worker (Collins, 1993). Regardless of gender, now it is clear that both men and women must balance the demands of their work and family roles.

In traditional bureaucratic organizations, workers were collocated in stable settings, where co-workers exchanged knowledge and other work resources. This division of labour spatially separated families from work. With few extended kin or community supports, caring for children outside of the job sphere took much of parents' personal time, especially the time of mothers in particular. With the rapid pace of organizational change in businesses and access to sophisticated communication media, the structure of organization is changing from traditional organization towards virtual organization (Castells, 1996; Nardi, Whittaker, & Schwartz, 2000).

In today's work environment, technology can be used by an employee, not only to accomplish their work related demands, but also help in the accommodation of their domestic responsibilities that are very important to them. Technology is continuing to alter the way the work is conducted. One form of technology-enabled work is telecommuting, whereby employees spend a consistent portion of their time working from home. These telecommuters, by virtue of their spatial and temporal distance from the employers' work location may experience an increased ability to adjust work activities to meet their own needs and desires, and this may play an important role in determining their level of work-family conflict (Hartman, Stoner, & Arora, 1992).

Apgar (1998) has reported that telecommuters have more available time due to absence of a commute, and they may conduct additional or alternative work or personal activities according to their own priorities and needs. It has been indicated that telecommuting is negatively related to work-family conflict.

Telecommuting motivations are likely to differ between men and women. Tingey, Kiger and Riley (1996) have suggested in their study that telecommuting would be more attractive to women than men. Because, working women still undertake a disproportionate share of domestic responsibilities. They hypothesized that the promise of telecommuting to save time and to offer greater flexibility would appeal even more strongly to women than to men (Gordon, 1976, Clark, 2000). Consistent with this study Mokhtarian, Bagley, and Soloman (1998) have identified gender related differences in the telecommuting motivations and constrains. They have reported that women on average rated the advantage of telecommuting more highly than men. Telecommuting appears to appeal more strongly to women as the solution of their problem which they face in their work and family domains (preferred by 83% men, compared to 92% of women). This study also revealed that women were more likely to than men cite family, personal benefits and stress reduction as advantage of telecommuting regardless of the presence of children.

Duxbury and Higgins (2003) have indicated that work to family interference increases when role demands creates conflict and women are more likely to suffer from role overload in comparison to male. In addition to this study, Hall (1972) has also revealed that working women are likely to report more conflict between their occupational role and family role than males. Working at home, shift is reducing the level of interrole conflict for women and enables them to obtain a better balance between the demands of the two roles (Gardon, 1976). Dimitrova (2003) adds that one of the most important changes with telework is the important temporal and spatial flexibility but the author observes that the gains were not dramatic and that they were often countered by longer working hours. Other research (Felstead and Jewson, 2000; Tremblay, 2003) have reported that there are minor adjustments at the beginning but that teleworkers manage to separate work and family life quite well over time. This is all the more so when teleworkers have a closed room from which to work (Felstead and Jewson, 2000). Several researchers have also examined that worker who telecommute extensively experienced and increased ability to meet the demands from both work and non-work related responsibilities (Riley & McClosky, 1997) and improve their work-family relationship by decreasing their work-family conflict (Golden, 2003; Grover & Crooker, 1995; Parasuraman, Greenhaus, & Greenrose, 1992; Rau & Hyland, 2002).

Many academicians and scholars view telecommuting as a good thing that leads to greater integration between the work and family roles (Duxbury, Higgins, & Neufeld, 1998; Gajendran & Harrison, 2007; Raghuram & Wiesenfeld, 2004). In a contemporary study Tremblay (2001 a), has shown that teleworkers identified several benefits of telecommuting including, a more flexible work-hours schedule (almost one-third of all respondents, men and women, recognized this feature, and among them 44% of full-time home workers), the avoidance of communicating with colleagues (one quarter of respondents). Other perceived advantages were: being more productive at work (10% men and 4% women); being able to spend more time with the family (8% women and 5% men), and to a lesser extent, savings on transportation and meals, peace of mind and quality of life.

Telecommuting provides psychological control or perceived autonomy at work. It comprises employees' personal assessments of the extent to which they can "structure and control how and when they do their particular job tasks" (Spector, 1986, p. 1006). Scholars asserting this view see telecommuting as a good thing that is thought to enhance perceived autonomy by providing employees with choice over the location, scheduling (at least for some), and means of work (e.g., DuBrin, 1991; Tremblay, 2003).

Researchers have speculated that, telecommuters require more communication with their supervisor due to their physical separation from workplace in comparison to non-telecommuters (Kinsman, 1989; Mahfood, 1992). In addition telecommuters are expected to communicate less with colleagues and their jobs may require more interdependence. Therefore, they can give more attention to their job and at the same time they can accommodate the needs of their family members. It is expected from these evidences that telecommuters experience less conflict than non-telecommuters (Shamir & Salomon, 1985).

Several disadvantages of telecommuting have also been reported by some researchers. First, the absence of colleagues' interaction and feedback comes first among the negative aspects of telework, followed by isolation and the difficulty to limit one's working hours (Cefrio, 2001; Tremblay 2001a, b). Actually, fewer men than women believe that working alone without colleagues scores first among the drawbacks associated with telework; people who work full-time at home are especially sensitive to this issue (Tremblay 2001a, b). Al Bcherrawy (1997) indicates that the feeling of isolation increases with age. Second, Teleworking typically increases the amount of interaction between the teleworkers and his/her family members (Galinsky, Bond, & Friedman, 1993; Nilles, 1994; Oslon & Primps, 1984). On the other hand, several other studies have reported that some mobile telework as having potential to blur the boundaries between work-life and family-life (Hill & Weiner, 1994) which may increase the level of conflict (Gurstein, 1991; Hartman *et al.* 1991; Pitt-Castouphes & Marchetta, 1991 ; Riley, 1994) and negative spillover (Duxbury, Higgins, & Neufield, 1988; Shamir & Salomon, 1985).

Conclusion and Implications

On the basis of the comprehensive review of existing studies pertaining to telecommuting and work-family conflict, the present chapter provides the following new insights. There have been very limited studies on the relationship between telecommuting and work-family conflict among working women. First, on the basis of the results generalized from these available studies, it has been found that despite of differences in responsibilities between men and women; women represent significant workforce segments and share similar problems, challenges and opportunities as the global economy approaches the new millennium. Second, telecommuting offers a way for employees (especially for the female employees) to more effectively balance competing demands from their work and family domains. Therefore, telecommuting increased the ability to meet the demands from both work and non-work related responsibilities and improve work-family relationship by decreasing the level of work-family conflict. It has been also found that telecommuting was found more attractive to women and they rated the advantage of telecommuting more highly than men. Women more likely want to telecommute from home in comparison to men, because from home they can accommodate the needs of their family also. Telecommuting is more strongly solution of the problems of working women which they face in their work and family domains and they get more advantage of telecommuting in comparison to men. It has been also found that telecommuting is extensively associated with lower work family.

Telecommuting permits women to better balance between key elements in their lives (i.e., work and family lives), increased their overall satisfaction and reducing the stress caused by conflicting responsibilities of their work and family. Further, women may allocate more time to pursuing their own individual career or leisure interests, resulting in enhancing the overall quality of life through increased self-satisfaction. Telecommuting also offers to women an opportunity to participate in the workforce while shouldering traditional responsibilities for family care.

Through telecommuting organizations can make their employees more satisfied with their jobs, reduce their turnover and their role stressors by offering them ability to adjust with their work demands and family activities. Telecommuting may also offer the opportunity to achieve greater balance between work and family roles. Another implication of the study that organizations offering telecommuting as a work-family benefit may find that their employees experience mild reductions in work-family conflict. Employers can maximize these reductions by allowing employees to spend most of their time away from their central work location. It also maximizes the stress lowering benefits of telecommuting.

Privilege of telecommuting may be reserved as reward for the more productive employees, but in long run managers may need to understand difference of telecommuters and regular employees. Discovery of these differences may be very helpful in the implementation of new activities and working alternatives.

Telecommuting may lead to improvement in quality of working life under certain conditions especially when a flexible option is included for individual who has special reason such as physically challenged, because they find difficult or impossible to work outside from home.

The general, implication of the finding suggest that telecommuting offers way for employees to efficiently balance the demands from their family and work areas so as to alleviate work's interference into their family lives.

Additional avenues of future research

Review of available research and theories raise several issues that represent substantial opportunity for future research. First, although there are many researches on the telecommuting and work-family conflict but there is practically no gendered feminist study. It is important that future research examines the specific household and caretaking responsibilities of teleworkers when examining the impact on women and men.

Second, although extensive research has explored the importance of telecommuting for the employees and organizations but only a handful of studies have examined the relationship of telecommuting and carrier success outcomes. Therefore, more empirical research based on theoretical framework on the relationship between telecommuting and carrier success outcome such as commitment satisfaction etc. is required. Further, there is a need to understand the outcome of the telecommuting programmes.

Third, although work-family interface is an important phenomena and telecommuting can have effects on various dimensions of work-family interface. Therefore, researcher should study the effects of technology on a variety of work-family outcomes, include multiple types and directions of work-family conflict (i.e., time-based, behaviour-based and strain-based conflict), work and life satisfaction, effectiveness and good performance at workplace and at home. In addition Research should also examine the prevalence of technology in the non-work domain that how and to what extent peoples using technology, and how this use is affecting them and their families.

REFERENCES

Ahuja, M., Kathrine, M., George, J.F., Kacmar, C., & Harrison (2002). Overworked and isolated? Predicting the effect of work-family conflict, autonomy and workload on organizational and turnover of virtual workers. Proceeding of the 35th Hawaii International Conference on System Science.

Al Bcherrawy, J.M. (1997). Travail a Domicile en tant que Nouveau Mode de Travail: Une Étude Empirique Exploratoire. Thesis M.Sc. Administration. Concordia University, Montréal.

Allen, T.D., Herst, D.E.L., Bruck, C.S., & Sutton, M. (2000). Consequences associated with work-to-family conflict: A review and agenda for future research. *Journal of Occupational Health Psychology, 5,* 278-308.

Apgar, M. (1998). The alternative workplace: Changing where and how people work, *Harward Business Review,* 121-136.

Ashforth, B.E. (2001). *Role transitions in organizational life: An identity-based perspective.* Mahwah, NJ: Erlbaum.

AT&T. (1997). *The 1997 EH&S report.* Retrieved November 8, 2005, from http://www.att.com/ehs/annual reports/ehs report/report97/common/l.html.

Bailey, D.S., & Foley, J. (1990). Pacific bell works long distance. *HR Magazine, 35,* 50-52.

Bailey, D.E., & Kurland, N.B. (2002). A review of telework: findings, new directions, and lessons for the study of modern work. *Journal of Organisational Behaviour, 23,* 383-400.

Barnes, K. (1994). Tips for managing telecommuters. *HR Focus, 71,* 9-10.

Barnett, R.C., & Hyde, J.S. (2001). Women, men, work and family. *American Psychologist, 56,* 781-796.

Baruch, Y. (2001). The status of research on teleworking and an agenda for future research. *International Journal of Management Reviews, 3,* 113-129.

Benchimol, Guy (1994). L'entreprise délocalisée ».Ed Hermés, Paris, pp. 67-103.

Beutell, N.J. and Greenhaus, J.H. (1980). *Some Sources and Consequences of Interrole Conflict among Married Women,* Proceeding of the Annual Meeting of the Eastern Academy of Management, 17, 2-6.

Beutell, N.J. & Greenhaus, J.H. (1983). Integration of home and non-Home roles: Women's conflict and coping behaviour. *Journal of Applied Psychology, 68,* 43-48.

Boivin, C., Rivard, S., Aubert, B.A. (1996). Le télétravail, un phénoméne en emergence. *Gestion, 21,* 68-75.

Boyar, S.L., Maertz, C.P., Pearson, A.W., & Kough, S. (2003). Work-family conflict: A model of linking between work-family domain variables and turnover intention, *Journal of Managerial Issues, 15,* 175-190.

Boyar, L.S., & Mosley, D.C. Jr. (2007). The relationship between core self-evaluation and work and satisfaction: The mediating role of work-family conflict and facilitation. *Journal of Vocational Behaviour, 71,* 265-281.

Burke, R.J. and Greenglass, E.R. (1987). 'Work and family'. In: Cooper, C.L. and Robertson, I. T. (Eds) *International Review of Industrial and Organizational Psychology,* Wiley, New York.

Brownson, K. (2004). The benefits of a work-at-home program. *Health Care Manager, 23,* 141-144.

Bureau of National Affairs (1992). Telecommuting: Its role and value in work and family programme: No. 50. The BNA special report series on work and family. Washington, DC: Author.

Callentine, L.U. (1995). The ecology of the mobile workplace: Influence of household composition and home workplace on satisfaction, stress and effectiveness. Unpublished master's thesis. Cornell University, Ithaca, NY.

Cardenas, R.A., Major, D.A., & Bernas, K.H. (2004). Exploring work and family distractions: Antecedents and outcomes. *International Journal of Stress Management, 11,* 346-365.

Carlson, D.S., & Frone, M.R. (2003). Relation of behavioural and psychological involvement to a new four factor conceptualization of work-family interface. *Journal of Business and Psychology, 17,* 515-535.

Carlson, D.S., & Kacmar, K.M. (2000). Work-family conflict in organization: Do life role values make a difference. *Journal of Management, 26,* 1031-1054.

Carlson, D.S., Kacmar, K.M., Wayne, J.H., & Grzywacz, J.G. (2006). Measuring the positive side of work-family interface: Development and validation of work-family enrichment scale. *Journal of Vocational Behaviour, 68,* 131-164.

Carlson, D.S., Kacmar, K.M., & Williams, L.J. (2000). Construction and initial validation of multidimensional measure of work-family conflict. *Journal of Vocational Behaviour, 56,* 249-276.

Castells, M. (1996). *The Rise of the Network Society.* Oxford: Blackwell. pp. 412, 477-78.

Cefrio (2001). Le télétravail : articuler qualité de vie et performance. Québec: Cefrio.

Christensen, K. (1988). *Women and home-based work: The unspoken contract.* New York, NY: Henry Holt and Company.

Clark, S.C. (2000). Work/family border theory: A new theory of work/family balance. *Human Relations, 53,* 747-77.

Collins, N. (1993). New IWPR study examines the economic benefits of alternative employment patterns for male and female workers. Research-in-brief, Institute for Women's Policy Research, Washington, DC.

Dannhauser, C.L. (1999). Who's in the home office? *American Demographics, 21*, 50-56.

Davis, E. (1994). Have modem, won't travel. *Management Review, 84*, 7.

Di Martino, V., & Wirth, L. (1990). Telework: A new way of working and living. *Internal Labor Review, 129*, 529-554.

Dimitrova, D. (2003). Controlling teleworkers: Supervision and flexibility revisited. *New Technology, Work* and *Employment, 18*, 181-194.

Ditlea, S. (1995). Home is where the office is: Technology improvement have made the home office an effective workplace alternative. *Nation's Business, 83*, 41-45.

DuBrin, A.J. (1991). Comparison of the job satisfaction and productivity of telecommuters versus in-house employees: A research note on work in progress. *Psychological Reports, 68*, 1223-1234.

Duxbury, L.E., & Higgins, C.A. (2003) Where to work in Canada? An Examination of Regional differences in Work-Life Practices. CPRN Research report commissioned by the BC Work-Life Summit 2003. 103 p. From: http://www.cprn.com/en/doc.cfm?doc= 1220

Duxbury, L., Higgins, C., & Neufield, D. (1998). Telework and balance between work and family: is telework part of the problem or a part of solution. In M. Igbaria and M. Tan (Eds.), *The virtual workplace.* Hershry, PA: Idea Group Publishing, pp. 218-225.

Duxbury, L.E., Higgins, C.A, and Thomas, D.R. (1996). Work and Family Environments and the Adoption of Computer-Supported Supplemental Work-at-Home, *Journal of Vocational Behaviour, 49*, 1-23

Dziak, M.J. (1993). Telecommuters do their best work at home. *Telephone Engineer and Management, 97*, 48-50.

Edward, J.R., & Rothard, N.P. (2000). Mechanism linking work and family: Clarifying the relationship between work and family constructs. *Academy of Management Review, 25*, 178-199.

Felstead, A., & Jewson, N. (2000). *In Home, at Work. Towards an Understanding of Homeworking.* London, Routledge, p. 196.

Feldman, D.C., & Gainey, T.W. (1997). Patterns of telecommuting and their consequences: Framing the research agenda. *Human Resource Management Review, 7*, 369-388.

Filipezak, B. (1992). Telecommuting: a better way to work? *Training, 29*, 53-61.

Frone, M.R. (2003). Work-family balance. In J.C. Quick & L.E. Tetrick (Eds.), *Handbook of Occupational Health Psychology* (pp. 143-162) Washington, DC.; American Psychological Association.

Frone, M.R., Russell, M., & Copper, M.L. (1992a). Antecedents and outcomes of work-family conflict: Testing a model of the work-family interface. *Journal of Applied Psychology, 72*, 65-78.

Frone, M.R., Russell, M., & Copper, M.L. (1992b). Prevalence of work-family conflict: Are work and family boundaries asymmetrically permeable? *Journal of Organizational Behaviour, 13*, 723-729.

Frone, M.R., Yardley, J.K. & Markel, K.S. (1997b). Developing and testing an integrative model of the work-family interface. *Journal of Vocational Behaviour, 50*, 145-67.

Fryxell, D.A (1994). Telecommuting. *Link Up, 11*, 18-19.

Fu, C.K., & Shaffer, M.A (2001). The tug of work and family: Direct and indirect domain specific determinants of work-family conflict. *Personal Review, 30*, 502-522.

Gajendran, R.S., & Harrison, D.A. (2007). The good, the bad, and the unknown about telecommuting: Meta analysis of psychological mediators and individual differences. Journal of Applied Psychology, 92, 1524-1541.

Galinsky, E., Bond, J.T. & Friedman, D.E. (1999). The changing workforce: Highlight the national study New York: Families and Work Institute.

Geurts, Sabine, A.E., Compier, Michel, A.J., Roxburg, Susan, & Houtman, Irene, L.D. (2003). Does work-home interference mediate the relationship between workload and well-being? *Journal of Vocational Behaviour, 63*, 532-559.

Golden, T. (2003). Technology and balance of work-family conflict: An investigation into the role of telecommuting. www.google.com

Goodrich, J.N. (1990). Telecommuting in America. *Business Horizen, 33*, 31-37.

Gordon, F. (1976). Telecommunication: Implications for women. Implication Policy 1.

Gordon, G.E., & Kelly, M.M. (1986). *Telecommuting: how to make it for you and your company.* Englewood Cliffs, N.J.: Prentice Hall.

Goode, W.J. (1960). A theory of strain. *American Sociological Review, 25*, 483-496.

Grandey, A.A., & Cropanzano, R. (1999). The conservation of resources model applied to work-family conflict and strain. *Journal of Vocational Behaviour, 5*, 350-370.

Greenhaus, J.H., (1988). The intersection of work and family roles: Individual, interpersonal, and organizational issues. *Journal of Social Behaviour and Personality, 3*, 23-44.

Greenhaus, J.H., & Beutell, N. (1985). *Sources of conflict between work and family roles.* Academy of Management Review, *10*, 76-88.

Greenhaus, J.H. and Parasuraman, S. (1986). 'A work-nonwork interactive perspective of stress and its consequences', *Journal of Organizational Behaviour Management, 8*, 37-60.

Grover, S., & Crooker, K. (1995). Who appreciates family responsive human resource policies: The impact of family friendly policies on the organizational attachment of parent and non-parent? *Personnel Psychology, 48*, 271-288.

Gurstein, P. (1991). Working at home and living at home: Emerging scenarios. *The Journal of Architectural and Planning Research, 8*, 164-68.

Hall, D.T. (1972). A model for coping with role conflict: The role behaviour of college educated women. *Administrative Science Quarterly, 17*, 471-486.

Hall, D.T. and Richter, J. (1988). 'Balancing work and home life: What organizations can do to help?' *Academy of Management Executive*, 2, 213-223.

Hammonds, K.H., Furchgoot, R., Hamm, S., & Judge, P.C. (1997). Work and family. *Bus. Week*, 96-99.

Hartman, R.I., Stoner, C.R., Arora, R. (1991). An investigation of selected variable affecting telecommuting productivity and satisfaction. *Journal of Business and Psychology, 6*, 207-225.

Hartman, R., Stoner, C., & Arora, R. (1992). Developing successful organizational telecommuting arrangement: Worker perception of managerial description. *SAM Advanced Management Journal, 57*, 35-52.

Higgins, CA. and Duxbury, L.E. (1992) 'Work-family conflict: A comparison of dual career and traditional career men', *Journal of Organizational Behaviour, 13*, 389-411.

Hill, E.J., & Winer, S. (1994). *Effective leadership in mobile environment*. Mt. Pleasant. NY: IBM.

Hobfoll, S.E. (1989). Conservation of resources: A new attempt at conceptualizing stress: *American Psychologist, 44*, 513-524.

Hochschild, A. (1997). When work becomes home and home becomes work. *California Management Review, 39*, 79.

Hooks, K. and Higgs, J.L. (2002). Workplace environment in a professional services firm. *Behavioural Research in Accounting, 14*, 105-127.

Hylmö, A. & Buzzanell, P. (2002). The phenomenon of telecommuting and changing organizations: An organizational culture examination. Paper presented at the International Communication Association, Seoul, Korea.

Igbaria, M., & Guimaraes, T. (1999). Exploring differences in employee turnover intentions and its determinants among telecommuters and non-telecommuters; *Journal of Management Information System, 16*, 147-164.

Jasperson, J., Carte, T., Saunders, C.S., Butler, B.S., Croes, H.J.P, Zheng, W.J. (2002). Power and Information Technology Research: A Metatriangulation Review, *Management Information Systems Quarterly, 26*, 397-459.

Jennifer, E.J., McDougald, M.S. (2007). Work-family interface experiences and coping strategies: Implications for entrepreneurship research and practice. *Academy of Management Review, 32,* 747-760.

Kim, J.L.S., & Ling, C.S. (2001). Work-family conflict of women entrepreneurs in Singapore. *Women in Management Review, 16,* 204-221.

Kinnunen, V., & Mauno, S. (1998). Antecedents and outcomes of work-family conflict among employed women and men in Finland. *Human Relations, 51,* 157-177.

Kinnunen, V., Feldt, T., Geurts, S. & Pulkkinen, L. (2006). Types of work-family interface: Well-being correlates of negative and positive spillover between work and family. *Scandinavian Journal of Psychology, 47,* 149-162.

Kinsman, F. (1989). Telecommuting: An idea where time has come. *Accountancy, 104,* 166-169.

Kraut, R.E. (1987). Predicting the Use of Technology: The Case of Telework, in *Technology and the Transformation of White-Collar Work,* R.E. Kraut (ed.), Hillsdale; NJ: Lawrence Erlbaum Associates, 113-133.

Li, E., & Shani, Y. (1991). Stress dynamics of information system managers: a contingency model. *Journal of Management Information System, 74,* 107-130.

Mahfood, P. (1992). *Homework: how to manage and monitor employees who work at home.* Chicago: Probus.

Major, V.S., Klein, K.J., & Ehrhart, M.G. (2002). Work-time, work interference with family, and psychological distress. *Journal of Applied Psychology, 87,* 427-436.

Matthews, K.A. and Rodin, J. (1989). 'Women's changing work roles: Impact on health, family, and public policy', *American Psychologist, 44,* 1389-1393.

Mokhtarian, P.L., Bagley, M.N., Salomon, I. (1998), "The impact of gender, occupation and presence of children on telecommuting motivations and constraints", *Journal of the American Society for Information Science,* Vol. 49, 1115-34.

Mokhtanan, P.L., & Salomon, I. (1996a). Modelling the choice of telecommuting: A case of the preferred impossible alternative. *Environment and Planning A, 28,* 1859-1876.

Nardi, B., Whittaker, S., Schwarz, H. (2000). It's Not What You Know, It's Who You Know Work in the Information Age http://firstmonday.org/issues/issue5_5/nardi/index.html

Netemeyer, R., Boles, J., & McMurrian, R. (1996). Development and validation of work-family conflicts and family-work conflict scale. *Journal of Applied Psychology, 81,* 400-410.

Nilles, J.M. (1994). *Making telecommunication happen a guide for telemanagers and telecommuters,* New York: Van Nostrand Reinhod.

O'Driscoll, M., Brough, P., & Kalliath, T. (2004). Work-family conflict and facilitation. *Applied Health Psychology Work Stress,* Chapter 6.

Oslon, M. H. (1988). Organizational barriers telework. In B. B. Korte, S., Robinson, & W. J. Steinle (Eds.). *Telework: Present situation and future development of a new form of organization* (pp. 77-100). New York; Elsevier Science Publishing.

Oslon, M., & Primps, S. (1984). Working at home with computers: work and non-work issues. *Journal of Social Issues, 40,* 97-112.

Parasuraman, S., & Greenhaus, J.H. (2002). Toward reducing some critical gaps in work-family research. *Human Resource Management Review, 12,* 3, 299-312.

Parasuraman, S., Greenhaus, J.H., & Granrose, C.S. (1992). Role stressor, social support and well-being among two career couples. *Journal of Organizational Behaviour, 13,* 339-356.

Perrone, M.K., Stefania, E., Webb K.L., Blalock, H.R. (2006). Work-family interface: commitment, conflict, coping and satisfaction. *Journal of Career Development, 32,* 286-300.

Pitt-Catsophes, M., & Marchetta, A. (1991). *A coming of age: telework,* Boston: Boston University, Center on Work and Family.

Raghuram, S., & Wiesenfeld, B. (2004). Work-non-work conflict and job stress among virtual workers. *Human Resource Management, 43,* 259-277.

Rau, B.L., & Hayland, M.M. (2002). Role conflict and flexible work arrangements. The effect on applicants' attraction. *Personnel Psychology, 55,* 111-136.

Reskin, B.F., & Padavic, I. (1994). *Women and men at work,* Pine Press, Thousand Oaks, CA.

Rice, E.P. (1993). *Intimate relationship, marriage, and, families,* Mayfield Publishing, London.

Riley, A.P. (1994). Teleworking: the keys to ensuring a successful programme. *Solutions,* 16.

Riley, F., & McCloskey, D.W. (1997). Telecommuting as a response to helping people balance work and family. In S. Parasuraman, & J.H. Greenhaus (Eds.), *Integrating work and family: Challenges and choices for a changing world,* 133-142. Westport, CT: Quorum.

Richter, J. and Meshulam, I. (1993). Telework at home: the home and the organization perspective. *Human Systems Management, 12,* 197-203.

Rothbard, N.P. (2001). Enriching or depleting? The dynamics of engagement in work and family roles. *Administrative Science Quarterly, 46,* 655-684.

Schipp, B. (1990). *Telecommuter's hard works: how to work for a salary without ever leaving the house.* New York: Pharos Books.

Schwartz, M.A., & Scott, B.M. (2000). *Marriage and families: Diversity and change,* Prentice Hall, Upper Saddle River, NJ.

Shamir, B., & Salomon, I. (1985). Work at home quality of working life. *Academy of Management Review, 10,* 455-463.

SHRM Foundation (2001). SHRM 2001 benefits survey. Society for Human Resource Management.

Singh, A.P., & Rai, S. (2004). Stress, social support and well-being among dual career couples. In A. Husain & T. Rashid (Eds.), *Stress Behaviour, vol-II, Sources & Effects.* Friends Publication, New Delhi.

Spector, P. (1986). Perceived control by employees: A meta-analysis of studies concerning autonomy and participation at work. *Human Relations, 39,* 1005-1016.

Steenbergen, E.F.V., Ellemers, N., & Mooijaart, A. (2007). How work-family can facilitate each other: Distinct types of work-family facilitation and outcomes for women and men. *Journal of Occupational Health Psychology, 12,* 279-300.

Sullivan, C., & Lewis, S. (2001). Home-based telework, gender, and the synchronization of work and family: Perspectives of teleworkers and their co-residents. *Gender, Work and Organizations, 8,* 123-145.

Tergesen, A. (1998). Making stay-at-homes feel welcome. Retrieved from http://www.businessweek.com/1998/41/b3599156.htm

Tingey, H., Kiger. G., & Riley, P.J. (1996). Juggling multiple roles: Perceptions of working mothers. *The Social Science Journal, 33,* 183-191.

Tiwari, P. (2003). Relationship of job and family involvement, family social support and work-family conflict with job and life satisfaction. Unpublished. Department of Psychology, Banaras Hindu University, Vanarasi.

Toffler, A. (1980). *The third wave,* New York: Morrow.

Tolbert, P.S., & Simons, T. (1994). The impact of working at home and career outcomes of professional employees (working paper 94-04). Ithaca, NY:Coronell University, Centre for Advanced Human Resource Studies.

Tremblay, D.G. (2001a). Télétravail : concilier performance et qualité de vie. *Rapport de recherche Cefrio,* p. 84.

Tremblay, D.G. (2001b). Le télétravail : definitions et enjeux. In Cefrio (Ed.) Télétravail : concilier performance et qualité de vie. *Montreal, IQ collectif et* CEFRIO: 23-32.

Tremblay, D.G. (2003). Telework: A New Mode of Gendered Segmentation? Results from a study in Canada. *Canadian Journal of Communication, 28,* 461-478.

U.S. Department of Transportation (1993). *Transportation implication of telecommuting.* Washington, DC; Author.

Voydanoff, P. (1987). *Work and Family Life,* Sage, Newbury Park, CA.

Voydanoff, P. (1988). Work role characteristics, family structure demand and work-family conflict. *Journal of Marriage and Family, 50,* 749-761.

Voydanoff, P. (2004a). The effect of work demands and resources on work-family conflict and facilitation. *Journal of Marriage and Family, 66,* 398-412.

Voydanoff, P. (2004b). Implication of work and community demands and resources for work-to-family conflict and facilitation. *Journal of Occupational Health Psychology, 9,* 275-285.

Voydanoff, P. (2005). The differential salience of family and community demand and resources for family-to-work conflict and facilitation. *Journal of Family Economic Issues, 26,* 395-417.

Wayne, J.H., Grzywacz, J.G., Carlson D.S., & Kacmar, M.K. (2007). Work-family facilitation: A theoretical explanation and model of primary antecedents and consequences. *Human Resource Management Review, 17,* 63-76.

Wayne, J.H., Musisca, N., Fleeson, W. (2004). Considering the role of personality in the work-family experience: Relationship of big-five to work-family conflict and facilitation. *Journal of Vocational Behaviour, 64,* 108-130.

Wilkes, R.B., Frolick, N., & Urwiler, R. (1994). Critical issues in developing successful telework programmes. *Journal of System Management, 45,* 30-34.

Williams, J. 2000. *Un Bending Gender: Why Family and Work Conflict and What to Do About it.* Oxford, New York: Oxford University Press.

Young, J.B. (1993). Ranks of "telecommuters" grow. *Christian Science Monitor.* Retrieved from the ProQuest database.

Zedeck, S. and Mosier, K.L. (1990). 'Work in the family and employing organization'. *American Psychologist, 45,* 240-251.

12

Glass Ceiling

Punam Midha

It is a fact that since time immemorial, gender has always played a significant role in the lives of human beings. Gender bias prevails in an overt or covert form, and is a global phenomenon. However, in the recent years considerable changes have occurred in the roles and status of women all-over the world. There is a common talk today that women have made the grade in many professions, that they have total freedom of opportunity. The new millennium provides an occasion to celebrate the remarkable progress made by women. That women now hold seats on corporate boards, run major companies, and are regularly featured on the covers of business magazines as prominent leaders and power brokers would have been unimaginable even a half century ago. But the majority of women are still left gazing at their goals and ambitious through an almost unbreakable glass ceiling.

The term 'Glass Ceiling' refers to invisible barriers that impede the career advancement of women. The situation is referred as a ceiling as there is a limitation blocking upward advancement and "glass" (transparent) because the limitation is not immediately apparent and is normally an unwritten and unofficial policy. This invisible barrier continues to exist run though there are not explicit obstacles. Keeping minorities from acquiring advanced job positions—there are no advertisements that specifically say "no" minorities nor are there any formal orders that say "minorities are not qualified". The "glass ceiling" is distinguished from former barriers to advancement such as education or experience, requirements. This invisible barrier seems to exist more in the developing countries, in those businesses, this effect is highly visible.

However, this glass ceiling tends to cripple working women the most. This barrier prevents large numbers of women from obtaining and securing the most powerful prestigious and highest - grossing jobs in the work. This barrier makes many women feel as they are not worthy enough to have these high ranking positions, but also they feel as if their boss does not take them seriously or actually see them as potential candidates. They feel either accurately or not, that men are deeply entrenched in the upper echelons of power and women try as they might find it nearly impossible to breakthrough.

In 1964, sexual discrimination was outlawed in the United States through the Civil Rights Act with the hopes of allowing women to rise in the working world, once proper experience has been achieved. In 1984, Gay Bryant wrote an article in 'Adweek' containing the first documentary use of the term "Glass Ceiling". Recently United States Senator Hillary Clinton used the term glass ceiling in her speech to endorse Senator Barack Obama for President. Her speech was "...... and although we were not able to shutter that highest, hardest glass ceiling this time, thanks to you, its got about 18 million cracks in it."

Glass ceiling actually exists as one can observe that men tend to be highly concentrated in the top professionals, such as supervisors, managers, executives and production operators. On the other hand, women tend to be overrepresented in the lowest ranking and lowest paid professionals in the workforce such as secretaries, sales associates, teachers, nurses and childcare providers. As a result, occupations became "sex typed" as either being specifically male or female jobs. The stereotypically male-characterized occupations in which at least 60-75 per cent of the workers are males, and no more highly paid than occupations in which 60-75 per cent of the job holders are women. This segregation and lower-ranked jobs also decrease a woman's chance of being promoted as well as the chance of having any type of power over others. Moreover, occupational segregation reduces women's success to insurance benefits and pension. Thus, occupational segregation is a vicious cycle that successfully continues to put women down.

Various surveys during recent years indicate that women holds meagre share of the top executive jobs in companies as follows:

1.3 per cent in Australia,
2.0 per cent in France
1 to 3.0 per cent in Brazil
3.6 per cent in U.K.
5.1 per cent in U.S.A.
3.0 per cent in Asia
3 to 5.8 per cent in India

The Mexican Government reported that in 1997 women held 12 per cent of executive management positions as Presidents, Director Generals and General Managers in the public and private sectors.

In U.K. (1998), a company survey showed a 15 per cent differences between tne average female and average male manager. At the director level, the gender gap was even greater at 42 per cent. Surveys in other countries during recent years reveal similar gaps such as follows:

35 per cent less women manager in Finland
50 per cent less women manager in Brazil
43 per cent less in Uruguay
16 per cent less in U.S.A.

The above data highlight the fact that women's presence at topmost job is definitely less than their male counterparts.

In India though women are involved in HR, IT and servicing activities, their presence in hard core production or marketing is much less and still lower at strategic policy-influencing levels.

There is also some evidence which shows sector-wise differences in career development of women in India, e.g., as 45 per cent women are in expansion of the Indian software industry, while a thick concentration of men exists in export software firms, whereas women are present in a higher proportion in domestic low end and IT enabled services (Suriya, 2003).

The Glass Ceiling effect can be seen in Indian Higher Education system, where women are severely underrepresented at senior academic management positions. The majority of women in the universities are also regarded as the "outsiders", "the disadvantaged", "tokens", "the others" and "double deviants" (Baglihole, 1994). All male networks are effective for lobbying and facilitate exchange of critical information. They are also the platforms for converting informal visibility "to formal visibility", that is, securing memberships of important committees and leadership roles (Chanana, 2003). There is an ample account of research that indicates that men tend to be promoted faster than women because of their rise of informal networks as opposed to women's greater reliance on formal processes alone (Gammie and Collahan, 1996). Women in educational field used to face two types of barriers (i) Internal, and (ii) External barriers. Internal barriers include emotionality, shyness, decency and lack of aggressiveness and rapid decision making. While external barriers are related to environment. They lack wide and vivid experiences as in comparison to males, the opportunities to experience the world are restricted for them, "The ego of the male colleagues even the peon is hurt in obeying a woman." Thus, our social system has the roots of these barriers. As males are not habituated to receive orders from females and females don't have habit of self-imposition.

Thus, males not only have superior status than women between jobs, but also within the jobs themselves. Women are concentrated into the lower ranked and down paid occupations within a given profession. If women are in management positions they are more likely to be in personnel than in marketing professions, there average salaries of each are $ 48,048 and $ 56,940 year respectively. Another example occurs within the medical field. Female doctors are much more likely to be heavily constricted in the family practice or pediatric specialities which average about $ 130,000 and $ 126,000 per year respectively. Whereas, men are more likely to become surgeon and highly specialized medical practitioners, with average salary of $ 2,40,000 or more per year.

The pay gap between men and women workers is still the cause for concern. In this way, pay differentials persist in all countries ranging from 10 to 30 percentage points. Further, the studies in this area show that women on an average work longer hours than men in nearly every country and they have to perform most unpaid work.

ILO (2003) research analysis suggests that disparity is greatest when the most power is exercised, the higher one goes, tbe larger is the gender gap. As women hold 1 to 3 per cent of top executive in the largest corporations worldwide. Only 8 countries have a woman head of the state, 21 countries have a deputy head, only 13.4 per cent of the world's Parliamentarians are women, only one per cent of trade union leaders are women though women are almost 40 per cent of their membership globally. Data show that women have the qualifications and work experience to take on responsibilities at the highest level, but the challenge is the slow pace in achieving a critical mass of women in top jobs with power.

It is a hard core fact that in many parts of the world the representation of women remains little more than a blip on the male political landscape. Powerful socio-economic, cultural and institutional barriers have blocked all but the most tenacious women from the public sphere, however the last four decades have witnessed the erosion of such barriers, the process has been painfully slow.

In 1997, the Inter-Parliamentary Union identified five countries that had national legislation establishing a compulsory quota of women MPs (Argentina, Belgium, Brazil, North Korea and Nepal), a further four had national legislation that reserved seats for women (Bangladesh, Burkina, Uganda. Tanzania and India). And in 36 nations, some or all of the political parties has quotas for women's candidatures for legislative elections.

A significant problem contributing to the difficulties facing women to reach the top seems to be the fact that few senior women are in the so-called "line" position that involve profit and loss or revenue generating responsibilities and which are critical for advancement to the highest levels, e.g, in 1999 men still held 93.8 per cent of line jobs in the U.S.A. and in Canada men held 93.6 per cent. Managerial women in developing countries often rely on extended family arrangements and the availability of inexpensive domestic assistance for childcare and household assistance.

In the financial sector, despite the fact that women are making same inroads in senior management in recent years, with few exceptions, they are not breaking through to the top positions. A survey of European banks published in 1999 showed increases between 1990 to 1995 in the proportion of women in executive positions except at the board level which remained static at around 5 per cent. There is evidence that the strong hurdle women accountant face in career development is even greater than in other areas (Gammie and Gammie, 1995).

Two professions in modern India are known to be woman friendly—banking and medicine. Unlike the early decades of the twentieth century, when women were largely employed in teaching and nursing (because both these vocations brought out the nurturing and mentoring instincts of women and more the best use of them); today women are seen in the higher echelons of all professions. But banking and nursing attract them for various reasons, thus 40 per cent of India's doctors are women. The third vocation which is fast gaining ground among educated women is entrepreneurship or flexi jobs. The former allows women to work at their own pace to a self-designed time schedule with the skills they have or can acquire. Thus, catering garment designing or tailoring, confectionery. stationery, designing, art work creation, graphics, desktop publishing, public relations, event management, media consultancy, guidance and insurance etc.—these are some of the favourite vocations of women, who are looking to earn money on a flexi-time work basis, yet others take part-time jobs or work as assignments from home.

All this information points towards one conclusion that women have to find job or vocation which fits in with their given life patterns rather than choose a vocation which itself defines their life graph as in the case of men. A man's life and achievement or success quotient is defined by what position—money and fame he achieves in his profession alone. While a woman's success is judged by a different yardstick altogether, such as—

— Has she performed her various roles well ?
— Does she manage her home and look after her family well ?
— Is she a good daughter, an efficient wife, and loving mother ?
— If she always there to hold up the sky when clouds darken the horizon?
— Is she always available when her family needs her?
— Over and above these, has she the right attitude to earning and self-reliance ?
— Does she handover her to the family kitty without caring about her personal security?
— Does she carry the role of culture bearer and religion teacher to her family?
— Has she carrying all this baggage achieved success in her carrier ?

Then alone is her triumph truly valued by the society particularly in the country like India. A fractured family, a broken marriage or unhappy motherhood devalue a women's performance, whereas man's professional excellence remains undiluted by any of these.

In this way, the major creator of glass ceiling (in India) is the dual personality she inherits by birth as a female in her parental home at least in urban educated homes, where she is encouraged to achieve excellence and high quality in anything she does. Yet, the same parents entreat her to put her husband and in-laws from the very first day of marriage, she has to change herself drastically to adjust herself in the new family. In many families her in-laws or her husband decide the scope of her work and success. She has to observe strictly and quietly the unseen line of control drawn by her matrimonial family.

Motherhood is the another event in her life which changes her completely. The road to motherhood is paved with surprises and embedded with (pit) falls. As in ILO (2005) report it was highlighted that 43 per cent of highly qualified educated women left their jobs voluntarily because of proper care of their children at some stage of their careers. Although 93 per cent wanted to return to their careers only 74 per cent did so and only 40 per cent went back to a full time position of those women who wanted to return to work, only 5 per cent desired to return to the position they had left.

There is a reflection of so-called "glass-walls", where women managers are concentrated in certain sectors such as in insurance, real estate, public administration and finance sectors with 42 per cent of women administrative and managerial employees being in the services sector compared with 30 per cent of men. However, in corporate jobs, peachy media assignments and hi-profile careers such as acting, art, dance or it need endless time for concentrated work. Among equals who may be brilliant and personable, those willing to give abundant time to the corporation or profession, have a better chance of making it to the top. Those willing to travel copiously and accept transfers linked to promotions, have more opportunities of reaching the top roof of the success ladder with jobs which fetch incredible incomes and perks. Obviously, women can't run fast in this race because they must give equal attention to homes and families. An unmarried woman can reach near this goal but insecure environment for a single woman unables her to live alone in cities, and in small towns and villages. Thus, due to the personal security, lack of mobility and inability to devote maximum time to a career, cause a further layer in the glass ceiling through which women can clearly see through their goals but cannot reach them. The world where they are working in which the dice is loaded against them in more ways than one. Sexual harassment and different treatment based on gender also keep them out of mainstream top jobs. They can't spend late nights with male clients or colleagues without causing wagging tongues. They can't join the club or bar life of men; because in our society particularly in India, women have to be more cautious than men in guarding their reputations. Only women who can beat all such circumstances and stand at the right time before the right door of opportunity with the right support structure can scale the heights of success and break the glass ceiling. Surely this combination of factors is hard to come by!

No doubt, modern era is called an era of "Human Rights" when we need to protect the rights of women and enable them to live freely in every walk of life without any discrimination. As once Pt. Nehru rightly stated, "Yon can tell the condition of a nation by looking at the status of its women." So it is a great surprise to see a woman who is considered as a "weaker vessel" do such multi task very diligently and happily. Her work is usually more arduous than her counterpart. She has got immense capabilities and qualities to do her work efficiently. But it is a sorry state of affair that no revolution can shatter this glass ceiling. In 1962, 1977 and even 1985, the women's movement used radical rhetoric and legal action to drive out overt discrimination, but most of the barriers that persist today are insidious—a revolution could not find them to blast away. Rather, gender discrimination now is so deeply embedded in organisation life as to be virtually indiscernible. Even the women who feel its impact are often hard-pressed to know what hit them.

One must be optimistic. This glass ceiling can be shattered in the new millennium through a strategy (Shattering the Glass Ceiling, Harward Business Review—Jan.-Feb. 2000). Small wins strategy is a powerful way of chipping away the barriers that bold women back without sparking the kind of sand and fury that scares people into resistance. And small wins strategy creates change through diagnosis, dialogue and experimentation, it usually improves efficiency and performance. The strategy benefits not only just women but also men and the organisation as a whole.

There was a time when it was easy to spot glass ceiling in terms of the criminalities and atrocities inflicted upon women in the corporate world. A talented female manager used to find herself demoted after her maternity leave. Today, such blatant cases are rare, they have been wiped out, by laws and by organisations increased awareness that they have nothing to gain, and much, to lose by keeping women out of the positions of authority, this does not mean that gender inequality has vanished. It has just gone underground (ILO's Yearbook of Labour Statistics, 2003). Still today, discrimination against women lingers in a plethora of work practices and cultural norms that really appear unbiased. They are common and mundane—and women *status quo* which is why most people don't notice them, let alone question them. But they create a subtle pattern of systemic disadvantage, which blocks all but a few women from career advancement.

There are continuous efforts put by women to break glass ceiling. Industries such as investment industry have suffered the burnt of criticism about legal judgments punishing Merrill Lynch and Morgan Stanley for their discriminatory practices. More recently, the huge efforts have been put to recruit and train women for top positions. Changes are slow, however, since currently though women represent 33 per cent of the best in the bank's analyst classes. Only 25 per cent of newly hired associates are women, only 14 per cent of the top executives in the banking industry are women and in 2005 one report showed that women make 80 cents for every one US dollar that men make. Many say that improvement no matter how small, shows that there are checks developing in the glass ceiling.

An important trend to note and which is providing other avenues for entrepreneurial women is that more women than ever before becoming employees and running their own businesses worldwide. By 1999, 38 per cent of all firms in the U.S.A. were run by women. In Australia, 35 per cent of the country's small business are female operators, in Ireland 35 to 40 per cent of new businesses are owned by women. Supporting women to gain more economic power through running their own business and employing others may well be a key strategy for reducing gender inequalities in the 21st century.

Certain strategies have been developed to speed up women's entry to the highest echelons of decision making. By working together with governments, employee's organisations, trade unions, the civil society and the U.N. family, the ILO intend to play a pivotal role in dismantling the so-called glass ceiling within its own walls and in the global and national labour markets. In order to curb glass ceiling, a new phenomenon known as The Reverse Glass Ceiling (RGC) has been taking shape in America over the past few years. More and more men have started their career in female-dominated industries, such as nursing, paralegal, travel and childcare. Many have been discriminated against because of this. Some experts question whether it actually exists because it is recent. Some others call this concept "The glass escalator" and describe it as the rapid advancement of men into positions of authority within female dominated occupations.

In India over years, a number of efforts have been initiated to support women. For example—Successive Five Year Plans have provided for resources in this regard. A significant event in the Indian Policy that can be seen as a landmark in the past two decades for women's development. The Equal Remuneration Act, 1976, provides for equal wages for the same work or work of similar nature for men and women workers and prohibits discrimination against women in matters of recruitment. The Maternity Benefits Act, 1961 and the Employees State Insurance Act, 1948 provide for among other matters, payment of maternity benefits.

Further 73rd and 74th Constitutional Amendments were carried out in 1992. These amendments provide for women's participation in local government by reservation of seats in "Village Panchayats", municipalities and local bodies. Women's wings of employer's Chambers have also worked for improving women's position in business management. The Sexual Harassment of Women Act, 1992 provide measures to prevent women from being subjected to harassment (Kothari, 2000). All major chambers of commerce including FICCI (Federation of Indian Chambers of Commerce and Industry), ASSOCHAM (Associated Chambers of Commerce and Industry) and IMC (Indian Merchants' Chamber) have also such wings. In the public sector, women managers have floated a forum called Women In the Public Sector (WIPS) for performing similar functions. Another public sector body SCOPE (Standing Conference On Public Enterprise) provides for counselling in training and development (Jain and Venkata Ratnam, 2002). Another non-govemmental organisations such as SEWA (Self Employed Women's Association) based in Ahmedabad, is known for organizing women in entrepreneurial managerial and related activities. Women managers bring with them a "unique style and attitude" to the workplace, this approach is adopted by ICICI Bank and Pepsi, while many of the organizations don't recogize this approach, which is considered to be a major hurdle in their career advancement (Fournier and Kelemen, 2001).

Thus, it is high time that serious attention to be paid to their unique needs and circumstances in an effort to raise both their self-worth and level of their contribution to the country's economic development.

For proper economic growth gender equality is to be maintained by having a balanced mix of so-called "masculine" and "feminine" attributes at all levels.

Other strategies for vanishing glass ceiling are :

— Meaningful change is required in diversification of occupation—meant for women and men.
— Foster greater sharing of family responsibilities.
— Cultivate and nurture women's entrepreneurial talents.
— Innovate with proven human resource and budget strategies.
— The lesson is that for companies and organisations to remain competitive must not utter these words that "we can't afford to lose out on women's talent." It is not only the right thing to do; but it's the most important action to do!

In a nutshell, the author of this chapter being herself a professional woman, takes a vow to put endless efforts to remove this glass ceiling effect. Woman who is a creator of this world, would not lag behind man in (an organizational) the professional world. Woman has strong willpower to achieve what she is determined to achieve. Even the Gods do not act without their female counterparts called 'Shakti'. They have always involved them while making important decisions. As Brahma did not work without Saraswati, Vishnu without Lakshmi and Mahesh without Parvati. I agree; it is not a easy job for women to jostle with men to reach the top position, still I will say that they are omnipresent, in every walk of life one can see them flourishing. Go ahead—Life is a big challenge—face it boldly and courageously.

REFERENCES

Appord, S. Siengthai, S. and Kasarla, J. (1998). The employment of women manager and professionals in an emerging economy; gender inequality as an organisational practice, *Administration Science, 43(3)*, pp. 538-561.

Anne, E.K. (2008). "Clinton urges Backer's to Look to Novembers." Washington Post AOI http://wwwpearsonschool.com index cfm7 10cater=PSZ3R98P.

Baglihole, B. (1994). Being Different is a very difficult Row to Hoe: Survival strategies of Women academics; in S. Davies *et al.* (eds.), *Changing The Subject: Women in Higher Education*, London : Taylor and Francis, pp. 15-28.

Bryant, Gay (1984). *Glass Ceiling*. Adweek Article, U.S.A.

Channana, K. (2003). Visibility, Gender and the Careers of Women Faculty in an Indian University, *McGill Journal of Education*, Vol. 38, No.3, Fall, pp. 381-90. Inter-Parliamentary Union (fu 27); 64-67.

Eagly, A.H. and Caeli, L.L. (2007). *Through the Labyrinth : The truth about how women became leaders.* Massachusetts: Harward Business Press.

Elder, S. and Schmidt, D.C. (2004). *Global employment trends for women employment.* Trends Unit, Employment Strategy Deptt., I.L.O.

Fournier, V. and Kelemen, M. (2001). The crafting of community: recoupling discourses of management and womanhood, *Gender, Work and Organization, 8(3)*, pp. 267- 290.

Gammie, T.N. and Coolaham, M. (1996). Career mobility in organisations. Implications for Career Development. *Journal of European Industrial Training*, Vol. 20, No. 4, pp. 30-40.

Hesse-Biber, Sharlene N. and Greg and L.C. (2005). *Working Women in America.* New York, NY : Oxford University Press.

Horton, S. (1999). Marginalisation revisited, Women's Market Work and Pay, an economic development, *World Development, 27(3)*, pp. 571-582.

Hymowitz, C. and Schellbardt, T. (1986). Glass Ceiling. *Wall Street Journal,* U.S.A.

ILO (2001). *Breaking through the Glass Ceiling: Women in Management* (Geneva : International Labour Office).

Jain, Harish C. & Venkata Ratnam, C. S. (2002). Gender equity in India, in: Carol Agocs (Ed.) *Workplace Equality—International Perspectives on Legislation, Policy and Practice* (The Hague. The Netherlands: Kluwer Law International).

Joshi, B. and Bhogayata, C. (2007). *Barrier Faced by Women Educational Managers at an Indian University,* E. Journal.

Judge, Timothy, A., and Beth, A. Livingston (2008). Is the Gap More Than Gender? A Longitudinal Analysis of Gender, Gender Role Orientation, and Earnings. *Journal of Applied Psychology, 93,* 994-1012.

Kothari, G.M. (2000). *A Study of Industrial Law* (Nagpur: Wadhwa & Company).

Kulkarni, S.S. (2002). Women and professiooal competency—a survey report, *Indian Journal of Training and Development,* XXXII(2), April-June, pp. 11-16.

Merritt, J. (2008). *Does the Reverse Glass Ceiling Exist?* MSN Encarta.

Meyerson, Debra, E., and Fletcher, Joyce, K. (2000). A modest manifesto for shattering the Glass Ceiling. *How and Business Review.*

Newman, D. and Smith R. (1999). The Architecture of Inequality, "Sex and Gender".

O'Shea, L. (1997). Asian Women in business debunking: a myth, *Asian Business.*

Pawans, Budhwar, Saini D., and Bhatnagar, J. (2005). Women in Management in the New Economic Environment : The Case of India, *Asia Pacific Business Review,* Vol. II, No. 2, 179-193.

Suriya, M. (2003). Gender' issues in the career development of IT Professionals: a goal perspective. Available at http://www.gisdevelopment.net/proceedings/mapasia/2003/papers/i4d/i4d002.htm

The Tribune Sunday (Oct. 14, 2001). Chandigarh, India.

Venkatasinbramanian, K. (2001). *Women ! Be Courageous, Other things follow;* A Convocation address, University News, *39(42),* 14-17.

Williams, C.L. (1992). The Glass Escalator : Hidden advantages for men in the "female" professions. *Soc. Problems, 39,* 253-267.

Wirth, Linda (2002). *Breaking through the Glass Ceiling: Women in Management.* First International Conference : Pay Equity between Women and Men—Myth or Reality, Luxembourg, Norway.

Zubaidah, Z. A., Azwan & A.R. Kamaruzaman J. (2009). The 'Glass Ceiling' Phenomenon for Malaysian Women Accountants. *Asian Culture and History,* Vol. 1, No. 1, Toronto:William Printing Inc.

13

Attitudes of Married Women towards Birth Restraints and Family Size in Relation to Personality

Rakesh K. Srivastava and *Madhu Seth*

Researches on fertility behaviour and related areas have been focus of attention in contemporary psychological research. Population is acknowledged as a critical variable in the development process. The sickness of Indian economy is mainly due to our excessive population growth. The population rapidly increases but the increase in the production of food and other necessities does not keep the pace. India is the first country in the South-East Asian region to introduce family planning in 1951 under Government auspices. In India, the population is increasing very rapidly, with a large and sustained excess of births over deaths. This is the most vital problem the country is now facing and population experts have a unique role to perform in analyzing these problems and devising suitable measures to reduce the birth rate and ensure better health and standards of living. In recent years, population growth has become one of the crucial human problems. The alarming increase in the size of population is due to many causes; as sharp fall in the death rate, due to modern medical and health facilities and excess of births over deaths, prevention and cure of diseases (Gowarikar, 1992; Chantia, 2008; Singh, 2008; Jain, 1989).

Mrinal (2004) observed that planning of the family is very much limited to higher and upper middle section of the society.

In developing countries like India, limited access to family planning results in higher rates of unintended pregnancy, millions of unsafe abortions and thousands of maternal death. In spite of sustained efforts to control the population many families in India still remain unplanned may be due to carelessness and largely due to religion as well as ignorance. Many families have 3-4 or 5 girl children because of the expectation factor that the next child may be a male child. He further commented that cultural and religious sentiments play a major role in the determination of the size of the family. They are aware that unintended size of the family may bring a lot of stress (Verma, 1990; Ramarao & Mohanan, 2003).

Rao (1978) reviewed significant researches on psychology of population and family planning during 1971-76. Furthermore, Tripathi (1988) in the third ICSSR survey of research in psychology commented that attitude towards family planning has continued to be a subject of interest. A. Srivastava (1999) observed that a grave social problem in India is that of overpopulation. Verma (1990) observed that fertility behaviour is complex and is determined by a host of biological, sociological, psychological and economic factors. These factors not only affect fertility behaviour directly but also a variety of combinations. Dave and Sadashivaiah (1981) have reviewed studies on family size. They concluded that lower social class urban men preferred a large family size than their wives. Rural men and women desired a larger family size. They also concluded that higher the education level and status of the women, the lower was the desired family size and also traditionalisation was associated with a higher family size. Biswas and Chakroborty (2008) studied the fertility behaviour and family planning measures of the Meches of North Bengal. They identified the fertility and family planning attributes of the population along with the direct and indirect factors of the same that may affect the fertility behaviour of the Meches of the North Bengal.

Mishra (1993) found in her study that most of the women agree that family size should be limited according to the physical, mental, emotional, and spiritual resources of the parents. Her study reveals that people now want less children because they want to provide better facilities and education to their children. Furthermore, 49.9 per cent males and 87.5 per cent females subscribe to this view. Increasing general education, lowering of the infant mortality rate, growth of the democratic idea that each individual is responsible for the welfare of himself and his family as well as of the society in which he lives are the important factors in achieving the goal of lower birth rates. This situation has definitely improved the life and conditions of women in Indian society. Earlier studies conducted in the area (Merchant, 1945; Rao, 1995) also confirm the view where it was found that not only that a very large majority of youth is awakened to the necessity of restricting the birth of the children due to the economic stress but there is a growing opinion emphasizing the right of the unborn to be wellborn. A sense of social responsibility seems to be growing ground among them. Verma (1990) also emphasized that the process of social change is likely to bring about changes in various aspects of individual personality may prove crucial from the viewpoint of fertility decisions.

Ramesh (1988) suggested that psychological characteristics such as the satisfaction of basic needs, developmental value orientation, and open attitude system operate as mechanism through which characteristics like place of residence, education, income and socio-economic status have their effect on fertility and family planning practice. Chung, Palmore, Lee, and Lee (1972) concluded that (a) the psychological factors are one of the mechanisms through which the social background factors operate to affect fertility behaviour, (b) the psychological factors are independently important beyond being operational mechanism of social background factors, and (c) in some socio-demographic conditions, the psychological factors are most important determinants of fertility behaviour than in other conditions.

Seth, Saksena and Srivastava (1979) conducted a study regarding socio-personal variables associated with attitude of Tharus (tribals) towards birth control. They remarked that intensive efforts are being made by the government to popularise the small family norm and several studies have been conducted to assess the attitude of the people towards the family planning programme. In any programme of change, the effectiveness in motivating them depends on the knowledge of personality characteristics and attitudinal level of the functionaries in the programme. The training to be effective it is also necessary to find out the personality characteristics of the functionaries and their attitudes towards the programme. This would also enable us to know the impact of the two dimensions of personality—Extrversion and Introversion towards birth restraints. Khan and Prasad (1980) compared the personality dimensions of acceptors and non-acceptors and have tried to establish that acceptors are more prone to change, possess rational thinking and their subjective efficiency is high. Kumar and Gairola (1981) also compared the personality traits of adopters and non-adopters and found that adopter women tended to be less anxious, more intelligent, and had a stronger need for dominance than the non-adapters.

The achievement of this objective among other things primarily requires a definite change in the attitudes and behaviour of people towards accepting the small family norms and plan and control births by telling the advantages of small families. Besides we have also to study the characteristics of the target population. Its customs, beliefs and practices related to sex life and marriage, child rearing (Seth, Saksena, & Srivastava 1978; Eagly 1995; Srivastava, 1989, 1984, 1979). Initiation of social mechanisms to create necessary environmental presses and measures to break down resistances in order to facilitate the adoption of new practices and value change later, the doctrination of non-fertile groups—children and older people—through the carefully planned educative programmes and the provision of self-oriented social incentives to make the small family norm a desirable and cherished value (Ramamurti, 1976). Intensive efforts are being made by the government to popularise this scheme among people and some studies have also been conducted to assess scientifically this scheme (Thakur Hazari & Thakur, 1977; Wadia, 1977).

Objectives

Keeping the above facts and review into consideration, the present study aimed at studying the following objectives:

(i) To study the attitudes of the extroverted and introverted men and women towards birth restraint.
(ii) To study comparatively the attitudes of the extroverted men and women towards birth restraint.
(iii) To study comparatively the attitudes of introverted men and women towards birth restraint.
(iv) To study the views of the extroverted and introverted men and women towards family size.

Method and Procedures

The participants of the present study were 400 individuals—200 men (100 extroverted and 100 introverted) and 200 women (100 extroverted and 100 introverted). The men and women chosen for the present study all were married, had more than one child and from the state of Uttar Pradesh, India. An extroversion-introversion inventory by Aziz & Agnihotry (1983) was administered upon larger sample of men and women to select 200 men (100 extroverted and 100 introverted) and 200 women (100 extroverted and 100 introverted).

The extroverted and introverted men and women selected were then interviewed to find out their attitudes towards birth restraints. This was done to see whether the personality characteristics of the individuals too have any effect on the attitudes of the individual towards birth restraints. They were asked whether they wanted to restrict the number of children if possible, whether they did not want to restrict the number of children and their opinion regarding the number of children a couple should have. Those few who showed no interest or were indifferent towards birth restraints were recorded separately. Non-parametric statistics were applied considering the nature of the data. For the attitude measure χ^2 was used and for views of family size percentage was calculated.

Results and Discussion

The results in Table 13.1 clearly indicate the attitudes of the extroverted and introverted women towards birth restraints. It was found that more extroverted than introverted women wanted to restrict the number of children if possible, while more introverted women than extroverted did not want to restrict the number of children and were also found to be more indifferent. The Chi-square value reached a significance level with p .001 showing that the two groups that is extroverted and introverted women differed significantly in their attitudes towards birth restraints. This suggests that women belonging to the extroversion group had a more favourable attitude towards birth restraints.

Table 13.1: Attitudes of Extroverted and Introverted Women towards Birth Restraints

Groups	*Those who want to restrict the number of children*	*Those who do not want to restrict the number of children*	*Those who are indifferent*	*Total*
Extroverted Women	80	13	07	100
Introverted Women	52	37	11	100
χ^2 Value		18.12		
p Value		.001 Significant		

From the nature of data (Table 13.2), it is clear that more extroverted men were in favour of birth restraints and more introverted men were not in favour of birth restraints and were also found to be more indifferent than the extroverted men. In this respect also both the groups differed significantly (p .001) in their attitudes towards birth restraints. It is further noted that the same trend was found between extroverted and introverted men as was noticed in the case of women, that is extroverted men too had a favourable attitude towards birth restraints than their introverted counterparts.

Table 13.2: Attitudes of Extroverted and Introverted Men towards Birth Restraints

Groups	*Those who want to restrict the number of children*	*Those who do not want to restrict the number of children*	*Those who are indifferent*	*Total*
Extroverted Men	90	08	02	100
Introverted Men	72	22	06	100
χ^2 Value		10.52		
p Value		.001 Significant		

From the data presented in Table 13.3, it can be known that there is no significant difference in respect of the attitudes of the extroverted men and women. The data in the table reveals that more extroverted men than women were in favour of restriction of the number of children if possible, while more introverted women than men were not in favour of restricting the number of children and were also more indifferent towards it, though not significantly so.

Table 13.3: Attitudes of Extroverted Men and Women towards Birth Restraints

Groups	*Those who want to restrict the number of children*	*Those who do not want to restrict the number of children*	*Those who are indifferent*	*Total*
Extroverted Men	90	08	02	100
Introverted Women	80	13	07	100
χ^2 Value		04.08		
p Value		0.10 Not Significant		

It is evident from our data also (Table 13.4) that there exists significant difference (p .05) between the two groups that is: the introverted men and women in their attitudes towards birth restraint. The data reveals that more introverted men and women were in favour of birth restraint while more introverted women than men did not want to restrict the number of children and were also more indifferent too. The significant sex differences observed between introverted men and women indicate that the introversion dimension of personality is associated with favourable attitudes towards birth restraint in case of men participants than women.

Table 13.4: Attitudes of Introverted Men and Women towards Birth Restraints

Groups	*Those who want to restrict the number of children*	*Those who do not want to restrict the number of children*	*Those who are indifferent*	*Total*
Introverted Men	72	22	06	100
Introverted Women	52	37	11	100
χ^2 Value		08.20		
p Value		0.05 Significant		

Thus, the attitudes one has towards birth restraint is found to be different in respect of the personality characteristics of the individuals interviewed. Persons with different dimensions of personality may be extroverted or introverted tend to hold different attitudes. As is evident from the results shown in Table 13.1 and 13.2 that the extroverted and introverted men and women differed significantly in their responses given towards birth restraint. This further clears that the two different dimensions of personality studied had a significant impact upon the attitudes of the men and women. Further, it can be suggested that to implement any programme and to create a positive attitude it is necessary to take into consideration the personality characteristics of the individuals.

Not only are there significant differences between extroverted and introverted men and women (Tables 13.1 and 13.2) but it is also evident (Table 13.3 and 13.4) that to some extent sex differences are also found in respect of the attitudes one has towards birth restraints. No significant differences were observed between the attitudes of the extroverted men and women. That is to say both extroverted men and women hold similar attitudes towards restriction of children. However, it is noteworthy that significant differences were observed between the attitudes of the introverted men and women towards birth restraints. More introverted men than women were in favour of the restrictions of children if possible. Hence, it can be suggested that we have to motivate and create a positive trend towards birth restriction more in introverted women. From the aforesaid results, it is clear that attitude towards birth restraints are the products of one's personality characteristics like introversion and extroversion. Hence, it is suggested that proper attention must be given to these personality characteristics in planning and implementing any programme for the restrictions of births.

Besides studying the attitudes of the extroverted and introverted men and women towards birth restraints, the present researchers also interviewed them to know their views towards family size, that is, their views as to the number of the children a couple should have. Results in Table 13.5 indicate the views of extroverted and introverted women towards family size. Out of the 100 extroverted women interviewed no one desired to have one child, 10(10%) desired to have two, 35(35%) of them desired to have three, 36(36%) to have four, 14(14%) to have five, and 5(5%) to have more than six children. While on the other hand, out of 100 introverted women interviewed no one desired to have one child, 2(2%) of them desired to have two, 21(21%) to have three, 43(43%) have four, 24(24%) to have five and 10(10%) to have more than six children. The results reveal the extroverted women are in favour of having a small family, that is, lesser number of children than the introverted women.

Table 13.5: Extroverted and Introverted Women's view of Family Size

Number of Children desired	*One*		*Two*		*Three*		*Four*		*Five*		*Six*		*Total*
	N	*%*	*N*	*%*	*N*	*%*	*N*	*%*	*N*	*%*	*N*	*%*	
Extroverted Women	-	-	10	10	35	35	36	36	14	14	05	05	100
Introverted Women	-	-	02	02	21	21	43	43	24	24	10	10	100

Table 13.6 reveals the views of the extroverted and introverted men towards family size. Out of the 100 extroverted men interviewed 2(2%) of them desired to have one child, 18(18%) to have two children, 42(42%) to have three, 30(30%) to have four, 3(3%) to have five and 3(3%) to have more than six children. On the other hand, out of the 100 introverted men no one desired to have one child, 13(13%) to have two children, 29(29%) to have three, 36(36%) to have four, 13(13%) to have five, and 9(9%) to have more than 6 children. This again reveals that more extroverted men are in favour having a small family with less number of children than their introverted counterparts.

Table 13.6: Extroverted and Introverted Men's view of Family Size

Number of Children desired	*One*		*Two*		*Three*		*Four*		*Five*		*Six*		*Total*
	N	*%*	*N*	*%*	*N*	*%*	*N*	*%*	*N*	*%*	*N*	*%*	
Extroverted Men	02	02	18	18	42	42	30	30	03	03	03	03	100
Introverted Men	-	-	13	13	29	29	36	36	13	13	09	09	100

Thus, on the basis of results obtained (Table 13.5 and 13.6), it is necessary to first find out the personality characteristics of the individuals and then motivate, educate, and convince them towards the benefits of having a small family size. It is also seen that such efforts are needed more in introverted men and women than their extroverted counterparts as those belonging to the extroverted group can easily be motivated to have a small family and to have a positive attitude towards the new methods of family planning practices.

Conclusion

Considering the limitations of the study, we may conclude that:

(i) Significant differences exist in the attitudes of the extroverted and introverted women towards birth restraints.
(ii) Significant differences exist in the attitudes of the extroverted and introverted men towards birth restraints.
(iii) No significant differences exist in the attitudes of the extroverted men and women towards the restriction of birth.
(iv) Significant differences exist in the attitudes of the introverted men and women towards birth restraints.
(v) More extroverted men and women are in favour of having a small family, that is lesser number of children than their introverted counterparts.

The overall findings suggest that the personality characteristics—Extroversion and Introversion are found to influence the attitudes of men and women towards birth restraints and also their views towards family size. In any programme of change involving various groups, the effectiveness in motivating depends on the knowledge of the personality characteristics and attitudinal level of the target group (Srivastava, 1996, 1990). It is also suggested that in implementing the family planning and welfare programmes proper attention should be given to the personality characteristics of the target population to check increase in population. Therefore, the findings of the present study may prove to be useful in effective implementation of any programme for population control and may also prove to be useful in the integration of cross-cultural research (Srivastava,

2009, 2005, 2003, 1999; Shobha, 1986; Singh & Shobha, 1986; Carlson, 1975; Kagitcibasi & Berry, 1989). Asthana (1992) also observed that population growth is a major social problem and efforts here have not been as effective and successful. Furthermore, he suggested that this problem has to be tackled at community level where a more direct interaction with the target population may be desirable since attitude and values change with considerable difficulty.

REFERENCES

Asthana, H.S. (1992). *Community psychology: Issues, relevance and directions,* Presidential address delivered at the 1st Convention of the Community Psychology Association of India, Kanpur, Sept. 27-28.

Aziz, P.F. and Agnihotri, R. (1993). *Manual for introversion-extroversion inventory in Hindi.* Agra: Sri M.D. Agnihotry.

Biswas S., and Chakroborty, D. (2008). *Fertility behaviour and family planning measures of the Meches of North Bengal: An observation,* Paper presented at the 95th Indian Science Congress. Visakhapatnam, Jan. 3-7.

Carlson, R. (1975). Personality, *Annual Review of Psychology, 26,* 393-414.

Chantia, A. (2008). *Population size and social changes: A study of Dhankut of District Bahraich (UP).* Paper presented at the 95th Indian Science Congress, Visakhapatnam, Jan. 3-7.

Chung, B.M., Palmore, J.A., Lee, S.J. and Lee, S.J. (1972). *Psychological perspective: Family planning in Korea.* Seoul: Hollyn Corporation Publishers.

Dave, C. and Sadashivaiah, K. (1981). Family size and quality of life. *Social change, 11,* 35-44.

Eagly, A.H. (1952). The science and politics of comparing women and men. *American Psychologist, 50,* 145-168.

Gowariker, V. (1992). *Science, population and development,* General Presidential Address delivered at the 79th Indian Science Congress, Vadodara, Jan. 3-7.

Hazari, A., Thakur, G.P. and Thakur, M. (1977). Attitudes of young and old people towards family planning. *Asian Journal of Psychology and Education, 1,* 1-4.

Jain, A.K. (1989). Fertility reduction and quaiity of family planning services. *Studies in Family Planning, 20(1),* 116.

Kagitcabisi, C. and Berry, J.W. (1989). Cross-cultural psychology: Current research and trends. *Annual Review of Psychology, 40,* 493-531.

Khan, M.E. and Prasad, C.V. S. (1980). *Fertility control in India: A critical evaluation of the role of incentive in promoting sterilization among individual workers.* New Delhi: Manohar Publications.

Kumar, P. and Gairola, L. (1978). An attitudinal and motivational study of early and late adopters of family planning among women. *Health and Population—Perspectives and Issues, 1,* 79-85.

Merchant, K.T. (1946). *Changing views on marriage and family,* Bombay: Popular Prakashan.

Mishra, S. (1993). *Status of women in changing urban Hindu family.* New Delhi: Radha Publications.

Mrinal, N.R. (2004). Mediation of stress in planned and unplanned Hindu families in India: A study of stress and copying resources. *Psycho-Lingua, 34(2),* 125-131.

Rao, C.V. (2005). *Human evolution and its uniqueness.* Visakhapatnam: Ravi Publishers.

Rao, T.V. (1981). Population and family planning. In U. Pareek (Ed.), *A survey of research in Psychology 1971-76 (Part-III).* Bombay: Popular Prakashan.

Ramarao, S. and Mohanan, R. (2003). The quality of family planning programmes: Concepts, measurements, interventions and effects. *Studies in Family Planning, 34(4),* 227-248.

Ramesh, B.M. (1988). Study of differentials in fertility and family planning behaviour: A psychological approach. In K. Srinivasan & S. Mukerji (Eds.), *Dynamics of population and family welfare.* Bombay: Himalaya Publishing House.

Seth, M., Saksena, N.K. and Srivastava, R.K. (1979). Socio-personal variables associated with attitudes of Tharus towards birth control. *Journal of Family Welfare, 24,* 34-39.

Shobha, S. (1986). *Achievement judgments by school teachers: An information integration analysis.* Ahmedabad: Gujarat University.

Singh, R. and Shobha, S. (1986). *Averaging model analyses of teacher expectations of performance from students varying in motivation and ability.* Working Paper No. 644. Ahmedabad: Indian Institute of Management.

Singh, S. (2008). *Population problem, education and reservation policy.* Paper presented at the 95th Indian Science Congress. Visakhapatnam, Jan. 3-7.

Srivastava, A. (1999). Role of social psychology in national development. In U.N. Dash and U. Jain (Eds.). *Perspectives on psychology and social developments* (Chapter 3, pp. 33-59) New Delhi: Concept Publishing Company (P) Ltd.

Srivastava, R.K. (2009). Culture and identity style preferences: Contexts and consequences. In A. Shukla (Ed.), *Culture, cognition, and behaviour* (Chapter 10, pp. 169-177). New Delhi: Concept Publishing Company (P) Ltd.

Srivastava, R.K. (2005). Consequences of acculturation for mental health of Indian tribals. In A. Shukla (Ed.). *Indian tribes: Psychological and social perspectives* (Chapter 3, pp. 12-18). New Delhi: Kanishka Publishers, Distributors.

Srivastava, R.K. (2003). Identity style preferences of adolescents of Hindu and Muslim communities in India. *Journal of Community Guidance and Research, 20,* 323-329.

Srivastava, R.K. (1999). *Psychology and social problems: Some issues and challenges for making psychology relevant for the masses.* Paper presented at the 10th Annual Conference of the National Academy of Psychology (NAOP), Lucknow, December 3-5.

Srivastava, R.K. (1996). *Tribal ego-identity in India.* New Delhi: Classical Publishing Company.

Srivastava, R.K. (1990). Culture contact and child-rearing attitudes of Indian (Tharu) tribals. *Indian Journal of Social Work, 51,* 425-436.

Srivastava, R.K. (1989). Acculturation and frustration—aggression patterns of Indian tribals. *British Journal of Projective Psychology, 34(2),* 12-30.

Srivastava, R.K. (1984). Rural-urban differences in authoritarianism among the Hindus in India. *Journal of Social Psychology, 122,* 291-292.

Tripathi, R.C. (1988). Applied social psychology. In J. Pandey (Ed.), *Psychology in India: The state-of-the-art* (Vol. 2, Chapter 3, pp. 95-157). New Delhi: Sage Publications.

Verma, R.K. (1990). Population research. In G. Mishra (Ed.), *Applied social psychology in India* (Chapter 15, pp. 279-294). New Delhi: Sage Publications.

14

Experiencing Satisfaction in life: *A Study on Paid and Unpaid Women*

Aradhana Shukla and *Shraddha Joshi*

Socio-psychological attempts to examine issues related to Indian women's entry into the employment market direct attention to important but the limited range of topics. More importantly, these attempts reflect gender's views of employment. As men's provided role is both socially accepted and valued, their employment is not seen to be in conflict with their provider status. Women, on the other hand, are primarily valued in their home-making and socializing roles and, therefore, their involvement outside the home is considered deviant behaviour, a problem and a source of stress in domestic life. Consequently, researchers mainly concern themselves with questions like how does women's employment status affect their performance of familial roles and quality of marital life? How does full-time employment of the mother influence children's psychological development and academic performance? How do working women combine their so-called "traditional" roles of home-maker and earner, and with impact, does it have on their stress levels". Clearly, the focus is on studying the effects of employment and less attention is paid to examining work related aspects of employed women. In short, researchers have continued to study working women in their roles as "wives" and "mother" rather than as "'workers" in gainful employment.

In addition to published research, there are a few review articles as source material on the theme of women in paid work (Agrawal, 1994; Parikh & Shah, 1994; Sastry, 1991). Outside the discipline, critical essays of sociological work are other recommended references (Desai & Annantram, 1985; Krisna Raj, 1986).

A drawback inherent in nearly all the studies is the lack of a theoretical perspective, and all the results are generally interpreted in a linear cause-effect manner. The complexity of working women's lives is not given due recognition. For instance, women in paid labour are treated as homogeneous group ignoring the socio-economic disparities, reasons for entering the labour force, quality of marital and family life, presence of kin, household or other support for childcare and domestic work, nature of the job and job demands. All these variables can be said to act as mediating factors influencing the outcome of mother's employment for children's development. In only one study by Vanaja and Venkataramaiah (1990), employed mother's marital satisfaction was considered as an important variable. Another drawback is that in most studies no rationale is provided for the dependent variables. For instance, Parvathi *et al.* (1985) did not explain the rationale for examining the relationship between children's locus of control, need of approval and mother's employment.

Women's Employment and Family Life Slightly Bold

Unlike male employment, women's employment is necessarily viewed in the context of their social, marital and familial roles and relationships. When women cross the threshold of their homes to enter the world of paid work, their employment is seen as intruding upon their primary responsibility of home-making. They are expected to recognize their "traditional" roles of wife, mother and home-maker in order to accommodate their "non-traditional" role as earner. A fair amount of sociological research exploring the work family interface in the case of employed women is available. Two major lines of enquire are discernible. First explores the balancing of role burden of employed women. Second examines the impact of women's earner role on their status within the family in terms of their decision-making power, sharing household labour, etc. in comparison to sociological literature, psychological research on these aspects is limited and thought-provoking.

In traditional Indian homes, the husband is considered to have greater power in decision making and the wife is merely expected to execute those decisions. In the context of women's involvement in paid work, the question arises, 'Do women gain more power at home when they are gainfully employed outside?' Shukla (1987a) compared the decision making patterns of single and dual career couples residing in a north Indian city. A decision making role with statements covering different decisions like finance and home decoration was used. The wives were employed as government officers, doctors, bank officers and lecturers. As hypothesized, employed women enjoyed more power than unemployed women and on the whole dual career couples were more egalitarian than single career couples leading to the conclusion, "since wives' employment is significantly associated with their marital power, their employment may be regarded as an important resource variable in Indian Context."

A sociological analysis of dual earner couples by Ramu (1989) also revealed the positive impact of wives' employment on their decision making power at home. Employed wives had significantly greater power than unemployed wives. However, these findings are partly at variance with western findings that although employed wives have more power, they still have less power than their husbands (Scanzoni & Polonka, 1980). In the light of this, decision areas in which working wives enjoy power are worth examining. Shukla (1987a) reported that employed wives enjoyed power in economically significant area like insurance and investments. A study by Bharat (1992) with career (N=190) and non-career women (N=136) revealed that even if women employed in high placed jobs gained power, they did so in seemingly less crucial areas like menu making or home decoration while decisions on matters involving finances were generally made by husbands.

The aim of this study was to find out the impact of chronological age level of employment and family type on life satisfaction. The objective and hypotheses of this study are as follows:

1. The first objective of this study was to find out the pattern of life satisfaction as affected by chronological age. It was contended that variation in age would cause variation in life satisfaction.
2. The second objective of this study was to find out the pattern of life satisfaction as affected by type of employment. It was hypothesized that employed and unemployed mothers would show variation in their magnitude of life satisfaction.
3. The third objective of this study was to find out the pattern of life satisfaction as affected by family type. It was hypothesized that variation in family type would cause variation in life satisfaction.

In order to test these hypotheses, the study was planned in 3×2×2 factorial perspective.

Method

Sample: One hundred and eighty women participants, in the age range of 25-50 years were taken in consideration and were arranged according to the requirements of 3×2×2 factorial design with 3 levels of age (25-30, 35-40 and 45-50), 2 levels of employment (employed and unemployed) and 2 levels of family type (joint and nuclear), i.e., 15 participants in each cell. The schematic presentation of experimental design is given in Table 14.1.

Table 14.1 : Schematic Presentation of Experimental Design

	A					
	A1		*A2*		*A3*	
	B1	*B2*	*B1*	*B2*	*B1*	*B2*
CI	25	25	25	25	25	25
C2	25	25	25	25	25	25

Tools: In this study one tool was taken in consideration and its description is as follows:

Life Satisfaction Scale

Constructed and standardized by Neugarten (1961) and adapted in India by Sharma and Saxena (1986), this scale includes five dimensions:

1. Zest
2. Resolution
3. Congruence desired and achieved goals
4. Self concept, and
5. Mood tone.

This scale consists of two short self-administered instruments, the life satisfaction index A (LSIA) and life satisfaction index B (LSIB). On the basis of the response to these scales an individual was regarded as being at the positive end of the continuum of psychological well-being to extent that he/she:

(a) Takes pleasure from the activities that constitute his everyday life,
(b) Regarded his life as meaningful and accept resolutely that which life has been,
(c) Feels that he has succeeded in achieving the major goals,
(d) Holds a positive self-image, and
(e) Maintains happy and optimistic attitude and mood.

Each of the five components was rated on a five point scale (with 5 high) and the ratings were summed up to obtain an overall rating with a possible range from 5 to 25. Ratings were made by two judges (the researcher and his supervisor) working independently. Average of the two ratings was used. The correlation between LSRS worked out to be 0.78. Spearman-Brown Coefficient of attenuation was employed and the coefficient rose to 0.87. The validity ratings confirmed those earlier works by Neugarten (1961)

Procedure: Data Collection was done individually or in group and best attempts were made to avoid external distractions.

Result

Obtained data were analyzed by 3-way ANOVA and interpreted in terms of chronological age, level of employment and family type as affecters of life satisfaction and it is presented in Table 14.2. It was found that the main effect of chronological age was significant ($F_{2, 168} = 7.96$ $P<0.01$) and it revealed that older women perceived better life satisfaction (X=41.75) as compared to middle age (X=56.47) and young age (X=69.08) women participants.

Table 14.2 : Summary table of analysis of variance showing the impact of chronological age, level of employment and family type on life satisfaction

Sources of variation	*SS*	*df*	*MS*	*F*
A	12.58	2	6.29	7.96
B	0.99	1	0.99	1.26
C	1.70	1	1.70	2.15
AB	11.99	2	5.99	7.59
AC	11.08	2	5.53	7.01
BC	5.21	1	5.21	6.59
ABC	15.96	2	7.98	10.10
Error		168	.79	
		179		

The next main effect of level of employment was significant ($F_{1, 168} = 2.15$ $P>0.05$) and it was found that participants of joint family (X=54.16) and nuclear family (X=57.37) were almost same in life satisfaction.

The last main effect of family type was insignificant (F1, 168=2.15 P> 0.05) and it was found that participants of joint family (X=54.16) and nuclear family (X=57.37) was almost same in life satisfaction.

The first two way interaction between chronological age and levels of employment was significant (F2, 168 = 7.59 P<0.01) and it is shown in Fig 14.1. The sense of life satisfaction was highest in oldest age group followed by middle and youngest age group respectively. However, the magnitude of discrepancy was highest in oldest age group followed by youngest and middle age groups respectively.

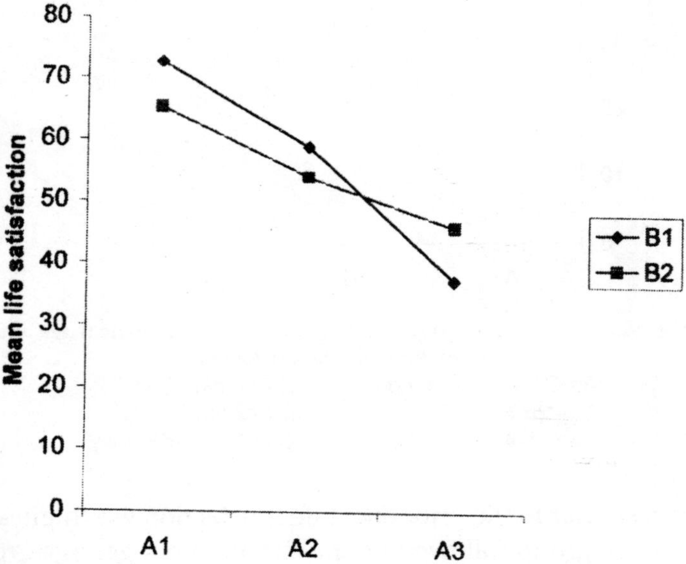

Fig. 14.1: Mean values showing the impact of chronological age and levels of employment on life satisfaction.

Legends : A= *Chronological Age*
A1= 25-30
A2= 35-40
A3= 45-50
C= *Family Type*
C1 =Joint Family
C2= Nuclear Family

B= *Levels of Employment*
B1 =Employed
B2=Unemployed

The next two way interaction of chronological age and family type was also significant (F2, 168 = 7.01 P<0.01) and it is shown in Fig 14.2. It was found that this interaction was

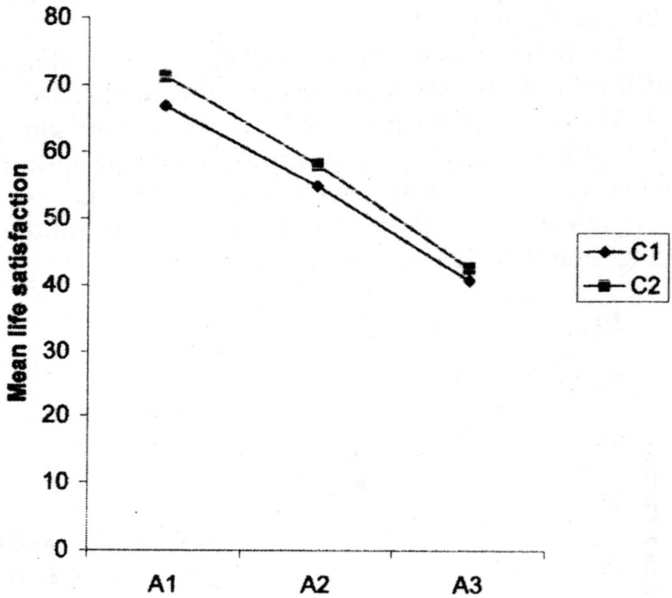

Fig. 14.2: Mean values showing the impact of chronological age and family type on life satisfaction.

Legends : *A= Chronological Age* — A1= 25-30, A2= 35-40, A3= 45-50; *C= Family Type* — C1 =Joint Family, C2= Nuclear Family

almost similar to the prior one. Life satisfaction was highest in oldest age group followed by middle and younger age group respectively. It was seen that the participants of joint family displayed higher level of life satisfaction than the participants of nuclear family. In addition it was also found that the discrepancy related to family type was highest at youngest age group followed by middle and oldest age group. Also it was seen that age related discrepancy was more pronounced between middle and younger age groups.

The last two way interaction between levels of employment and family type was significant (F1, 168 = 6.59 P<001) and it is shown in Fig 14.3. It was found that the discrepancy of life satisfaction as affected by family type was varied between the participants of joint and nuclear family. This discrepancy was higher in the unemployed participants as compared to the employed participants.

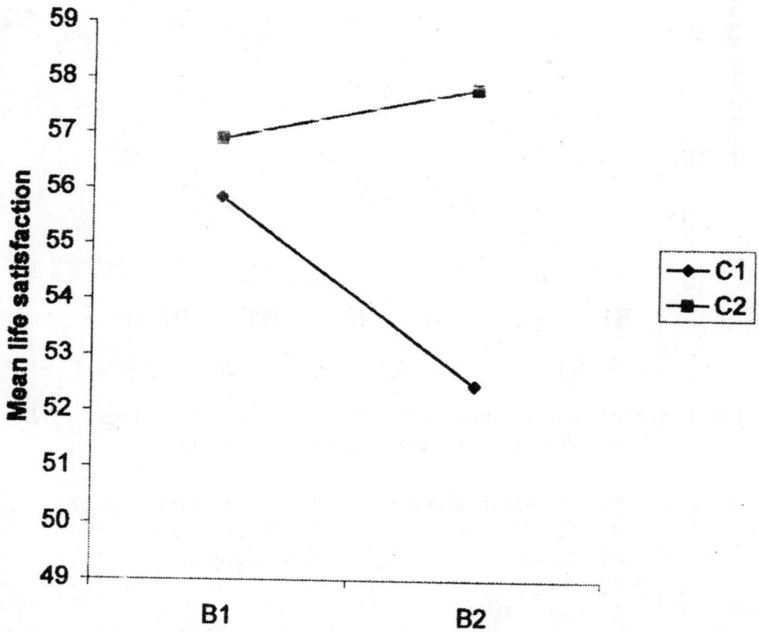

Fig. 14.3: Mean values showing the impact of levels of employment and family types on life satisfaction

Legends : *B= Levels of Employment* B1 =Employed B2=Unemployed

C= Family Type C1 =Joint Family C2= Nuclear Family

The three way interaction of chronological age, levels of employment and family type was significant (F2, 168 = 10.10 P<0.01) and it is shown in Fig 14.4. All the variables laid their impact on life satisfaction.

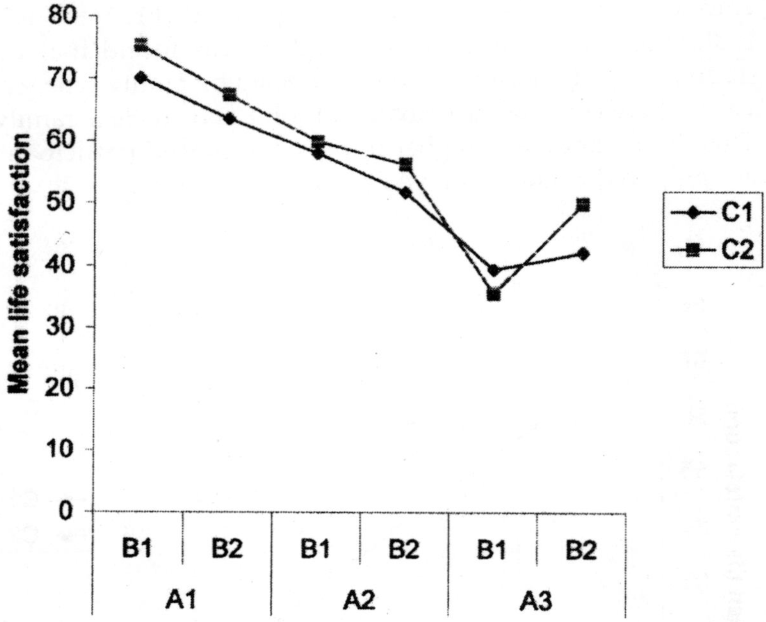

Fig. 14.4: Mean values showing the impact of chronological age, levels of employment and family type on life satisfaction.

Legends : A= *Chronological Age*
A1= 25-30
A2= 35-40
A3= 45-50
C= *Family Type*
C1 =Joint Family
C2= Nuclear Family

B= *Levels of Employment*
B1 =Employed
B2=Unemployed

Findings in sum are as follows:

1. Increase in age caused increase in life satisfaction.
2. Level of employment and family type were unable to yeild their impact on life satisfaction.

Co-relational analysis of life satisfaction scale

In order to get the profile of co-relational analysis, data were pooled across all independent variables and findings obtained are given in Table 14.3.

Table 14.3: Co-relational analysis of life satisfaction

Sl. No.	*Name of areas*	*1*	*2*	*3*	*4*	*5*
1.	Zest	-	0.49	0.48	0.57	0.62
2.	Resolution		-	0.61	0.51	0.41
3.	Congruence desired and achieved goals			-	0.62	0.59
4.	Self concept				-	0.49
5.	Mood tone					-

Table 14.3 reveals that all areas were highly correlated with each other.

Discussion

Obtained data were analyzed by 3 way analysis of variance and interpreted in terms of age level of employment and family type as affectors of life satisfaction. Prior to the inception of this work some hypotheses were made and the findings will be interpreted accordingly.

(i) Variation in age would cause variation in life satisfaction

Our first notion was related with the impact of age on life satisfaction. It was formulated that variation in life satisfaction would be influenced by chronological age. It was found that middle aged women were more satisfied with their life compared to young and old aged women. Moreover, it was also noticed that the related age was highly discrepant.

Meaning of life is a concept which has central importance for existential psychiatry and psychology, and more recently the main stream of psychology. It has been defined as '...... the cognizance of order, coherence, and purpose in one's existence, the pursuit and attainment of worthwhile goals, and an accompanying sense of fulfilment' (Reker and Wong, 1988). A person's sense of meaning is believed to be generally stable, and undergoing gradual transformation across the lifespan in conjunction with hanging beliefs and value system (Reker and Wong, 1988).

The writing of Frankl made a substantial contribution towards the development of a theoretical foundation of meaning in life, as well as suggesting clinical implications that arise from loss of meaning. Frankl's idea and insights emerged out of his experiences as a prisoner in a concentration camp. Frankl (1959, 1967) described a similar condition, existential neurosis which he suggests has cognitive, affective and behavioural components. According to Maddi, the syndrome '.... is characterized by the belief that one's life is meaningless, by the affective tone of apathy and boredom, and by the absence of selectivity in actions.' Further, a person suffering from existential neurosis experience alienates from self and society. The writings of Frankl, Maddi and others inspired some researches to investigate life-meaning concepts, although many of these early studies are unpublished developed by Cambaugh and Maholick (1964) to assess Frankl's construct of meaning in life. After reviewing this body of research, Yalom (1980) concluded that meaning was associated with psychopathology, whereas positive life high related to strong religious beliefs, self-transcendent values, membership in dedication to a cause, and clear life goals. Yalom also concluded that the meaning change over a person's life, and need to be viewed from the developmental perspective.

Until very recently elderly women were not considered a subject worthy of serious investigation in gerontological research. In recent years, social gerontological research has focused attention on elderly widows and their plight. A closer look at the difficulties faced by elderly people reveals that women suffer more and in greater numbers. Like African women Indian older women too traditionally been subjected to cultural limitations and socio-economic deprivation and this could have an influence on developmental and manifestation of PWB. Older age of women was related to higher levels of purpose in life, personal growth and positive relationships (Heidrich, 1993). Wissing (2002) mentions in her research work that women may have less access to resources that could help to buffer stress and maintain wellness. The Indian Vedic inscriptions gave deep thoughts to the problems of old aged and evolved a social order which provided security and respect to elders.

The satisfied body may not always make the mind happy but a satisfied mind can definitely pass on the feeling of well-being to the body. In the globalized society more and more factors being found to affect personal well-being of elderly women.

(ii) Variation in the type of employment would lay its impact on life satisfaction

Our second notion was related with the pattern of life satisfaction as affected by type of employment. It was formulated that there would be significant difference in the participant in relation to their score to life satisfaction. It was resulted that employed women were more satisfied than unemployed women.

Immediate consequence of unemployment: The immediate consequences of unemployment have (usually) reduced income and an increased amount of time spent in non-labour market activities. Concerning the satisfaction level with vocational activity, unemployment trends have negative psychological consequences, including the loss of identity and self-esteem, increased stress from family and social pressures, along with greater future uncertainty with respect to labour market status. The psychological effects—of unemployment are fewer if future job prospects are better or if one has greater moral support from family and society. There are some evidences that family and social support promotes satisfaction and physical health, while social isolation is detrimental (Berkman and Glass, 2000). The duration of unemployment is one important variable that affect the satisfaction level among the unemployed. How the duration of unemployment affect the satisfaction level? The theory of adaptation and habituation, proposed mostly by psychologists, suggests a recuperation of satisfaction over unemployment spells as and adapts to the situation (Diener and Lucas, 1999). Lack of adaptation is around with respect to unemployment in some studies that use panel data (Winkelmann and Winkelmann, 1988; Clark and Osward, 2002; Clark, Diener, Georgellis and Lucas, 2003).

Well-being is associated with the general level of satisfaction and happiness. The importance of general well-being as a construct refers to the harmonious functioning of the physical as well as psychological aspects of personality, giving satisfaction to the self and benefit to society. Psychological well-being is an important part of general well-being, which conceptually measures only the subjective feeling of an individual, in sum total. Operationally, psychological well-being contains the various components of adjustment, like freedom from health concern, worry, distress, energy level, satisfying energy life, cheerful, relaxed, emotional behaviour control etc. (Verma, Dubey and Gupta, 1988). Therefore, psychological well-being is not a simple unitary entity but has multiple facets that must be assessed through global judgments, momentary mood reports, physiology, memory and emotion expression. Though some might argue that being subjective in nature, it nevertheless depends upon reactions in multiple psychological and psychological systems. Thus, it is believed that subjective experience can also be measured by psychological characteristics, behavioural reactions and memories. Taking this perspective, the study was planned to examine and compare the well-being of employed and unemployed youth.

(iii) Variation in marital status would influence life satisfaction

Our third notion was concerned with the impact of marital status on life satisfaction. It was contended that magnitude of life satisfaction would be influenced by marital status. It was noticed that widows experienced less satisfaction from life as compared to husbanded women. Widowhood among the elderly probably is the most stressful part of life event since the loss of spouse is the major emotional trauma involving termination of the central attachment. Many elderly could undergo a sense of shock and numbness followed by an intense agonized yearning for the lost partner. This is followed by a long period of despair and depression, until the individual can begin to reorganize his or her life. Elderly widowed with their disabilities in their social world, psychological state, economical conditions, physical health, and spiritual well-being find greater problem in reorganizing his or her life after the loss of his or her spouse. As the widowed individuals are likely to experience a long period of despair and depression, elderly who passed through such situation are also likely to experience more intense feeling of loneliness and despair as his or her social world crunched or reduced to their immediate neighbours and friends. Following widowhood there is usually a sudden loss of financial support or either affected their financial status and consequently lowering the standard of living. Hiltz (1981) observed that widowhood has been conceptualized as a negatively evaluated social category where the individual loses the central sources of identity, financial supports and social relationship and thus widowhood is a role-less-role.

Mansharamani, *et al.* (1988) found that spouse is the main source of physical, psychological and financial supports and boosts the morale in the time of illness. Contacts with the valued relatives and friends and coping with a reduced and declining budget are becoming the significantly important problems reported by the elderly. Each gender of this elderly personal life is likely to be complicated by the death of spouse due to absence of skills and knowledge of works or tasks as before each spouse knowledge of works and tasks are complemented by the other. As to when to perform the other role without knowledge, life would be probably complicated and disruptive. Dooghe, Vanderleyden and VanLoon (1980) reported from their study that widowhood and being alone seem to have considerable influence on social adjustment. Gallagher, Thompson and Peterson (1981-82) observed that the death of spouse is consistently found as a major life stressor requiring more readjustment than any other life event. They also made critical review of the existing literature and suggest that widowhood experienced multiple problems. The impact of widowhood can be attenuated through the operation of a number of complex psychological variables such as social network, coping strategy, and religious commitment.

Parker and Brown (1972) reported that bereavement is characterized by gender disturbances of sleep, appetite and weight and by complaints of depression, restlessness, indecisiveness, excessive strain and by an increased consumption of alcohol, tobacco and tranquilizers. The authors found significant difference between the bereaved and the controlled group on self-reported general health status, although the widows were significantly more likely to have been admitted to a hospital during the preceding years.

Income meditates the effects of widowhood for both male and female on subjective evaluation of health life satisfaction and especially for male on social participation (Elwell and Malfbie-Crannell, 1978). Lopata (1969) and Belle (1987) observed that loneliness was marked by lack of friends and on impoverished social network. Aggrawal and Chadha (1990) assessed the psychological health of the aged and found that elderly persons living with spouse were low on hopelessness and high on life satisfaction than widows and widowers. Easwaramoorthy and Chadha (1995) from a sample of 900 aged, found that significant differences exist between widowed and elderly living with spouse on family income, health awareness, physical distress, mental status, loneliness, hopelessness, life satisfaction, psychological distress, leisure activities, family integration, social integration, perception of social support, social network size and self-rated quality of life (QOL). Chao and Chadha (2002) found the difference between the elderly widowed and the elderly living with spouse on loneliness, health awareness, daily activities, social support, social networks and self-rated QOL among the elderly Nagas.

However, Mullins, Elston and Gutkowsky (1996) found that marital status of the elderly persons does not directly influence and related with the cause of loneliness but have indirect influence. Abaster, *et al.* (1998) also found that marital status does not associate with the outcome of perceived QOL in a sample of Hispanic and non-Hispanic elderly persons.

Quality Of Life (QOL) of the elderly is considered relatively somewhat different from the generalized QOL. The definition of QOL has undergone a revolutionary change. In recent years and decades, the concepts of QOL is diverting from the conventional to the post-modernistic derivation. Bowling *et al.* (2002) defined the constituents and indicators of QOL in the old aged to offer a more dimensional and useful model of quality based on perspective of the older people by themselves. The main focuses are self-evaluation of global QOL including health, psychological and social variable and social circumstances. The main independent predictors are social comparisons and expectation, personality and psychological characteristic (optimism-pessimism), health and functional factors (status) and personal and neighbourhood social capitals. Some of the researchers viewed that QOL be best determinant through multi-dimensional approach including the aspects of social culture, psychological, physical, economical and spiritual dimensions of the individual. Holland and Kornbith (1994) listed seven dimensions of QOL commonly agreed to be important. The lists are of physical, social, psychological, emotional and spiritual dimensions of the individual. WHO defines QOL as "an individual perception of his/her position in life in the context of culture and value system in which he/she lives and in relation to his/her goals, expectation, standard and concerns." Chadha, Easwaramoorthy, and Kanwara (1993) observed that QOL for the elderly is a function of physical health, psychological well-being, good social relationships, in his/her social environment and its well-being. Unlike general, QOL of the elderly probably would not mean the reaching any specific desired goal, or proceeding towards it by themselves, but concerned professionals probably can help enhance their QOL. Therefore, understanding of QOL of the elderly is very important as the elderly population is growing faster so also their problems growing faster. Spousal relationships are considered closest and the most shared relationships. Death of spouse tremendously influenced the pattern of elderly lifestyle. This could bring to a total change of life ranging from role erosion and change to the extent of feeling of emptiness and loneliness. Those conditions are consequently likely to affect the well-being of many elderly persons. In contrast, those elderly living with their spouse expected to have better satisfaction of life (Chao, 2004).

Peplu and Pertman (1982) found that widowhood is accompanied with loneliness markedly perceived in deficiency in social relationship and characterized by poor health. Mullins and Dugan (1990) analyzed the association between the experience of the indicators of QOL and the marital status and found that the indicators of QOL were related to gender, age, health, marital status, and socio-economic condition, need of affection and security and desire to be part of the social network. Chao and Chadha (2002) found significant differences between the widowed and living with spouse elderly happiness, health awareness, disabilities in daily activities, leisure activities, social supports, social network and self-rated QOL.

REFERENCES

Abaster, *et al.* (1998). Self and adaptation in later life. *Journal of Gerontology, 34,* 841-851.

Agarwal, V., & Chadha. N.K.. (1990). *Hopelessness, alienation and life satisfaction among aged.* Paper presented at the 78th Session of the Indian Science Congress Association. Indore, 2-7 Jan.

Agarwal, V. (1994). Stress and multiple role of women. *Indian Journal of Social Science. 1 (3&4),* 319-334.

Belle, D. (1987). Gender differences in social modulator of stress. In R.C. Barrett, L. Liener, and G.K. Baruch (eds.), *Gender and stress.* New York: Free Press.

Berkman, L.F. & Glass, T. (2000). Social integration social networks. Social support and health, In L.F. Berkman and I. Kawachi, (eds), *Social Epidemiology,* Oxford: Oxford University Press, 137-173.

Bharat, S. (1992). *The two pay cheque couples: An analysis of their housework, decision making, sex-role perception and attitudes.* Bombay: Tata Institute of Social Sciences.

Bowling, A., Barrister, D., Sutton, S., Evans, O., *et al.*, (2002). A multi-dimensional model of quality of life in old age. *Aging and Mental Health, 6*, 355-371.

Cambaugh, C.J. and Malolick, L.T. (1964). An experimental study in existentialism. The psychometric approach to Frank's concept of naozenicnureses. *Journal of Clinical Psychology, 20*, 200-207.

Chadha, N.K., Easwaramoorthy, M. and Kanwara, P. (1993). Quality of life among aged. *Journal of Psychology, 68*, 15-21.

Chao, D. (2004). *Quality of life of the elderly in Nagaland.* Unpublished Ph.D. Thesis. Delhi University, Delhi.

Clark, A.E. & Osward, A.J. (2002). *Well-being and Panels*, Mimeo, DELTA, Paris.

Clark, A.E., Diener, E., Georgellis, Y. & Lucas, R.E. (2003). *Lags and leads in iife satisfaction: A test of baseline hypothesis*, DELTA Working Paper No. 2003-14, DELTA, Paris.

Desai, N. & Anantram, S. (1985). Middle class women's entry into the world of work. In K. Saradamoni (Ed.), *Women, work and society: Proceedings of the ISI Symposium.* Calcutta: Indian Statistical Institute.

Diener, E. & Lucas, R.E. (1999). Personality and Subjective Well-being. In D. Kahneman, E. Diener and N. Schwarz (eds), *Well-being: The Foundation of Hedonic Psychology*, New York: Russell Sage Foundation, 213-227.

Easwaramoorthy, M., & Chadha, N.K. (1995). Aging: issues and rehabilitation strategies. In N.K. Chadha and S. Nath (eds.) *Issues and trends of rehabilitation research*, New Delhi: Friends Publication.

Elwell, F., & Malfbie-Crannell, A. (1978). *The impact of interaction of widowhood: Two models and empirical tests.* Paper presented at Gerontological Society Meeting. Dallas. Nov.

Frankl (1959). *Men search for meaning*. London; Hodder and Stoughton.

Frankl (1967). K.L. *Psychotherapy on existentialism.* New York, Symon, Schuster .

Holland, J.C. & Kornbirth, A.B. (1994). Handbook of measures for psychological, social and physical functions in cancer patients, Vol. 1, *Quality of life.* New York: Memorial Sloankeffusing Cancer Centre.

Krishna Raj, M. (1986). Research on women and career: Issues of methodology. *Economic and Political Weekly, 21*, WS67-74.

Lopata, H.Z. (1969). Loneliness: Forms and Component. *Social Problems, 17*, 243-261.

Mullins, L.C., Elston, C. H. & Gutkowsky, S. (1996). An examination of loneliness among the elderly Canadian residents in Florida. *Journal of Gerontology, 44*, 580-586.

Parikh, I.J. & Shah, N.A. (1994). Women managers in transition: From homes to corporate offices. *The Indian Journal of Social Work, 55*, 143-160.

Peplau, L.A. & Pertman, D. (1982). *Loneliness: A source book of essent theory, research and therapy*. New York: John Wiley and Sons.

Raker, G.T. and Wong, P.T. (1988). Aging as an individual process; towards a theory meaning. In J.E. Berren, and V.L.Bankston, E.D.S. *Emergent theory of aging, psychology*. New York, Springer.

Ramu, G.N. (1989). *Women, work and marriage in urban India: A study of dual and single career couples*. New Delhi: Sage.

Sastry, N. (1991). Women employees: An emerging issue of HRM in organizations. *The Indian Journal of Social Work, 52*, 493-514.

Scanzoni, J. & Polonka, K. (1980). A conceptual approach to explicit marital negotiation. *Journal of Marriage and the Family, 42*, 31-44.

Shukla, A. (1987a). Decision making in single and dual career families in India. *Journal of Marriage and the Family, 49*, 621-630.

Vanaja, M. & Venkataramaiah, S.R. (1990). Effects of marital satisfaction and employment status of mothers on behavioural problems of their children. *Indian Journal of Clinical Psychology, 17*, 8-11.

Varma, S.K. and Dubey, B.L. & Gupta, D. (1998). Post Graduate Inventory (PGl) general well-being scale: Some correlates. *Indian Journal of Clinical Psychology, 10*, 299-304.

Winkelman, L., and Winkelman, R. (1998). Why are unemployed so unhappy? Evidence from panel data. *Economica, 65*, 1-15.

Yalom, I.D. (1980). *Existential Psychotherapy*. New York, Basic Books.

15

Mental Health of Adolescent School Girls in Relation to Anger

Nitu Jain, Nov Rattan Sharma and *Amrita Yadava*

Introduction

In the past two decades, comparative studies of the health, well-being, and social functioning of adolescents and youths have been focused in developing countries where rapid social, cultural and economic changes have been associated with dramatic increase in the rates of social problems indicative of poorer mental health. Young people in many societies suffer from some of the highest rates of social problems like suicide and substance abuse in the world. It is generally agreed that the increase in the rates of social problems among the youth result from increase in psychological stress, anger, and frustration surrounding intergenerational conflict within the family. Everyday experiences of young people can lead to some psychosocial stress and the angry episodes of interpersonal conflict often precede suicide attempts, binge drinking or create mental health problems.

With changing time, definition of health has also changed and once again health is defined in a manner, which is similar to the ancient Indian concept of health. Charaka and Sushruta Samhita has clarified that the meaning of health is a state of accommodation and trying to stable oneself. Health is defined and appreciated in three important dimensions, i.e., physical, mental and social, and during the last decade, a fourth one, i.e, spiritual dimension has also been added to the concept of total health. This fourth dimension had been described in the age-old Ayurvedic texts. World Health Organization (WHO) also defined health in the same manner in 1986. "Health is a state of complete physical, mental and social well-being and not merely, the absence of disease or infirmity". Mere absence of diseases doesn't indicate health. If one is not ill, then it is not necessary that the person is healthy. However, if someone has perfect health, there would be no disease. Considered in this way, health is a much broader concept. Actually, health is the complete functioning of body, mind and soul. Today, it is accepted that spiritual and social health is necessary at the same level as the physical or mental health. That is why health is an integration, balance, and harmony between body, mind, soul and society.

A variety of factors influence health. These include social factors, emotional factors, cognitive factors, perceived symptoms, and factors relating to access to medical care (Leventhal; Leventhal, and Nguyen, 1985). As mentioned earlier, mental health is an essential part of health. It can be explained in terms of physical, biochemical and psychological factors. Mere absence of mental disorder cannot be considered as mental health. It is a harmonious condition in which all the physical, mental, social and even spiritual elements merge with each other. It is a known fact that 450 million people worldwide are affected by mental, neurological or behavioural problems at any time. Mental illnesses are common to all countries and cause immense suffering. People with these disorders are often subjected to social isolation, poor quality of life and increased mortality. These disorders are the cause of staggering economic and social costs With the growth of scientific knowledge over the centuries, the medical concern in the realm of mental health has also grown. Currently, the field of mental health and illness is understood in relation to three major orientations: (a) the biomedical, (b) the psychological, and (c) the psychosocial. The range of these three contemporary professional and scientific orientations suggest that mental health problems may be generated from diverse causal factors, ranging from the biochemical to the social. Mental health is also affected by several psychological factors that include hostility, personality, self-efficacy, and social support, locus of control, stress, tension, anxiety, frustration, aggression, depression and anger. There are more than 200 classified forms of mental illness. Some of the more common disorders are depression, bipolar disorder, dementia, schizophrenia and anxiety disorders. Symptoms may include changes in mood, personality, personal habits and/or social withdrawal. Mental health problems may be related to excessive anger due to a particular situation or series of events. Similar to physical disorders like diabetes and heart disease, mental illness often have a physical emotional as well as psychological component. Mental illness may be caused by a reaction to environmental stresses, genetic factors, biochemical imbalances, or a combination of these all. With proper care and treatment many individuals learn to cope or recover from a mental illness or emotional disorder.

Friedman and Booth-Kewley (1987) have indicated the existence of a generic "disease-prone" personality that involves depression, anger/hostility, anxiety, and possibly other aspects of personality. Although, there is extensive psychological research on aggressive behaviour but there is surprisingly little work on the emotion of anger. It is now clear that psychologists must separate the emotion of anger from the behaviour pattern associated with aggressive behaviour. Therefore, it is useful to look upon aggressions an overt act that involves an attempt to harm other people or at least to damage their property (Kaufmann, 1970). The terms anger and hostility are often used interchangeably to describe a set of negative emotions, but they are not the same. Hostility, on the other hand, is not a temporary emotion, but rather an attitude. It is anger that is expressed in aggressive behaviour motivated by animosity and hatefulness. Anger is an emotion. It's temporary. It combines physiological arousal with emotional arousal. Anger has been defined as a temporary but basic human emotion that may or may not be accompanied by outward expressions (physical or verbal). Behavioural anger consists of assault, aggressive, hurtful or rebellious behaviour. Assault behaviour implies a physically destructive attack on the perceived source of the anger. Hurtful behaviour is typified by gossips, stealing trouble making, etc. Rebellious behaviour reveals open defiance, refusal to talk, in effect, attacking authority in a somewhat subtle fashion.

Verbal and cognitive signs of anger include open hatred and insults, expressing contempt, criticism, suspicion, accusing, or name-calling. While many types of anger are overt, some are slightly suppressed, and reveal them in ways different. Veiled anger can emerge as distrust, skepticism, argumentation, irritation, resentment, jealousy, envy, disruption, and sullenness, of a superior attitude. This can lead or be accompanied by veiled anger in speech patterns. Undermining the credibility of others with catty, untrue remarks are typical of this.

People use a variety of both conscious and unconscious processes to deal with their angry feelings. The main approaches are expressing, suppressing and calming. Expressing angry feelings in an assertive manner are the healthiest way to express anger. Anger can be suppressed, and then converted or redirected. This happens when hold in anger, stop thing about it, and focus on something positive. The aim is to inhibit or suppress anger and convert it into more constructive behaviour. The danger in this type of responses is that if it is not allowed outward expression, anger can turn inward on oneself. Anger turned inward may cause hypertension, high blood pressure or depression. Unexpressed anger can create other problems. It can lead to pathological expressions of anger, such as passive-aggressive behaviour or personality that seems perpetually cynical and hostile. People who are constantly putting others down, criticizing everything, and making cynical comments haven't learned how to constructively express their anger. Not surprisingly, they are not likely to have many successful relationships. The cause of that anger is usually within the angry person, not in the situation that trigger the anger.

It is experienced in a distinctive way and is expressed by a definable facial expression and by muscular and physiological body responses. Anger is aroused by extreme persisting frustration of one's intentions or by the continuation of circumstances in which one cannot assimilate a mass of information or cannot match up new information with one's well-established plans or the programmes for coping and organizing. In rare cases, anger may play a valuable role in self-defense or in the physical defense of a loved one. Any other time, an angry assault is considered today, a violation of both legal and moral ethics, and while the victim may suffer physical harm, the aggressor almost always gets in serious trouble (Izard, 1977). Anger does not necessarily lead to aggressive actions. It is well recognized that anger is a negative emotion or affect, an unpleasant experience that can lead to hostile thoughts, but it is separate from direct or even indirect acts of aggression. The awareness of an obstacle in the attainment of a goal, which cannot be easily explained away or dealt with in any obvious manner, leads to many mental associations in an attempt to make sense of the situation. As these associations, thoughts of remedies, memories of previous similar frustrations pile up without any solution, they lead to the emergence of the affect of anger. A research has shown that, to be healthy, people need to express anger. It is a mandate to confront the things that are making people angry and to work through the anger. Daldrup in 1989 said that there are two classic ways of expressing anger in an unhealthy way: misdirecting it or suppressing it completely. People who misdirect their anger seem to be expressing it; they are just burying the real problem and creating more problems along the way. There are many other unhealthy ways of expressing anger (Tavris, 1984). Some of the most common ones are miscommunication, emotional distancing, escalation of the conflict, endless rehearsals of grievances, assuming a hostile disposition, acquiring angry habits, making a bad situation worse, loss of self-esteem, and loss of the respect of others. Izard (1977) has pointed out that the frustration of intentions is a major cause of anger. Zillman and Bryant (1974) found that people who are already emotionally aroused and who are then subjected to provocation are much more likely to become angry. Anger is the most frequently experienced emotion, which leads to a variety of negative consequences for personal and social lives and has damaging effects on mental health.

Spielberger (1988) who has produced master pieces on the experience and expression of anger, defined it as an emotional state that consist of feelings that vary in intensity, from mild irritation or annoyance to fury and rage. Further, he talked of experience of anger as having two major components, i.e., experience of anger as an emotional state (State anger) and individual differences in anger-proneness (Trait anger). He also conceptualized anger-expression as having three major components, (i) expression of anger towards other people or objects in the environment (anger-out), (ii) holding in or suppressing anger feeling (anger-in) and expects to control expression of anger (anger-control). At one time anger was probably important in human survival because it led to a rapid mobilization of energy and preparation for self-defense but in day to day life in modern society, anger is not so useful except in rare instances involving self-defense. Some researches often links hypertension to a lifestyle that involves a recurring suppression of anger (Glass, 1977). A study conducted by Neighbors, Vietor and Knee (2002) provides support for the author's motivational framework suggesting that individuals who generally feel controlled tend to experience more pressure and ego-defensiveness, which leads to more anger and aggression while driving. Adolescents with higher eating disorders symptom scores have been found to have significantly higher levels of anger inhibition and silencing the self-scores. (Zaitsoff, Geller and Srikameswaran, 2002). Researches also suggest that the Type A are indeed carrying around with them a continuing set of expectations of being angered and a higher level of intensity so that, given a new provocation, they respond with an excessive reaction.

According to researchers, anger rarely exits in isolation. When researchers at the University of Tennessee studied eighty-seven middle-aged women to determine their anger levels, they found that the women who were angry also tended to be pessimistic, to lack social support, to be overweight, to sleep poorly, and to lead sedentary lives. The angriest women were also more likely to have existing health problems and to feel they could do nothing to control their problems (Tavris, 1992). High neurotic group experience intense anger feelings which may be suppressed, expressed or both more than low neurotic or emotional stables (Sharma, Hooda, and Yadava, 2004). The type A personality is increasingly being defined as a person who can't manage anger (Weisinger, 1988). The angry women in the study also showed lower optimistic and a greater number of daily hassles, had less social support, and had lost an important relationship during the previous year (Sandra and Madge, 1991).

A study conducted by Sharma, Sharma and Yadava (2003) reveals that high caste people directed their anger more outwardly, suppress it less, show less control and at the same time express the anger more than the low caste people in a significant manner. These findings may be attributed to the view that low caste people felt insecurity, powerlessness with frustration and depression (Berkowitz, 1989; Mathew and Ram, 1999; Sharma, Sunita, Yadava and Yadava, 1999).

Medical research shows that no matter how many times you work out at gym or how careful you are to eat correctly (Weisinger, 1988) anger has broad consequences, considering physiological reactions as changes in muscle tension, scowling, grinding of teeth, glaring, clenching of fists, flushing (redness of face), goose bumps, chills and shudders, prickly sensations, numbness, choking, twitching, sweating, losing self-control, or feeling hot or cold. Common reactions associated with chronic anger include fatigue, teeth clenching, pain in the neck or jaw, ringing in the ears, lowered skin temperature, excessive sweating, redness, hives, acne, itching, severe headache, migraine headache, belching, hiccupping, peptic ulcers, chronic indigestion, diarrhoea, constipation, loss of appetite and frequent colds (Weiss, 1984). The results of repressed, chronic, or prolonged anger can be devastating and almost any part of body can be harmed. Mismanaged anger, anger that is either suppressed or misdirected, has also been shown to be a major factor in bulimia and anorexia (Weisinger, 1988). One of the major physiological effects of anger is on the release of chemicals and hormones, principally adrenaline and non-adrenaline. Observations in the 1960s by mental health specialists led to a proposal that males with an extra Y chromosome in their gene structure, the so-called XYY chromosomal type, which occurs only about once in one thousand newborn males, were especially prone to violence. Moreover, the angry feelings may be experienced or expressed for assorted durations but if the issue is not resolved it may lead to hostility and can even turn to aggression (Segall, Dasen, Berry and Porrtinge, 1990). Preliminary research has shown that bottling up anger can lead to many health consequences, among them heart disease, cancer, rheumatoid arthritis, hives, acne, psoriasis, peptic ulcer, epilepsy, migraine, Raynuaud's disease, and high blood pressure (Izard, 1977). And most researches agree that expressing anger is essential to good health as long as the expression itself is healthy. In her book *Anger: The Misunderstood Emotion*, Tavris (1982) adds ventilating is cathartic only when it restores one's sense of control, reducing both the rush of adrenaline that accompanies an unfamiliar and threatening situation and the belief that you are helpless and powerless. According to studies, suppressed anger is especially dangerous for women. Researches at the University of Michigan conducted an eighteen-year study of 700 persons. They found that women who suppress their anger are three times likelier to die early of any cause than those who expressed it. Men, they found, were at high risk from suppressed anger only if they had high blood pressure or chronic bronchitis. New research has found that people who sometimes express anger, sometimes repress are most prone of all to coronary heart disease (Pennebaker and Traue, 1993). Studies show that people who suppress anger tend to exercise less and have poorer cardiovascular capacity than those who let it out. Those who were angry generally got inadequate sleep and too little exercise and used a greater than average number of over-the-counter drugs.

Most of the studies described so far have been conducted on males. The reason may be that direct aggressive acts are far less common in girls and women (Maccoby, 1980). However, evidence (Eron, 1980; Singer and Singer, 1980) suggests that aggression in preschool or elementary schoolgirls is on the increase, and some of these changes have been attributed to greater emphasis on female assertiveness and the increase of female superheroes on television. There is also evidence that girls show a good deal of indirect aggression and do not differ from boys in this form of activity (Maccoby, 1980). However, this is one area where there is paucity of research on women. There is also lack of awareness among the Indian women regarding their mental health needs. Most of the research available in the area of health focuses on the physical aspects, while less focus has been on research concentrating on the mental health aspect of women and the factors affecting it. In Indian setting, it appears that the mental health aspect of women's well-being has not been considered as a serious issue. While linkage between women's reproductive functions has received some professional attention, it is only in the 1990s that a need was realized for a more pragmatic attention on women's mental health (Davar, 1995ab). Researches have indicated that anger influences general health, psychological distress both depression and anxiety. In order to study how the experience and control of anger influences the psychological distress amongst the adolescent schoolgirls, the present investigation was planned and conducted.

Problem

To study the mental health of adolescent schoolgirls in relation to their experience, expression and control of anger.

Method

Sample

In order to carry out the present investigation a purposive sample of one hundred normal adolescent schoolgirls 15 to 18 years was selected from Rohtak city on the basis of availability.

All the participants were XI or XII class students with a low socio-economic class background. It was also ensured that participating schoolgirls had not experienced any critical life change in recent two months.

Tools

For the purpose of data collection following two tests were used:

The State Trait Anger Expression Inventory (STAXI: Spielberger, 1988) was administered to measure the experience, expression and control of anger. The STAXI is a 44-item inventory, consisting of six subscales, namely, State Anger, Trait Anger, Anger-in, Anger-out, Anger-control and Anger-expression. The factor structure of the STAXI has received strong empirical support in a number of studies. Internal consistency of coefficient for the subscales range from 0.70 to 0.89 indicating strong relationships among the scales items. The anger experience and expression scales have good test-retest reliability, internal consistency, and content, concurrent and discriminate validity and have a factor structure which is relatively uniform across criterion groups.

General Health Questionnaire (GHQ): In order to study the mental health of the subjects, General Health Questionnaire of Golberg and Hillier (1979) was used. This is a self-administered screening test designed for detecting non-psychotic psychiatric disorders in the general population. It is designed to identify short-term changes in mental health (general psychological strain, distress, depression, inability to cope, social dysfunction, somatic symptoms etc.). The respondents are asked to indicate the extent to which they have experienced change in the particular symptom or feeling in question. **Lower the score better is general and psychological health and vice versa.** Hindi version (Mohal, 1991) of the GHQ was used in the present study. The 12 items version of GHQ supplemented by 7 items of anxiety and depression scale each consist of 23 items (3 being common). Three scores were thus available for each respondent (i.e. GHQ-12, anxiety and depression) but scores on individual items are summed to produce a total severity scores. All the scores reported here are with a four-point response scale, from 0 to 3. The possible scores could vary from 0 to 69. Scoring weightage are 0, 1, 2 and 3 respectively for each item except few items where scoring was 3, 2, 1 and 0. Reliability and validity coefficients for GHQ are well established.

Procedure

The present study was conducted to study the possible association between the anger dimensions and the psychological health. For this purpose, a State Trait Anger Expression Inventory and GHQ were administered on a sample of 100 adolescent schoolgirls who had not experienced any critical life change during the preceding two months to ensure that recent particular life circumstance had not undesirably affected their psychological health. The respondents were assured of confidentiality of their responses so that they could provide free, frank and honest information. The data was collected in small groups of 12 to 15 participants. The tools were administered one by one after obtaining the personal information (like age, class etc.) and on establishing the good rapport. On the completion of the scale, it was ensured that every participant has answered all the items. The data thus collected were placed for statistical treatments like means, SD, pearson correlation and mean comparisons by t-test. The results have been presented in respective tables.

Results and Discussion

The purpose of the investigation was to study the relationship between mental health as indicated by psychological distress and expression of anger. Psychological distress scale and a state-trait anger expression inventory were administered to a total of 100 adolescent girl students. As mentioned earlier STAXI provides scores on various dimensions of anger. The mean and SD scores of the subjects on all the components of anger, i.e., state-anger, trait-anger, anger-in, anger-out, anger-control and anger-expression along with scores on psychological distress, i.e., depression, anxiety and GHQ were worked out and analyzed statistically.

Table 15.1: Mean and SD Scores on the Various Components of Anger and Psychological distress

	State-Anger	Trait Anger	Anger-in	Anger-out	Anger-control	Anger-expression	GGQ	Anxiety	Depression	Psychological Distress
Mean Scores	11.75	16.25	12.67	11.81	23.16	17.32	11.44	5.13	2.21	16.32
S.D	2.43	4.05	2.62	2.68	5.27	6.94	4.93	3.35	2.56	8.06

It is indicative from Table 15.1 that the female subjects suppressed the anger more and also controlled it more in comparison to directing their anger outwardly and also expressing it. It is also evident from the result tables that mean score of subjects is higher on trait anger as compared to scores on state-anger. It implies that females have a greater tendency of anger as a trait. In an earlier study conducted by Sharma, Sharma and Yadava (2003), it was observed that male subjects directed their anger outwardly and they also expressed it more in comparison to female subjects. Present findings are also in line with those obtained by Buntaine and Costenbader (1997) who observed superiority of females in suppression of anger. Present findings are also supported with the study conducted by Pennebaker and Traue (1993) that reveals suppressed anger is especially dangerous for women. They found that women who suppress their anger are three times likelier to die early of any cause than those who expressed it. New research has found that people who sometimes express anger, sometimes repress are most prone of all to coronary heart disease.

In order to see the possible association between/amongst various components of anger and different psychological distress measures, an inter-correlation matrix was prepared. These inter-correlations have been presented in Table 15.2.

Table 15.2: Inter-correlation between /amongst the Components of Anger and Psychological distress measures

	State-Anger	*Trait-Anger*	*Anger-in*	*Anger-out*	*Anger control*	*Anger expre-ssion*
GHQ	.573**	.370**	.257**	.291**	-.259**	.407**
Anxiety	.461**	.277**	.241*	.188	-.250*	.354**
Depression	.470**	.388**	.250*	.207*	-.193	.322**
Psychological Distress	.549**	.362**	.221*	.444**	-.194	.403**

**Significant at 0.01 level, *Significant at 0.05 level

Results presented in Table 15.2 indicate that psychological distress measures are significantly correlated with almost every component of anger. Correlation between depression, psychological distress and anger-control are found to be non-significant. On the other hand, the co-efficient of correlations obtained between the state-anger, trait-anger, anger-in, anger-out, and anger-expression scales with GHQ, anxiety, depression and psychological distress are reported to be positive as well as significant, although, correlation, between anxiety and anger-out is also not significant.

The correlations between the state-anger and trait-anger with GHQ were positive and highly significant. It reveals that higher the level of state-anger or trait-anger higher the health problems, because higher the scores on GHQ means poor the health. Similarly, the correlations between the state-anger, trait-anger with anxiety, depression and psychological distress measures were also positive and highly significant. It also reflects that individuals having high scores on state-anger and trait-anger are more prone to suffer more anxiety, depression and even psychological distress too.

The correlation co-efficient between the anger-in with GHQ, anxiety, and depression and psychological distress was positive as well as significant. It implies that girls those suppress their anger have anxiety, depression and psychological distress and in turn poor health. At the same time, the correlation between anger-out and GHQ, depression and psychological distress were significantly positive but this was not significant with anxiety level. This means that girls with high anger-out may experience high depression, psychological distress but not the anxiety.

The values of correlation between anger-control with GHQ and anxiety were significant although, the same were negative. At the same time, there were negative but non-significant correlation of anger control with depression and psychological distress. It shows that girls with high control on their anger tend to invest a great deal of energy in monitoring and preventing the experience and expression of anger. While controlling anger is certainly desirable, it may result in significantly good health and less anxiety.

The correlation between anger-expression with GHQ, anxiety, depression and psychological distress were positive and significant. It reflects that girls who expressed their intense angry feelings resulted in more poor health, anxiety, depression and psychological distress. They are likely to experience extreme difficulty in interpersonal relationships and are also at risk for the development of psychosomatic disorders. From the above discussion, it is clear that there are strong relationship between mental health and anger.

Finally, the entire data was classified into two groups (low and high) on the basis of their scores on anger-control by identifying those who have below (Mean - 1 SD) as low group and those who have above (Mean + 1 SD) as high group on their control on anger. In order to compare the means on the general health, anxiety level, depression and psychological distress of low and high groups t-test was applied.

Table 15.3: Application of t-test to mean scores of low and high groups (Anger Control) on GHQ, Anxiety, Depression and Psychological Distress measures

	Mean-I (Low)	*Mean-2 (High)*	*t-value*	*Probability*
GHQ	14	10.29	2.11	<.05 Level
Anxiety	6.11	4.12	1.53	>.05 Level
Depression	3.44	1.41	1.92	<.05 Level
Psychological Distress (Total)	21	14.12	4.79	<.05 Level

According to result of Table 15.3, the two groups has significantly different scores on general health, depression and psychological distress measures, as the three obtained t-values are significant except the scores on anxiety. The low anger control group has significantly higher scores on GHQ, anxiety, depression and psychological distress. It can be inferred that low anger control certainly invite more general health problems as compared to those on high group of anger control. It further means that good control on anger is a healthy sign and definitely it leads to better psychological health.

Similarly, the entire data was again classified into two groups (low and high) on the basis of their scores on anger expression by identifying those who have below (Mean - 1 SD) as low group and those who have above (Mean + 1 SD) as high group on their expression of anger. In order to compare the means on the general health, anxiety level, depression and psychological distress of low and high groups t-values were computed.

Table 15.4: Application of t-test to mean scores of low and high groups (Anger Expression) on GHQ, Anxiety, Depression and Psychological Distress measures

	Mean-1 (Low)	*Mean-2 (High)*	*t-value*	*Probability*
GHQ	9.6	14.42	2.74	<.05 Level
Anxiety	4.15	7.26	2.68	<.05 Level
Depression	1.00	3.78	3.19	<.05 Level
Psychological Distress (Total)	12.95	22.74	7.19	<.05 Level

As per result of Table 15.4, low expression group has significantly lower scores on general health, anxiety and depression and psychological distress measures as all the four obtained t-values are significant. It can be inferred that high expression of anger certainly invite more general health problems, greater anxiety, enhanced depression level and higher level of psychological distress as compared to those on the low group of anger expression. It further means that anger expression is not a healthy sign and it only leads to mental health problems.

From the above discussion, it is clear that anger control is better way than the anger expression. It may be because of the view that expression of anger is not considered to be a good sign in the society. On the basis of present findings, it can be concluded that adolescent schoolgirls have greater tendency of trait anger and suppress the anger in wards. It may be further concluded that anger-control is far better option than the expression of angers amongst the schoolgirls as anger-control has shown positive effect on mental health. The present study may have the implication on developing anger-control strategies in schools/colleges for enhancing mental health of students.

REFERENCES

Berkowitz, L. (1989). Frustration-aggression hypothesis: examination and reformulation. *Psychological Bulletin, 106,* 59-73.

Buntaine, R.L. and Costenbader, V.K. (1997). Self-reported differences in the experience and expression of anger between boys and girls. *Sex Roles, 36,* 625-637.

Daldrup, R. (1989). How a good dose of anger therapy can restore peace of mind. *Your Personal Best,* 8.

Davar, B.V. (1995a). Mental illness among Indian Women. *Economic and Political Weekly, 30,* 2879-86.

Davar, B.V. (1995b). *The mental health aspects of socialization, from the gender perspective.* Paper presented at the Symposium on Socialization, Theory and Research. Department of HDFs, MS University of Baroda.

Eron, L.D. (1980). Prescription for reduction of aggression. *American Psychologist,* 345-348.

Friedman, H.S. and Booth-Kewley, S. (1987). The 'disease-prone personality': A meta-analytic view of the construct. *American Psychologist, 42,* 539-555.

Glass, D.C. (1977). *Behaviour Patterns, Stress and Coronary Disease.* Hillsdale, NJ: Erlbaum.

Goldberg, D.P. and Hillier, V.F. (1979). A scaled version of the General Health Questionnaire. *Psychological Medicine, 9,* 139-145.

Izard, C.E. (1977). *Human emotions.* New York: Plenum Press.

Kaufmann, H. (1970). *Aggression and altruism.* New York: Holt, Rinehart & Winston.

Leventhal, H., Leventhal, E.A. and Nguyen, T.V. (1985). *Reactions of families to illness: Theoretical models and perspectives.* In D.C.Turk and R.D. Kerns (Ed.), Health, illness and families: A lifespan perspective (pp. 108-145). New York: Wiley.

Maccoby, E.E. (1980). *Social Development.* New York: Harcourt Brace Jovanovich.

Mathew, P. and Ram, U. (1999). Anger in relation to gender, religion and marital status. *Indian Journal of Applied Psychology, 36,* 10-13.

Mohal, K.S. (1991). *A study of the effect of unemployment on attributional Style: Self-esteem, and depression among educated youth.* Unpublished doctoral thesis, Kurukshetra University, Kurukshetra.

Neighbors, C., Vietor, N.A. and Knee, C.R. (2002). A motivational model of driving anger and aggression. *Personality and Social Psychology Bulletin 28(3),* 324-335.

Pennebaker, J.W. and Traue, H.C. (1993). Inhibition and Psychosomatic Processes. In Harald, C. Traue and James W. Pennebaker (Ed.) *Emotional Inhibition and Health,* pp. 152-153. Seattle, Washington: Hogrefe and Huber Publishers.

Sandra, P.T. and Madge, M.D. (1991). Correlates of anger symptoms in Women in middle Adulthood. *American Journal of Health Promotion, 54,* 267-272.

Segall, M.H., Dasen, P.R., Berry, J.W. and Porrtinge, Y.H. (1990). *Human behaviour in global perspective: An introduction to cross-cultured psychology.* New York: Pergamon.

Sharma, N.R., Hooda, D. and Yadava, A. (2004). Study of anger in relation to personality. In R. Singh, N.R. Sharma and A. Yadava (Ed.) *Psychology of Individual Differences* (pp. 106-112). Delhi: Wisdom Publications.

Sharma, N.R., Sharma, S. and Yadava, A. (2003). A study of anger expression among college students. *Journal of Personality and Clinical Studies. 19,* 243-248.

Sharma, N.R., Sunita, Yadava, A. and Yadava, N. (1999). Level of general depression among Scheduled Caste/Scheduled Tribe and non-Scheduled Caste/Scheduled Tribe students. *Indian Psychological Review, 52,* 64-68.

Singer, D.G., and Singer, J.L. (1980). Television viewing and aggression behaviour in preschool children: A field study. In F. Wright, C.Bahn, and R. Riebe (Ed.), *Annals of New York Academy of Sciences* (Vol. 347). New York: New York Academy of Sciences, 343.

Spielberger, C.D. (1988). *Professional manual for the State-Trait Anger Expression Inventory.* Odessa, Florida: Psychological Assessment Resources.

Tavris, C. (1982). *Anger: The Misunderstood Emotion.* New York: Touchstone.

Tavris, C. (1984). On the wisdom of counting to ten. In P. Shaver, (Ed.) *Review of Personality and Social Psychology* (pp. 170-191). Sage Publications.

Tavris, C. (1992). How Anger Affects Your Health. *Wellness Letter.*

Weisinger, H. (1988). *Mad? How to work out your anger.* Shape Publications, 86-93.

Weiss, E. (1984). *How anger affects our bodies.* New Women, 98-103.

World Health Organization (1986), *Chater der j, International Konferenz fur gesund Heitsfordering,* Ottowa: Author.

Zaitsoff, S.L., Geller, J. and Srikameswaran, S. (2002). Silencing the self and suppressed anger: Relationship to eating disorder Symptoms in adolescent females. *European Eating Disorders Review, 10,* 51-60.

Zillmann, D. and Bryant, J. (1974). Effect of residual excitation on emotional response to provocation and delayed aggressive behaviour. *Journal of Personality and Social Psychology, 30,* 787-91.

16

Impact of Cultural Variation, Age and Climateric Variation on Emotional Disturbance

Akanksha Lall and *Aradhana Shukla*

Emotion is derived from the Latin word *"Emover"* which means the spirit that moves us. That energy is the transmitter and recorder of all feelings, thoughts and action. In other words, emotions are the currents of energy that are within us. It activates our lives, shapes our perceptions and bebaviour[9] which then emanate outward and influence others. The Oxford English Dictionary defines motion as *"any agitation or disturbance of mind, feeling, passion, and any vehement or excited mental state."*

Thus, it is apparent that emotions are primarily motivating forces; they are processes which, arouse, sustain and direct activity. Emotions are reported to influence learning, in addition to influence a range of behaviours such as helping, negotiating, altruism, risk-taking, and compliance (Isen, 1983).

The terms emotionally disturbed and adolescents have been widely treated in different sources. Emotionally disturbed child has been defined by Bower (1959) as, *"One having a higher degree of vulnerability to behaviour problem and who as an adult will exhibit this vulnerability in general health problems or interpersonal relationship, inability to function sexually or economically, inability to profit from experience or lead a happy life....*

a child who is unable or will be unable to take the strings and arrows of life without craving in. becoming immobilized or exploding." Kvarceus and Miller (1959) have mentioned that when behaviour of individual is unlike that of his peers and it is on apparent how the behaviour was learned, it usually comes under the category of emotionally disturbed. Valet (1963) stated these *"for the purpose of education, emotionally handicapped pupil is a child who is suffering from as affectional disturbance, which interferes with the establishment of normal human relationship and results in an impairment of learning."*

According to Dunn (1964) *"a child is emotionally disturbed when his relations to life-situations are so personally unrewarding and so inappropriate as to be unacceptable to his peers and adults."* Emotionally disturbed children have also been characterized as having unusual difficulty in maintaining satisfactory interpersonal relationship (Magary & Eichorn, 1964). Telford and Sawrey (1967) have mentioned that emotionally disturbed children are children with emotional problems severe enough to prevent them from making necessary adjustments for effective functioning in the culture. Kirk (1970) referred the term to those *"who have inner tensions and show anxiety, neuroticism and psychotic behaviour."* Good (1973), mentioned that emotional disturbance is a deep rooted problem, involving the control and expression of feelings, emotionally disturbed children are described by Kauffman (1974) as those *"whose behaviour may at odds with others' expectations or with their own expectotions for themselves ... children... Who chronically and markedly respond to their environment in socially unacceptable and/or personally unsatisfying ways?"* Hallahn and Kauffman (1978) have summarized that there is no universally accepted definition of emotionally disturbed adolescent.

Characteristics of Emotionally Disturbed Persons

Thc causes of emotional disturbance have not been adequately determined. Although various factors such as heredity, brain disorder, diet, stress, and family functioning have been suggested as possible causes, research has not shown any of these factors to the direct cause of behaviour or emotional problems. Some of the characteristics and behaviours seen in children who have emotional disturbances include:

- Hyperactivity *(short attention span, impulsiveness);*
- Aggression/self-injurious behaviour *(acting out, fighting);*
- Withdrawal *(failure to initiate interaction with others; retreat from exchanges of social interaction, excessive fear or anxiety);*
- Immaturity *(inappropriate crying, temper tantrums, poor coping skills);* and
- Learning difficulties *(academically performing below grade level).*

Children with the more serious emotional disturbance may exhibit distorted thinking, excessive anxiety, bizarre motor acts and abnormal mood swings. Some are identified as children who have a severe psychosis or schizophrenia.

Many children who do not have emotional disturbance may display some of these behaviours at various times during their development. However, when children have an emotional disturbance, these behaviours continue over long periods of time. Their behaviour thus, signals that they are not coping with their environment or peers.

In this study, an attempt was made to find out the developmental impact of climateric variation and age on emotional disturbance in cultural perspective. The objectives and hypotheses were as follows:

- The first objective of this study was to find out the pattern of emotional disturbance affected by age. It was contended that variation in age would influence the level of emotional disturbance.
- The second objective of this study was to find out the pattern of emotional disturbance as affected by cultural variation. It was hypothesized that cross-cultural variation would influence the level of emotional disturbance.

- The third objective of this study was to find out the pattern of emotional disturbance as affected by home climate. It was formulated that variation in home climate would influence the level of emotional disturbance.
- The fourth objective of this study was to find out the pattern of emotional disturbance as affected by school climate. It was thought that variation in school climate would influence the level of emotional disturbance.
- The fifth objective of this study was to find out the impact of the level of home climate supportiveness or emotional disturbance. It was hypothesized that variation of the supportiveness of home climate would influence the level of emotional disturbance.
- The sixth objective of this study was to find out the impact of the level of school climate supportiveness on emotional disturbance. It was hypothesized that variation of the supportiveness would influence the magnitude of emotional disturbance.

In order to examine these objectives and hypotheses this study was planned in factorial perspective:

Method

Sample: Four hundred eighty participants were taken. They were placed according to the requirement of 3×2×2×2 mixed model factorial with 3 levels of the (8-9-10-1 and 12-13 years) ×2 levels of cross-cultural variation Tribal (Tharu and Buxa) and Non-tribal (General Kumauni and Punjabi) × 2 types of climateric variation (home and school) × 2 levels of climateric supportiveness (High/Low) climate support. The schematic presentation of experimental design is given in Table 16.1.

Table 16.1: Schematic presentation of experimental design used in study two

	A											
	A1				A2				A3			
	B				B				B			
	B1		B2		B1		B2		B1		B2	
	C		C		C		C		C		C	
	C1	C2	C1	C2	C1	C2	C1	C2	C1	C2	C1	C2
D1	20	20	20	20	20	20	20	20	20	20	20	20
D2	20	20	20	20	20	20	20	20	20	20	20	20

Legends:
A— ***Chronological Age:*** A1—8-9 Years; A2—10-11 Years; A3—12-13 Years
B— ***Types of Cultural Variation:*** B1—Tribal (Tharu, Buxa); B2—Non-Tribal
C— ***Types of Climateric Variation:*** C1—Home; C2—School
D— ***Levels of Climateric Supportiveness***—D1—Low Level of Climateric Suportiveness; D2—High Level of Climateric Supportiveness.

Measure: In this study only one tool was taken and it is described below:

Emotional Disturbance Scale

This scale is developed by Shukla and Dhami (2000). It consists of 90 five point items which represent the area of life when a person can feel emotional disturbance. There are 10 domains of emotional distrubance in this scale namely:

- **Withdrawal from the society:** It is defined in a defense mechanism with which we protect ourselves and escape from the society.
- **Isolation:** Separation from others of the same species, used for groups or organism existing separate from other groups of the same species, either geographically, or with respect to reproductive maturity, in either case with the effect of preventing interbreeding.
- **Rejection:** A Type of avoiding behaviour on the part of an organism, throwing out something that has

already been taken into the body; mentally negative attitude a judgment, or belief.

- **Day dreaming:** Type of Phantom, in which the individual allows his mind to wander aimlessly among pleasant imagery, wishes which are ungratified in real life.
- **Guilt Feeling :** Sense of wrong-doing, as an emotional attitude, generally involving emotional conflict, arising out of real or imagined contravention of moral or social standards, in act of thought.
- **Inferiority complex :** A hypothetical complex arising from conflict between the impulse to seek recognition (positive self-impulse), and fear of the hurt arising from frustration frequently experienced in similar situation in the past, resulting in defensive, compensatory, or often aggressive behaviour, unconsciously determined.
- **Conflict:** Opposition between contradictory impulses or wishes, a rule producing emotional tension, often highly disagreeable. According to psychoanalytic theories, to repress of one of the impulses.
- **Low confidence:** Less determination of a person over himself/herself for any activity termed as low confidence. It is deferent with inferiority complex.
- **Nervousness:** Nervousness is a state of perplexion and sorer which blacknes the behaviour of a person, as a result, he either hesitates to express himself or wrong response are produced by him.
- **Anxiety:** A chronic complex emotional state with apprehension or dread as its most prominent component, characteristic of various nervous and mental disorders.

Scores range between 90-450. Low score indicates low emotional disturbance and high score *vice versa.*

Results

Data analysis was done in three phases and they are given below·

(i) Developmental impact of cultural variation, types of and levels of climateric variation on emotional disturbance: Obtained findings were analyzed by four way analysis of variation and interpreted in terms of chronological age, cultural variation types and levels of climateric supportiveness as affectors of emotional disturbance. They are shown in Table 16.2.

Table 16.2: Summary table showing the impact of chronological age, type of cultural variation, types of climateric variation and levels of climateric supportiveness on emotional disturbance

Sources of variation	*SS*	*df*	*MS*	*F*
A	18.74	2	9.37	14.64
B	4.94	1	4.94	7.71
C	4.08	1	4.08	5.74
D	6.98	1	6.98	10.11
AB	19.28	2	9.64	15.06
AC	16.88	2	8.44	13.19
AD	17.94	2	8.97	14.01
BC	6.34	1	6.34	9.91
BD	6.21	1	6.21	9.71
CD	1.40	1	1.40	2.19
ABC	12.14	2	6.07	9.49
ABD	12.50	2	6.25	9.76
ACD	13.51	2	6.72	10.56
BCD	6.80	1	6.80	10.64
ABCD	14.83	2	7.41	11.59
Error	291.84	456	.64	
(Within)		479		

It was found that the main effect of age was significant (F, 2,479 = 14.64 P < .01). Mean value pooled across cultural variation types and levels of climateric supportiveness were: 171.14, 218.18, 262.47 respectively for youngest to oldest age group. Mean value showed that magnitude of emotional disturbance was relatively high in the participants of oldest age group. The next main effect of cultural variation was also significant (F, 1,479 = 7.71 P < .01) and it was found that emotional disturbance was relatively high in tribals as compared to non-tribals. The third main effect of types of emotional disturbance was also significant (F, 1,479 = 5.74

P < .01) and it showed that emotional disturbance was lower in home than school. Similarly, the main effect of levels of climateric supportiveness was also significant (F, 1,479 = 10.91 P < .01) and it was evinced that there was a drastic change in the magnitude of emotional disturbance in highly supportive and low supportive participants.

The two way interaction of age and cultural variation was significant (F, 2,479 = 15.06 P < .01). Similarly, the age X types of cultural variation was also significant (F, 2,479 = 13.19 P < .01). The age X levels of climateric supportiveness interaction was also significant (F, 2,479 = 14.01 P < .01) and it was found that all variables laid their impact on emotional disturbance.

The cultural variation X types of climateric supportiveness interaction was significant (F, 1,479 = 9.91 P < .01). Same story was repeated in cultural variation X levels of climateric supportiveness interaction which was also significant (F, 1,479 = 9.71 P < .01).

The type of cultural variation X level of climateric supportiveness was insignificant and it was found that both the variables were not able to lay their effect on emotional disturbance (F, 1,479 = 2.19 P < .05).

The age X cultural variation X types of climateric supportiveness interaction was significant (F, 2,479 = 9.49 P < .01) and it is mentioned in Fig. 16.1. Figure shows fine interaction. The age X cultural variation X levels of climateric supportiveness interaction was significant (F, 2,479 = 9.76 P < .01) and it is appeared in Fig. 16.2. The age X type of climateric supportiveness X levels of climateric supportiveness interaction was also significant (F, 2,479 = 10.56 P < .01) and it is mentioned in Fig. 16.3.

The chronological age X types of climateric supportiveness interaction was significant (F, 1,479 = 10.64 P < .01) and it is presented in Fig. 16.4.

The four way interaction of age, cultural variation, types of climateric supportiveness and levels of climateric supportiveness was also significant (F, 2,479 = 11.59 P < .01) and it is shown in Fig. 16.5.

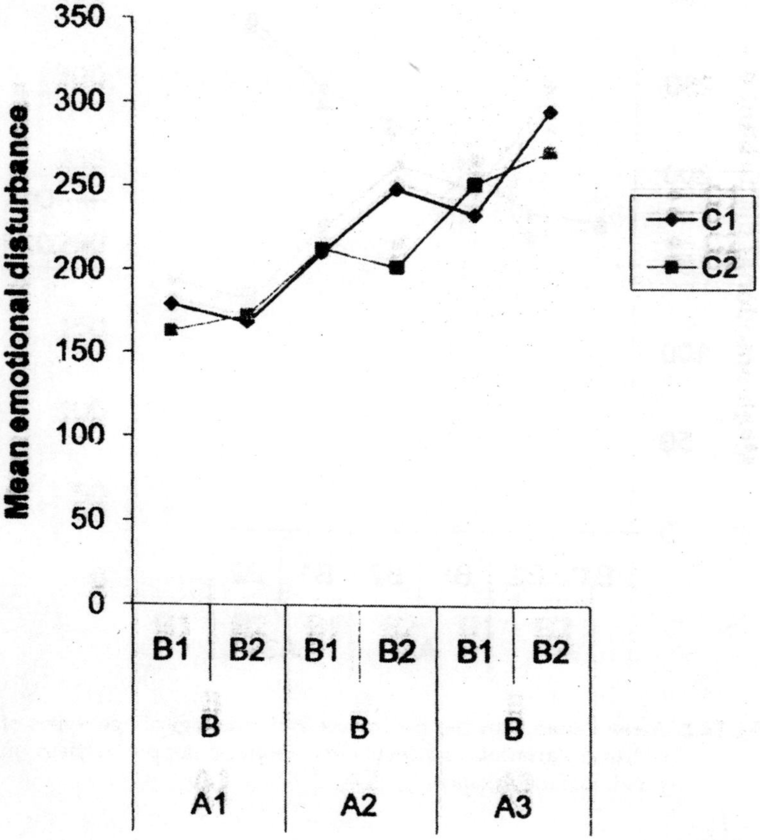

Fig. 16.1: Mean values showing the impact of chronological age, types of cultural variation and types of climateric variation on emotional disturbance

Legends:

A— Chronological Age:
A1—8-9 Years;
A2—10-11 Years;
A3—12-13 Years

B— Types of Cultural Variation:
B1—Tribal (Tharu, Buxa);
B2—Non-Tribal

C— Types of Climateric Variation:
C1—Home climate;
C2—School climate

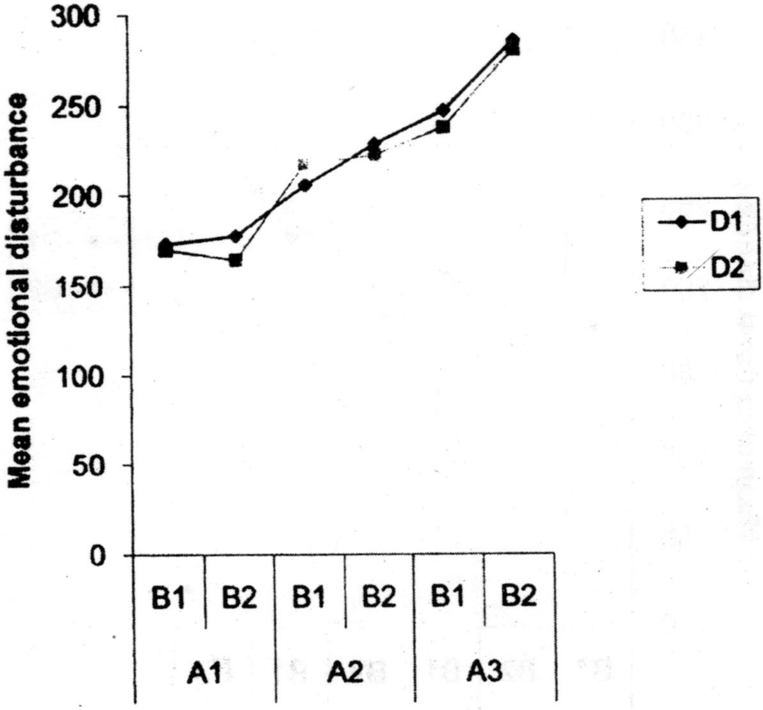

Fig. 16.2: Mean values showing the impact of chronological age, types of cultural variation and levels of climateric supportiveness on emotional distrubance.

Legends:

A— Chronological Age:
- A1—8-9 Years;
- A2—10-11 Years;
- A3—12-13 Years

B— Types of Cultural Variation:
- B1—Tribal (Tharu, Buxa);
- B2—Non-Tribal

D— Levels of Climateric Supportiveness
- D1—Low Level of Climateric Supportiveness;
- D2—High Level of Climateric Supportiveness.

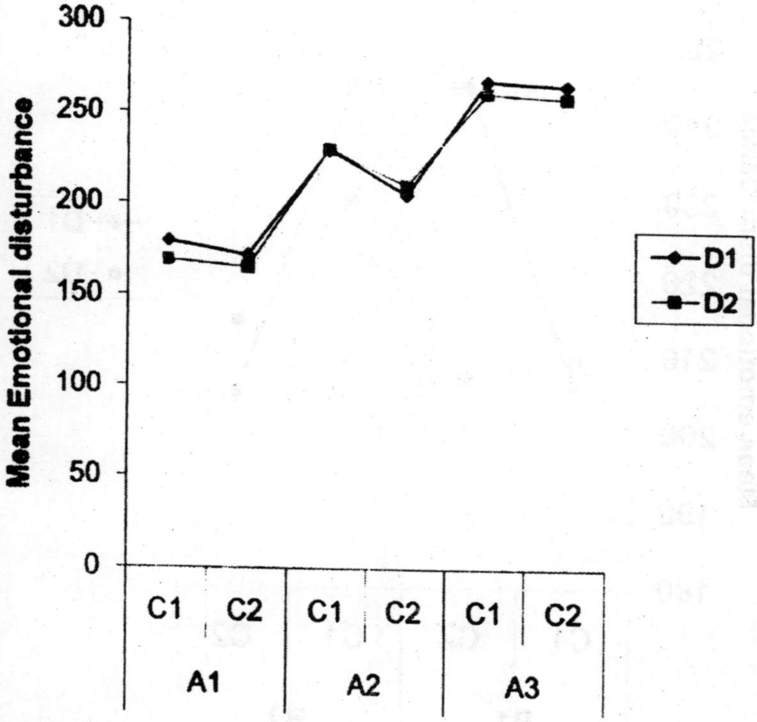

Fig. 16.3: Mean values showing the impact of chronological age, types of climateric variation and levels of climateric variation on emotional disturbance.

Legends:

A— Chronological Age:

A1—8-9 Years;

A2—10-11 Years;

A3—12-13 Years

C— Types of Climateric Variation:

C1—Home climate;

C2—School climate

D— Levels of Climateric Supportiveness

D1—Low Level of Climateric Supportiveness;

D2—High Level of Climateric Supportiveness.

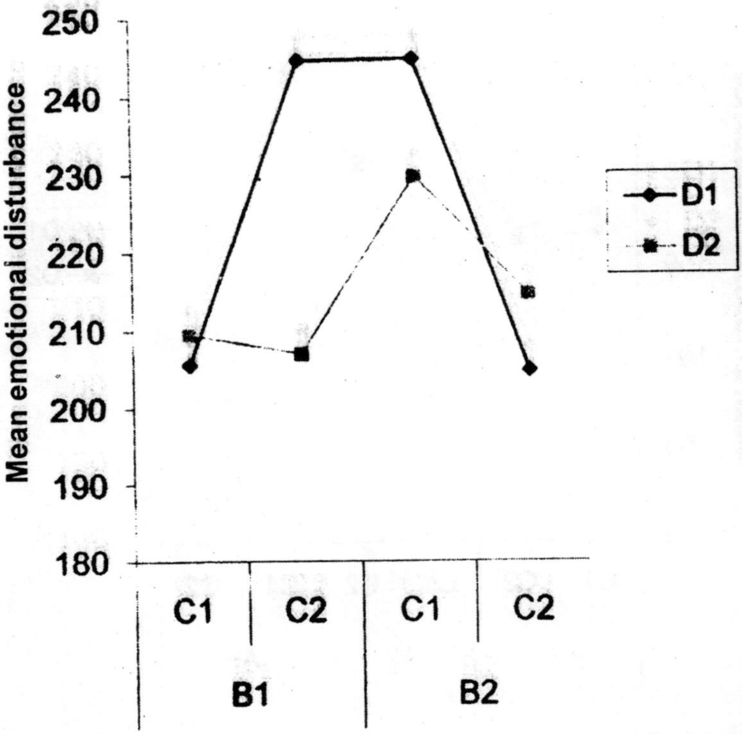

Fig. 16.4: Mean values showing the impact of types of cultural variation, types of climateric variation and levels of climateric supportiveness on emotional disturbance.

Legends:

B— *Types of Cultural Variation:*

B1—Tribal (Tharu, Buxa);

B2—Non-Tribal

C— *Types of Climateric Variation:*

C1—Home climate;

C2—School climate

D— *Levels of Climateric Supportiveness*

D1—Low Level of Climateric Supportiveness;

D2—High Level of Climateric Supportiveness.

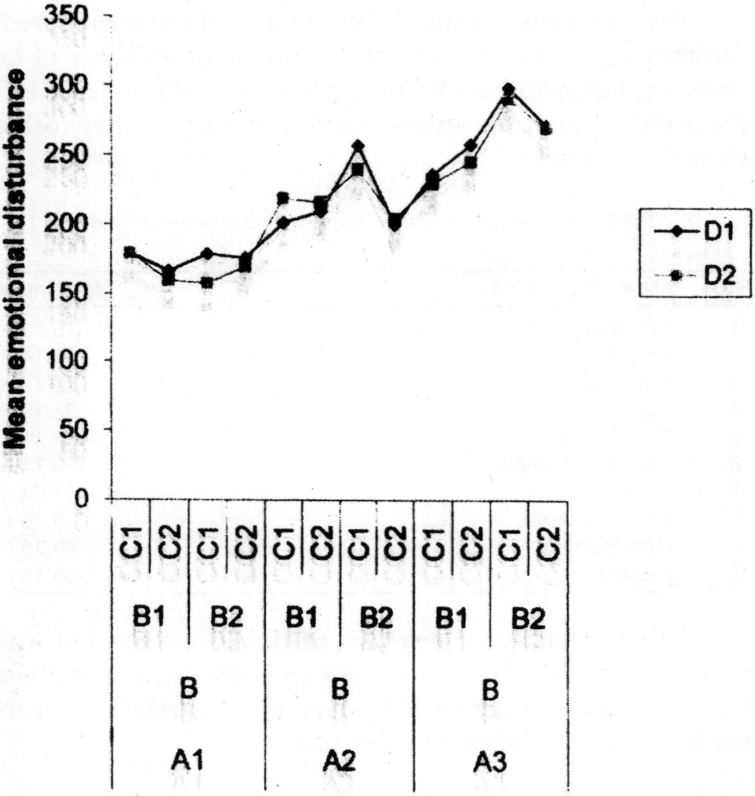

Fig. 16.5: Mean showing the impact of chronological age, types of cultural variation, types of climateric variation and levels of climateric supportiveness on emotional disturbance.

Legends:

A— Chronological Age:

A1—8-9 Years;

A2—10-11 Years;

A3—12-13 Years

B— Types of Cultural Variation:

B1—Tribal (Tharu, Buxa);

B2—Non-Tribal

C— Types of Climateric Variation:

C1—Home climate;

C2—School climate

D— Levels of Climateric Supportiveness—D1—Low Level of Climateric Supportiveness; D2—High Level of Climateric Supportiveness.

(ii) Area-wise analysis of emotional disturbance: In addition to the above analysis, the area-wise analysis of the scale was made and the findings are mentioned in Table 16.3. A close perusal of the table indicated that a good network of areas was revealed.

Table 16.3: Mean Values of Emotional Disturbance Scale

S.No.	*Name of the Area*	*Mean values*
1.	Withdrawal from the society	15.39
2.	Isolation	36.14
3.	Rejection	35.78
4.	Day dreaming	32.19
5.	Guilt feeling	21.16
6.	Inferiority complex	56.74
7.	Conflict	41.54
8.	Low confidence	38.75
9.	Nervousness	29.76
10.	Anxiety	39.15

(iii) Correlational analysis of data: Last but not least analysis was this in which area-wise correlation was computed. Data were pooled across all independent variables and the findings are mentioned in Table 16.4.

Table 16.4: Area-wise Correlation of Emotional Disturbance Scale

S. No.	*Name of the Area*	*1*	*2*	*3*	*4*	*5*	*6*	*7*	*8*	*9*
1.	Withdrawal from the society	.70	.64	.64	.54	.49	.50	.50	.56	.56
2.	Isolation		.63	.54	.56	.49	.56	.60	.61	.64
3.	Rejection			.59	.54	.46	.76	.66	.56	.57
4.	Day dreaming				.56	.49	.48	.69	.56	.66
5.	Guilt feeling					.41	.61	.60	.69	.76
6.	Inferiority complex						.66	.56	.46	.60
7.	Conflict							.41	.56	.62
8.	Low confidence								.68	.50
9.	Nervousness									.59
10.	Anxiety									—

Findings in sum are as follows:

1. All independent variables laid their impact on emotional disturbance.
2. All interactions were quite significant.
3. Area-wise analysis also exhibited good relationship between the areas.

Discussion

Obtained data were analyzed by analysis of variance and it was found that the pattern of emotional disturbance laid its impact everywhere.

Emotion is derived from the Latin word "*Emover*" which means the spirit that moves us. That energy is the transmitter and recorder of all feelings, thoughts and action. In other words, emotions are the currents of energy that are within us. It activates our lives, shapes our perceptions and behaviour, which then emanate outward and influence others. The Oxford English Dictionary defines motion as *"any agitation or disturbance of mind, feeling, passion, and any vehement or excited mental state."*

Emotions are primarily motivating forces; they are processes which, arouse, sustain and direct activity. Emotions are reported to influence learning, in addition to influence a range of behaviours such as helping, negotiating, altruism, risk-taking, and compliance (Isen, 1983).

Researchers continue to argue over precisely, which emotions can be considered primary—the blue, red and yellow of feeling from which all blends come—or even if there are such primary emotion at all. Some theorists propose basic families, though not all agree on them. The main characteristics and some of the members of their families are given as under:

Anger: Fury, outrage, resentment, wrath, exasperation, indignation, vexation, acrimony, animosity, annoyance, irritability, hostility, and perhaps at the extreme, pathological hatred and violence.

Sadness: Grief, sorrow, cheerlessness, melancholy, gloom, self-pity, loneliness, dejection, despair, and pathologically severe depression.

Fear: Anxiety, apprehension, nervousness, concern, consternation, misgiving, worries, qualm, edginess, dread, fright, terror; as a psychopathology, phobia and panic.

Enjoyment: Happiness, joy, relief, contentment, bliss, delight, amusement, pride, sensual pleasure, thrill, rapture, gratification, satisfaction, euphoria, whimsy, and at the far edge, mania.

Love: Acceptance, friendliness, trust, kindness affinity, devotion, adoration, infatuation.

Surprise: Shock, astonishment, amazement, wonder.

Disgust: Contempt, disdain, scorn, abhorrence, aversion, distaste, revulsion.

Shame: Guilt, embarrassment, chagrin, remorse, humiliation, regret, mortification and contrition.

Emotion and Cognition

Every emotion has a cognitive component and every thought is influenced by emotional factors. Both emotion and thought are basic attributes, which in the human being are intimately mashed, in a dialectical unity. Differentiated psychological traits of older children and adults clearly state the interaction processes that involve emotion and thought. Feelings reinforce ideas and ideas in true reinforce feelings.

When we remember incidents that made us feel angry and sad when we thought about these incidents, did our mood also change? Did recalling memories of these events influence the way we felt? The chances are good that it did. If our thought seems to extent/exert strong effects on our emotions, this relationship works in the other directions as well. Being in a happy mood often causes us to think happy thoughts, while feeling sad tends to bring negative memories and images to mind. In short, these appear to be important links between emotion and cognition—between the way we feel and the way we think.

Most researchers on the relationship between emotion and cognition indicate that: Our moods, or emotional states, strongly influence our perception of ambiguous stimuli. In general we perceive and evaluate these stimuli more favourably when we are in good mood than when we are in a negative one.

- Positive and negative moods exert a strong influence on memory. In general, information consistent with our current mood is easier to remember than information with it.
- Our current moods often influence the process of decision making. Would anyone be more willing to adopt relatively risky course of action when in a good mood or when in a bad mood? Informal observation suggests; when in a good mood.
- The emotions or feelings we experience are strongly determined by the interpretation or cognitive labels we select.
- Activation of a strong racial, ethnic, or religious schema or stereotype may exert powerful effects on our current feelings or mood (Isen, 1987).
- Our thoughts can often influence our reactions to emotion provoking events by determining how we interpret to appraise those events.

The terms emotionally disturbed and adolescents have been widely treated in different sources. Emotionally disturbed child has been defined by Bower (1959) as, *"One having a higher degree of vulnerability to behaviour problems and who as an adult will exhibit this vulnerability in general health problems or interpersonal relationship, inability to function sexually or economically, inability to profit from experience or lead a happy life.... a child who is unable or will be unable to take the strings and arrows of life without craving in, becoming immobilized or exploding."* Kvarceus and Miller (1959) have mentioned that when behaviour of individual is unlike that of his peers and it is on apparent how the behaviour was learned, it usually comes under the category of emotionally disturbed. Valet (1963) stated these *"for the purpose of education, emotionally handicapped pupil is a child who is suffering from an affectional disturbance, which interferes with the establishment of normal human relationship and results in an impairment of learning."*

According to Dunn (1964) *"a child is emotionally disturbed when his relations to life-situations are so personally unrewarding and so inappropriate as to be unacceptable to his peers and adults."* Emotionally disturbed children have also been characterized as having unusual difficulty in maintaining satisfactory interpersonal relationship (Magary & Eichorn, 1964). Telford and Sawrey (1967) have mentioned that emotionally disturbed children are children with emotional problems severe enough to prevent them from making necessary adjustments for effective functioning in the culture. Kirk (1970) referred the term to those *"who have inner tensions and show anxiety, neuroticism and psychotic behaviour."* Good (1973), mentioned that emotional disturbance is a deep-rooted problem, involving the control and expression of feelings, emotionally disturbed children are described by Kauffman (1974) as those *"whose behaviour may at odds with others' expectations or with their own expectations for themselves...children... Who chronically and markedly respond to their environment in socially unacceptable and/ or personally unsatisfying way?"* Hallahn and Kauffman (1978) have summarized that there is no universally accepted definition of emotionally disturbed adolescent.

Emotional disturbance and social maladjustment have been the two terms, which are sometimes used interchangeably. This has confused demarcation between socially disturbed from emotional disturbed. Barber (1963) had distinguished the socially disturbed child "as one who is maladjustment in his relationship with others, while the emotionally disturbed child is maladjusted in his relationship with himself. Further, the socially disturbed denoted such groups as juvenile delinquents, while the emotionally disturbed includes neurotics and psychotics who may not behave anti-socially." Dunn (1964) states *"some members of socially maladjusted gangs are also emotionally disturbed, but this is not to say that emotional disturbance and social maladjustment are identical. Gang membership requires high degree of sociability, conformity and purposefulness, which can rarely be achieved by emotionally disturbed youngsters."*

Telford and Sawrey (1967) mentioned that when socially or personally unsatisfactory modes of behaviour are acquired in the course of living and the manner of acquisition is relatively easy to discern, we generally refer to this as *'social maladjustment'*. While, when the reinforcements are subtle and the behaviour not obviously adaptive, the individual is said to be emotionally disturbed. Kirk (1970) labels the term socially maladjusted to children causing trouble at home or school, incorrigible, truants, per-delinquents or delinquents, while the term emotionally disturbed children refers to those who have inner tension, anxiety and neuroticism. Thus, emotional disturbance is a psycho-emotional state of withdrawal, isolation, fear, anxiety and pessimism.

In this way, we can say that emotional disturbance is the key of behavioural disturbance and it can be seen in many sorts of behaviour like withdrawal, guilt, fear, and pessimism etc.

Many terms are used to describe emotional, behavioural or mental disorders. Currently, students with such disorders are categorised as having an emotional disturbance, which is defined under the individuals with Disabilities Education Act as follows:

"... a condition exhibiting one or more of the following characteristic over a long period of time and to a marked degree that adversely affects a child's educational performance:

1. An inability to learn that cannot be explained by intellectual, sensory, or health factors.
2. An inability to build or maintain satisfactory interpersonal relationship with peers and teachers.
3. Inappropriate types of behaviour or feelings under normal circumstances.
4. A general pervasive mood of unhappiness or depression.

5. A tendency to develop physical symptoms or fears associated with personal or school problems." [*Code of Federal Regulations, Title, 34, Section 300.7(c) (4)(i)]*.

As defined by the IDEA, emotional disturbance includes schizophrenia but does not apply to children who are socially maladjusted, unless it is determined that they have an emotional disturbance [*Code of Federal Regulation, Title 34, Section 300.7(c)(4)(ii)*].

Characteristics of Emotionally Disturbed Persons

The causes of emotional disturbance have not been adequately determined. Although various factors such as heredity, brain disorder, diet, stress, and family functioning have been suggested as possible causes, research has not shown any of these factors to the direct cause of behaviour or emotional problems. Some of the characteristics and behaviours seen in children who have emotional disturbances include:

- Hyperactivity (*short attention span, impulsiveness);*
- Aggression/self-injurious behaviour (*acting out, fighting*);
- Withdrawal (*failure to initiate interaction with others; retreat from exchanges of social interaction, excessive fear or anxiety*);
- Immaturity (*inappropriate crying, temper tantrums, poor coping skills*); and
- Learning difficulties (*academically performing below grade level*).

Children with the more serious emotional disturbance may exhibit distorted thinking, excessive anxiety, bizarre motor acts and abnormal mood swings. Some are identified as children who have a severe psychosis or schizophrenia.

Many children who do not have emotional disturbance may display some of these same behaviours at various times during their development. However, when children have an emotional disturbance, these behaviours continue over long periods of time. Their behaviour thus, signals that they are not coping with their environment or peers.

In this way, it is surely fair to say that the relative efficacy of emotional disturbance can not be denied.

REFERENCES

Bower, E.M. (1959). The Emotional Handicapped Child and the School, *Exceptional Child, 26,* pp. 6-11.

Dunn, L.M. (1964). *Exceptional children in the school.* Holt Rinehart and Winston, New York, 242.

Good, C.V. (1973), *Dictionary of Education,* IIIrd Ed., Mc-Graw Hill Co., New-York.

Hallahan, Q.R. and Kauffman, J.M. (1978). *Exceptional Children Introduction to Special Education.* Prentice Hall, Englewood Cliff, New York.

Isen, A.M. (1987). Positive effect, cognitive processes and social behaviour. *Advances in Experimental social psychology. 20,* 203-253.

Kvaraceus, W.C. and Miller, W.B. (1959). *Delinquent Behaviour: Culture and the Washington.*

Kirk, S.A. (1970). *Educating Exceptional Children,* IBH Pub. Co., New Delhi.

Kauffman, J.M. (1974). *Characteristics of children behaviours disorder.* Carles, E. Marill, Ohio.

Magary, J.F. and Elichorn, J.R. (1964). *The Exceptional Child: A Book of Reading,* Holt, Rinehart and Winston, New York.

Shukla, A. and Dhami, S. (2000). *Emotional disturbance Scale. Unpublished Manuscript.* Department of Psychology, Kumaun University, Nainital.

Telford, C.W. and J.M. Sawray (1967). *The Exceptional Individual: Psychological and Educational Aspects,* Prentice-Hall, Englewood Cliffs, New Jersey.

Valett, R.E. (1963). The Practice School of Psychology: *Professional Problems,* John Wiley and Sons, New York.

17

Gender Equality and Equity

Punam Midha

Gender shapes the lives of all people in all societies. It influences all aspects of our lives, the schooling we receive, the social roles we play, and the power and authority we command. Here the term 'gender' refers to the behaviors or patterns of activities that a society or culture deems appropriate for men and women. In some way, it is a socio-cultural construct and underscores the social relations between men and women in which women are systematically subordinated. The family is the powerful force in shaping women's lives.

There are a number of gender concepts but the one which assumes greater importance in macroeconomic policies and programs is the gender equality. Equality in reference to gender means equality between men and women; choices unhindered by gender stereotype roles and prejudice, where the different behaviors, aspirations and needs of women and men are considered, valued and favoured equally. It does not mean that both of them have to become the same, but that their rights, responsibilities and opportunities do not depend on whether they are born male or female(http:/portal.unesco.org).

World bodies have defined gender equality as related to human rights, especially women's rights and economic development. UNICEF defines gender equality as "Levelling the playing field" for girls and women by ensuring that all children have equal opportunity to develop their talents. The United Nation's Fund declared gender equality "first and foremost a human right". Which in way asks for treating both men and women the same during the legal proceedings irrespective of sex.

Equity denotes equality of opportunities to pursue a life of one's choice and protection from extreme deprivation. In this sense, equity is complementary to long-term prosperity. The gender equity is the process of being fair to both men and women. Though, often used interchangeably with gender equality, it is a very distinct concept. Equity programs favour treating women and men differently in order to achieve the equal status of men and women. Such programs are based on the idea that if women and men were treated the same there would be a risk of reaching unfair outcomes due to original disparities.

Gender equity is one of the goals of the United Nations Millennium project to end world poverty by 2015, the project claims: "Every single goal is directly related to women's rights and societies where women are not afforded equal rights as men can never achieve development in a sustainable manner".

There are empirical evidences that the promotion of gender equity leads to better economic performance of the concerned societies. Gender gaps undermine the ability of women to be effective agents of economic process (Stephen Klasen, 2006) and that the societies with greater female employment opportunities are less prone to corruption and poor governance. In China gender equity is considered as a "luxury good", The demand for female schooling is more income elastic than that of male schooling (Sang *et al.*, 2006) Shellenbarger, S. (2006) observed that even parents who fight for gender equity in their own marriages find themselves splitting their children's task along traditional gender lives. If a society maintained gender equity which will no doubt will lead to gender equality.

The notion of gender equality is based on the concept that no individual should be less equal in opportunity to access to resources and benefits or in human rights than others. All people are created equal, therefore, should have equal share of the world's resources and benefits. In this case, therefore, women and men have an equal right to access and control over resources and benefits, participation in politics, and decision making, gainful employment and so forth. But the reality is quite different. The afflicted world in which we live is characterized by deeply unequal sharing of the burden of adversities between men and women. It exists in most parts of the world and is an universal phenomenon. United Nations sponsored report (2008) highlighted that women's disempowerment in 'Arab Countries' is a critical factor crippling the Arab Nations' quest to return to the first rank of global leaders in commerce, learning and culture.

Among all nations in the world Sweden is unique in its valuing of gender equality and its social programs that translate this commitment into action. Over a century ago, Sweden's ruling political party adopted equality as a central unit. The Swedish "equal roles family model" maintains that husband and wife should have the same opportunities to pursue a career and be equal responsible for housework and child care. As per the World Economic Forum's latest Gender Gap Index (GGI) Report (Nov., 2007) Sweden has been at the top position in gender equality with a 81.5 per cent followed by Norway, Finland, Iceland and New Zealand. India has been placed at the 114th position after taking into account economic, political, educational and health parameters among a total of 128 countries. According to the Report, India has an overall 59.4 per cent gender equality while for economic participation and opportunity it stands at 39.8 per cent.

Social structures are responsible for producing gender inequality. In most countries, women and girls are at disadvantage in terms of males access and control over facilities and services and other resources as well as influence and control over decision making processes that determine quality of life. Around 100 million women are missing in the world due to gender inequality. Some of the main factors which are considered to be major hurdles in bringing gender equality are:

Mortality inequality: In some regions of the world inequality between men and women directly involves matters of life and death and takes the brutal form of unusually high mortality rates of women and consequence preponderance of men in the total population as opposed to preponderance of women found in societies with little or no gender bias in health care and nutrition. It is observed extensively in North Africa and in South Asia.

Natality inequality: Given a preference for boys over girls that many male dominated societies have gender inequality which manifests itself in the form of parent's desire the newborn to be a boy rather than a girl. This has become possible with the availability of modern techniques to determine the gender of the fetus, consequently sex selective abortion has become common in many countries. It is prevalent in East Asia, such as in China, South Korea and in India. Some researchers have also reported that the inequalities in mortality vary in response to birth order and sex composition of siblings (Das Gupta, 1987; Kishor and Parasuraman, 1998). In India, female/ male ratio in 1991 was 976/1000 and in 2001 it was 927/1000. Data of National Family Health Survey-2 (1998-99) confirmed that 33 per cent of women prefer sons than daughters and over 85 per cent wanted at least one son among their children. The greatest decline of female child sex ratio has been observed in the states of Punjab, Haryana, Gujarat, Maharashtra and Delhi. It clearly indicates the strong preference for male children or "Son Syndrome", as male children are considered assets while females are considered liability. Christians display the lowest level of son preference, Sikhs and Hindus the hightest and Muslims are somewhere in between.

Basic Facility Inequality: Even when demographic characteristics don't show much or any anti-female bias, there are other ways in which women can have less than a square deal. This inequality may be seen even in the most developed country like U.S.A. where voting right to women was given much later than male. However, in India the voting right was given simultaneously to men and women. In the present era, Afghanistan is the only country in the world, which is keen on actively excluding girls from schooling. There are other differences in basic facilities which are not available to women such as encouraging to cultivate one's natural talents to fair participation in rewarding social functions of the community.

Special Opportunity i.e. Education Inequality: Education is widely recognized as the gateway to economic security and opportunity particularly for girls and women. The opportunities for higher education may be far fewer for young women than for young men. Gender bias for higher education can be seen even in some of the richest countries of the world i.e. in Europe and North America. World figures in literacy relate a sorry tail of the 130 million 6-11 years old children not in school – majority i.e. 60 per cent are girls. The figures only go to show how in most regions of the world especially the developing societies gender bias impinges on girl's education. All this despite the fact that educating girls is one of the best investments a society can make. An educated women has the skills, the self-confidence and the information she needs to become a better parent, worker and citizen. Combating the high rate of illiteracy among women and girls remains an urgent global need. According to UNESCO Institute of Statistics, it is now estimated that among two-third of world's 875 million illiterate half of them are women found in Africa and Arab region. Similarly in South Asia, women have only half as many years of schooling as men.

Professional Inequality: In terms of employment as well as promotion in work and occupation women often face greater handicap than men. Women face many more barriers than men in their quest to reach top leadership positions in organizations, sex stereotyping and systemic barriers are responsible for it (Morrison and Van Glinow, 1990). Despite the tremendous increase of women in work force generally, and in management and entrepreneurial endeavours specifically, women remain conspicuously absent among the most powerful corporate positions (Davidson and Cooper, 1992; Morison *et al.*, 1992). Only 2 to 5 per cent of top executive positions (e.g. Corporate officers) are held by women (Powell, 1993). This is what is called 'Glass Ceiling'. It has been discussed as a barrier so subtle that it is transparent, yet so strong that it prevents women on moving up the management hierarchy (Morison and Von Glinow, 1990). This professional gender inequality can be seen in terms of salary paid to women registered dieticians in U.S.A.

earned $ 45,258/year while men on the same post earned $ 50,250/ year. Thus gender equality and the advancement of women at the workplace still remains a 'utopian dream'! . In the United Nations General Assembly Special Session discussing "Women 2000, Gender Equality Development and Peace for the Twenty-First Century", concluded that "...The commitments made by government of 189 states and despite advances women have made in many societies, progress made towards achieving gender equality has been slow and erratic":

- Their concerns are still given second priority almost everywhere.
- They continue to face discrimination and marginalization, both subtle and blatant at home, workplace and society.
- Women constitute 70 per cent of the world poor (UNDPI, 2000) or almost 900 million of the 1.3 billion people who live in absolute poverty.

Ownership inequality: In many societies, the ownership of property can also be very unequal. Even basic assets such as home and land may be asymmetrically shared. The absence of claims to property not only reduce the voice of women, but also make it harder for women to enter and flourish in commercial, economic and even in some social activities. In much of sub-Saharan Africa women obtain land rights, chiefly through their husbands as long as marriage evolves.

Household inequality: In the present scenario, both men and most of the women go outside home to do work. And female is overburdened with roles and responsibilities at home and work area. So men must share work load of women to enhance the health and status of them in home, farm, field and in any workplace is quite heavy and is seldom recognized. They do much more work than their counterpart.

Thus, there are a few segments of society who recognize the real worth of the female. No doubt, during the Vedic period, in India, female was considered as "Devi" or Goddess as there is a well-known saying 'Naaree Tum Poojneeya ho..." Gender equality is possible only when economic and social policies should be made for the development of women and enable them to realize their full potential. They should be given equal access to participation and decision making in social, political and economic life .They should be given equal rights of health care and quality education at all levels, career and vocational guidance, employment and equal remuneration etc. Female feticide should be strictly banned. Thus, women commissions' national and international policy for women empowerment should be developed to bring them at par with men. Social structures that reproduce gender inequality should be addressed by acknowledging the complexity of social and cultural norms and by challenging them. UNESCO's ultimate goal in reaching gender equality is to make fundamental changes in gender relation and create new partnerships based on mutual respect, dialogue and sharing public and private roles and responsibilities. As of March 2002, women held just 14.2 per cent of representative posts in national parliament around the world. As of 1999, women occupied more than 30 per cent of parliamentary positions only in just five countries worldwide. In 31 countries at the same time, they held less than 5 per cent of positions. The women's position in the political scenario is miserable throughout the world.

In India, a "National Movement" under the leadership of Mahatma Gandhi was started, who called women to step out of the confines of their home to join the *Prabhat Pheris, Satyagraha* etc. In 1918, Gandhi ji said " women is the companion of man. Gifted with equal mental capacities, she has the right to participate in the minutest details of the activities of the women and she has the same right of freedom and liberty as he." In 1989, India has started National Commission for Women (1990). Year 2001 was observed as a year of "Women Empowerment". National policy for women empowerment has been evolved and similarly World Population DAY July 11, 2001, focused on gender imbalance (Sunderlal, 2002). Recent gender specific interventions in the realms of woman's health are setting up of a committee to review and assess women's health needs. Committee's task focuses on suggesting innovative measures to improve women's health. Other than this, Government has given higher priority to mental health prohibited gender verification in the use of new reproductive technology and strengthened health care for pregnant women. Though the Prenatal Diagnostic Technique Act was enacted by the Parliament in 1994 to reduce imbalance in sex ratio but its implementation is quite tardy in most of the states but in May 2001 the Government of India has decided to implement strictly the order of Honourable Supreme Court decision regarding the Prenatal Diagnostic Technique (PNDT) Act, 1994 (Thakur, 2001). Interventions to increase women's participation in politics, as at present women accounts for only ten per cent of seats in parliament worldwide. Certain measures are also being taken to include women in leading positions in the public sector. India is recognizing the dire need for an active policy to consider the problem of violence against women. The interventions are setting up of DNA registers, the violence alarm system and creation of resource centres to address the problem. In a landmark judgement, the Honorable Supreme Court of India on 12th August, 1997 ruled that sexual harassment, whether verbal or non-verbal, of women at workplace will constitute a crime against women.

On the whole two main trends of feminist activism have been identified in India. Of these one emphasis on rights and equality and other focuses on empowerment and liberation. Both types of activism are relevant in the task of lobbying for gender sensitive reforms, the ability of feminist groups to unite women on the issue of legislative reform for greater participation in the process of government and more just family laws is crucial, yet these remain one of the major stumbling blocks to the creation of gender equality in India. In spite of all these plan and policies, the debate on giving 33 per cent reservations for women in Parliament is not only surprising but tragic. The number of female ministers in national governments worldwide increased two-fold from a mere 3.4 per cent to still just 6.8 per cent. As of 1996, 48 countries had no female ministers in their national government at all.

Whether the measures would be able to redefine the status of women and would generate new relationships between men and women can't be stated at this juncture, because the dimensional new relationship and image of new status of women are blurred. It is, perhaps, men and women's joint federations which can play better role in bringing desirable changes in the status of women.

In a nut shell, the continuance of a journey depends on the equal strength and speed of both wheels of the chariot.

REFERENCES

D.O. Letter No. 1183/HEM/2001 of Padamshree Dr. C.P. Thakur, Hon'ble Minister of Health and Family Welfare, Govt. of Indian, 5 July, 2001.

Davidson, M.J., Cooper, C.L. (1992). *Shattering the Glass Ceiling—The Women Manager,* U.K.: Paul Chapman.

Gupta, Das, M. (1987), *Selective discriminates against female children in rural Panjab, India.*

International Institute of Population Science (1999). *National Family Health Survey (NFHS-2) 1998-99.* Mumbai: IIPS.

Kishor, S., and Parasvraman, S. (1998). *National Family Health Survey Subject Reports, No. 8.* Mumbai: India, IIPS.

Morison, A.M., Randall, P.W., Allen, V. (1994). *The Centre for Creative Leadership,* U.S.A.: Perseseus Publishing.

Morison, A.M., Vonglinow, M.A. (1990). *American Psychologist,* 45.

Powell, G.N., Butter field, D.A., Parent, J.D. (2002). Gender and Managerial Stereotypes: Have the times changed? *Online Sage Journals,* 28.

Sen Amartya (1992). Missing Women. *British Medical Journal.* 304.

Sen, Amartya (2001). Many faces of gender inequality. *Frontline.* Vol. 18, India: *The Hindu.*

Shallenbanger S. (2006) Employers Step UP Efforts to Kishor, S, and Parasvraman, S. (1998). *National Family Health Survey Subject Reports, No. 8.* Mumbai: India, IIPS.

Shallenbanger S. (2006) Employers setup efforts to lure stay at-home moms back to work; *Wall Street Journal*—Eastern edition, 248, issue 134.

Sunderlal (2002). Down with Low Child Sex Ratio. *Indian Journal of Comm. Med.* 27, 3-8.

United Nation's Department of Public Information (UNDPI), April, 2000.

Index

Abortion, 114, 142, 147–148
  sex-selective, 145
  unsafe, 143, 147–148, 250
Abuse characteristics, 32
Academic goals, 36
Access to Health Care, 153
Adjustment problems, 6
Adolescent girls, 24, 43
Adolescent school, 283
Advertisements, 117, 235
  recent television, 113
African-American women, 29, 197
Aggression, 285, 287–288, 290–291
Aggressive actions, 287
Aggressive behaviours, 285, 306
Agricultural labour, 149
Agricultural technology, 179
Agriculture department, 163, 167
Alcohol, 196, 199, 278
Alcoholic husbands, 22
Almora, 80, 83, 129, 136
Altruism, 65, 199, 301, 315
American Psychological Association, 19
Amusement, 316
Analysis of variance, 131, 268, 273, 315
Anger
  behavioural, 285
  components, 294
  -control, 288, 291–292, 294–298
  dimensions, 10, 293
  emotion of, 285
  excessive, 285
  experience of, 288, 292
  expressing, 287, 290
  expression, 6, 10, 288, 292–294, 296–298
  -expression scales, 295
  prolonged, 289
  suppress, 286, 290, 294
  trait, 288, 292, 294, 298
  unexpressed, 286
  veiled, 286
Angriest women, 289
Antenatal stress, 193
Anxiety, 6, 10, 31, 106, 181, 183, 189, 192–193, 285, 291–292, 294–297, 302–303, 306, 316, 318–320
Anxiousness, 105–106
Appalachian women, 197
Aryan caste system, 2
Assertiveness, 42–43
Associated Chambers of Commerce and Industry, 245
Association of Radical Midwives, 196
Attributional process, 66–67, 71
Awareness movies, 120

Bank of India, 170
Banking industries, 244
Behaviour Change Communication (BCC), 113–114, 125–126
Behaviour modification programmes, 154

Behavioural problems, 284
Behaviour-based conflict, 214–215
Biobehavioural mechanism, 40
Biological factors, 141
Biological process, 144, 193
Bipolar disorders, 285
Bookkeeping, 171–172
Brain disorders, 302, 320
Breed intolerance, 19
Broken marriage, 241
Buddhism, 3
Buddhistic practices, 3
Buffer stress, 274
Bureaucratic organizations, traditional, 220
Business experiences group, 175

Career development, 237, 240
Career goals, 29
Caretaking responsibilities, 225
Cerebral Blood Flow (CBF), 24
Characters, dynamic, 166
Child care, 219, 324
Child marriage, 3, 145
Child prostitution, 145
Childbearing, 144, 193, 198
Childhood Sexual Abuse (CSA), 32, 39
Chronic stress, 26, 190
Chronic stressors, 24
Civil Rights Act, 236
Civil society, 245
Civilian jobs, 2
Climateric supportiveness interaction, 308
Clinical intervention projects, 43
Co-curricular groups, 90
Code of Federal Regulations, 320
Cognitive factors, 284
Cognitive trauma therapy, 32
Columbia International Film Festival, 123
Commodification of Women, 117
Communication media, 220
Community development, 178
Competitive industries, 94
Compulsory Education, 138
Concentration camp, 274
Constructive behaviours, 286
Co-relational analysis, 272
Corporate
  jobs, 242
  threshold, 112
  world, 14, 243
Correlation matrix, 87
Counteract hopelessness, 188
Crime Against Women (CAW), 117, 119, 122, 329
Critical information, 238
Critical life change, 292–293
Cross-cultural research, 259
Cultural variation, 301, 303, 307–308
  impact of, 301

Day dreaming, 306
Decision-making process, 36
Decision-making scale, 8
Decisive factors, 40, 188
Declining budget, 277
Defeatist attitudes, 113
Demographic characteristics, 325
Depression, 6, 9, 12, 26, 31, 183, 187–188, 190–194, 198, 277–278, 285–286, 289, 291–297, 316, 319
  and psychological distress, 296–297
  antenatal, 194
  incidence of, 189
  mental, 142
  scale, 292
  women experience, 9
Development of Women, 328
Developmental Analysis, 78
Developmental impact, 303
Developmental perspectives, 129, 274
Disabilities Education Act, 319

Discriminatory practices, 244
Distress symptoms, 193
Domestic labour, 5
Domestic life, 263
Domestic responsibilities, 220
Dose-response relationships, 195
DRDA funds, 168
Dual career family lifestyles, 13

Early marriage, 3, 143
Eating disorders, 142
Economic
  development, 160, 246, 322
  factors, 3, 141–142, 155, 159, 250
  power, 244
  process, 323
  stress, 251
Education of Muslim women, 4–5
Educational factors, 193
Educational institutions, 5
Educational leadership programmes, 30
Educational resilience, 44
Electronic briefcase, 213
Electronic media/films, 120
Emotional
  conflicts, 306
  disorders, 21, 285
  distress, 192
  disturbance scale, 305, 314
  disturbed persons, characteristics of, 302, 320
  problems, 302–303, 318, 320
Employed women, 6–8, 10–11, 13, 15, 263, 265, 275
Employee Assistance Programme, 108
Employees State Insurance Act, 245
Employment market, 263
Entrepreneurial women, 244
Environmental awareness, 217
Environmental impoverishment, 136–137
Environmental stress, 285
Epidemiological association, 194
Episodic stress, 25
Equal Remuneration Act, 245
Equity programs favour, 323
Explorative analysis, 95
Exposure of Children to Media, 117
Extra marital sex, 146
Extrinsic factors, 12

Factorial design, 129, 266
Familial adjustment, 6
Families decisions, 168
Family climate, 78, 80, 82, 85, 87
  scale, 80, 84–85
Family conflict, 7
Family domains, 211, 213, 215, 221, 223–224
Family planning, 72, 143–144, 151, 249–250, 252, 259
Family reorganization, 31
Family responsibilities, 6, 29, 165, 246
Family-centred function, 26
Family-work conflicts, 6, 215–216
Feasibility factors, 178
Federation of Indian Chambers of Commerce and Industry, 245
Female-dominated industries, 245
Feminine sex, 12
Feminist activism, 329
Fertility
  behaviours, 249–251
  decisions, 155, 251
Fetal development, 194
Film festivals, 123
Film-making industries, 122
Financial sectors, 240
Financial stressors, 19
Flexi jobs, 240
Formal
  orders, 235
  process, 238
Framing process, 160
Full-time employment, 263

Functional factors, 279
Fundamental human rights, 142
Funeral pyre, 3

Gender
-based violence, 145
concept, 322
differences, 41, 94
discrimination, 158, 243
disparities, 148
equality, 5, 322–324, 327–329
gap index, 324
imbalance, 328
inequality, 244, 324–325, 328
orientation, 12
-planned health services, 154
-related inequality, 150
sensitisation, 119
sensitivity programmes, 108
violence, 145
Gene-environment interaction, 44
General Health Questionnaire (GHQ), 292–297
Genetic factors, 285
Gerontological research, 32, 274
Gestational age, 195–196
Glass ceiling policy, 113

Handicraft corporations, 170
Harvard Business Review, 243
Health awareness, 278, 280
Health care, 143, 149–150, 152–153, 325, 328
delivery, 200
inadequate, 144
providers, 154
strengthened, 329
Health checkups, 108
Health education, 200
Health life satisfaction, 278
Health of women, 142
Health problems, 19, 103–106, 142, 145, 295
mental, 192, 283–285, 297
sexual, 150
Health status, 28, 32, 141, 151
mental, 9
reproductive, 143
self-reported general, 278
Health symptoms, 95
Health-risk behaviours, 196–197
High neurotic group experience, 289
High-risk factors, 21
Hinduism, 3
HIV/AIDS campaigns worldover, 125
Home climate, 78–79, 81, 304
Home decoration, 8–9, 265–266
Home environment scale, 82–85, 88
Home-based work centres, 218
Homogeneous group, 15, 264
Honest information, 293
Human problems, crucial, 249
Human Resource Development, 108
Hyperactivity, 303, 320

ICSSR survey of research, 250
Illicit relationships, 124
Images of women, 120
Impact assessment, 171
Implicit personality theory, 128
Impoverished social networks, 278
Impoverishment, 179
Inclusive organizations, 109
Income generation activity, 171
Indecent Representation of Women (Prohibition) Act, 120
Indian Penal Code (IPC), 118
Influence stress-vulnerability equilibrium, 188
Informal campaigns, 158
Information
gaps, 158
revolution, 125
technology, 211
Informational support, 68

Institutional barriers, 239
Institutional marriage, 64
Interactive relationships, 159
Inter-correlation matrix, 294
Intergenerational conflicts, 283
International Children Film Festival, 123
International Conference on Population and Development (ICPD), 143
International Federation of Gynecology and Obstetrics, 143
International Gender Day, 108
International women's day, 107–108
Inter-Parliamentary Union, 239
Interpersonal conflicts, 105, 283
Interpersonal interaction, stressful, 188
Interpersonal relationships, 296, 301–302, 317–319
Interpersonal stress, 24
Inter-role conflicts, 213, 221
Intrinsic factors, 12
Introverted women, 254–259
Investment industries, 244

Jainism, 3
Jewish women, 198
Job satisfaction, 11–13
Joint family, 219, 268–270
Juvenile sex ratio, 113

Kama Sutra, 123
Kumauni women, 129

Lactating women, 149
Latina women, 27
Latino culture, 197
Lesbian relationships, 123
Life expectancies, 141–142
  women's, 142
Life graph, 241
Life satisfaction, 184–187, 199, 225, 266, 268–273, 275–276, 278
Life satisfaction index, 267
Life transforming, 199
Life-events stress, 195
Lifestyles
  elderly, 280
  healthy, 154, 199
  promiscuous, 148
Literary pursuit, 3
Lower-ranked jobs, 236

Mahatma Gandhi, 328
Male-dominated society, 112, 124, 325
Management hierarchy, 326
Managerial
  problems, 96
  research, 95–96
  stress, 94–95
  women, 240
Manila International Film Festival, 122
Marital life, 263
Marital power, 8, 265
Marriage counsellors, 74
Maternity Benefits Act, 245
Menopausal women, 28
Menstrual cycle disorders, 142
Menstrual problems, 146
Mental association, 287
Mental disorders, 22, 284, 306, 319
Mental distress, 188
Mental health, 109, 183, 185, 188, 190–192, 196, 200, 283–285, 288, 291–293, 296, 298, 329
Mexican-American women, 36, 197
Ministry of Rural Development, 162
Molestation cases, 115–117
Montreal student film festival, 125
Mormon women, 198
Motivational factors, 159–160
Motivational process, 181

Muslim women, 3–5

National Award for Best Direction and Best Cinematography, 122
National Commission for Women (NCW), 121
National Crime Records Bureau (NCRB), 115
National Film Festival, 122, 124
National Programme of Nutritional Support to Primary Education, 163
Negative association, 185, 187
Nervous disorders, 148
Neuroticism, 6, 302, 318–319
New reproductive technology, 329
Non-govemmental organisations, 246
Non-labour market activities, 275
Non-professional jobs, 5
Non-Resident Indian (NRI), 114
Non-tribals children, 83
Nuclear family, 5, 164, 268–271
Nurturing activities, 40

Occupational stress, 94, 213
Operational mechanism, 251
Operational programmes, 154
Operationalized resilience, 33
Optimism, 35, 37, 182, 197
Optimism-pessimism, 279
Organism, 305
Organizational change, 220
Organizational levels, 218

Parent responsibilities, 211
Parental teacher expectancy, 78
Parent-child interaction, 44
Passive-aggressive behaviours, 286
Pastoral tribes, 1
Patriarchal society, 117
Peachy media assignments, 242
Personal development, 61
Personal goals, 69
Personal information, 69, 293
Personal religious activity, 186
Personality characteristics, 252–253, 256–259
Personality development, 90, 108, 130
Personality tests, 16
Pessimism, 319
Physical distress, 278
Physiological process, 25, 148
Planned educative programmes, 252
Political problems, 179
Poor education, 179
Positive association, 187
Positive information, 67
Post-abortion problems, 148
Post-menopausal women, 28
Postpartum stress, 39
Post-traumatic stress disorders, 24
Poverty reduction, 158
Powerlessness, 95, 289
Predispositional factors, 18
Pregnant women, 10, 44, 181, 191, 197–198, 329
Prenatal Diagnostic Technique (PNDT), 329
Prenatal Diagnostic Technique Act, 114, 329
Pre-school children, 25
Professional jobs, 15
Pro-social goals, 188
Protective mechanism, 41
Protective process, 34
Psycho-immunodoctrinological research, 191
Psychological conflicts, 6, 214, 216
Psychological development, 263
Psychological distress, 195, 278, 291, 293–297
  measures, 294–297
  scale, 293
Psychological factors, 28, 195, 251, 284–285

Psychological health, 278, 292–293
Psychological literature, 182
Psychological problems, 124, 147
Psychological stress, 193, 195, 283
Psychological system, 276
Psychosocial factors, 195
Psychosocial stressors, 195
Psychosomatic disorders, 296
Psychotherapeutic principles, 45
Psychotic behaviours, 302, 318

Quality education, 328
Quality of Life (QOL), 142, 146, 154, 222, 224, 278–279, 284, 324

Rebellious behaviours, 285–286
Regional development agencies, 178
Relationship development, 70
Religion
  codifies, 181
  commitment, 191
  sustains, 198
Religious belief system, 193
Religious participation, active, 191
Representation of women, 239
Reproductive health, 142–145
Reproductive system, 144
Reproductive tract infections, 142
Resilience, 18–20, 26–28, 30–35, 37–39, 41–45
  academic, 29, 39
  body image, 28
  building, 32
  defined, 19
  developed, 30
  factors, 24, 27, 37, 43
  improving, 27
  psychological, 22
  research, 21, 27
  symbolize, 33
  theory, 20, 45
Reverse Glass Ceiling (RGC), 245
Role conflict, 6–8, 147
Rotation work, 94
Rural development, 160, 162, 178

Sampooran Grameen Swarojgar Yojana (SGSY), 162, 166, 168, 171–172, 175
Satellite work centre, 218
School Meal Programme, 163
School-related stress, 24
Screening test, self-administered, 292
Self Employed Women's Association, 246
Self-esteem, Measure of, 130
Sensitisation Programme, 120
Services sectors, 242
Sex composition, 325
Sex disorderliness, 57
Sex orientation androgynous, 12
Sex stereotyping, 326
Sex typed, 236
Sex-related crimes, 118
Sexual abuse, 31–32
Sexual assaults, 39, 118–119
Sexual discrimination, 236
Sexual happiness, 58
Sexual harassment, 108, 119, 145, 242, 329
Sexual Harassment of Women Act, 245
Sexual health, 142, 145
Sexual minorities, 44
Sexual orientation, 141
Sexual pleasure, 117
Sexual purpose, 121
Sexual relations, 145, 150
Sexual relationships, 79
Sexual violence, 122, 146
Sexually transmitted diseases (STDs), 143, 146, 150
Single career husbands, 72
Situationism, 3
Skepticism, 286
Skill development, 171–172, 176

Slow-acting poison, 62
Small-scale entrepreneurship, 160
Social awareness, 120
Social gerontological research, 274
Social health, 284
Social mechanisms, 252
Social penetrating theory, 66
Social psychological research, 160
Social research, 125–126
Social responsibilities, 178, 251
Social structural processes, 15
Social support system, 103, 183
Social withdrawal, 285
Socialization process, 23
Societal factors, 126
Societal problems, 114
Socio-economic
  development, 142, 152
  disparities and health, 151
  groups, 142, 151
Sociological literature, 8, 265
Sociological research, 6, 8, 265
Software firms, 238
Software industry, 237
Somali women refugees, 43
Spielberger's scales, 10
Spousal relationships, 279
State Trait Anger Expression Inventory, 292–293
Strain-based conflicts, 214, 225
Stress
  perceptions, 197
  reactivity, 25
  reduction, 221
  responses, 40–41
  situations, 196
  -vulnerability models, 188
Stressful events, 23, 40, 190
Supportiveness scale, 84–86
Surat District Cooperative Bank, 170
Systematic problems, 142
Systemic barriers, 326

Target resilience factors, 43
Technological learning, 42
Technology-enabled work, 220
Technology transfer, 167
Teenage pregnancy, 22
Telecommuting, 210–213, 216–225
  benefits of, 218, 222
  organizations, 224
  privilege of, 224
  programmes, 216, 225
Tend-and-befriend theory, 40
Test retest reliability, 82, 130
Thematic Apperception Test, 6, 11
Therapeutic support groups, 27
Therapeutic values, 182
Time-based conflict, 214
Tourism industries, 118
Tourist industries, 121
Tourist wardens, 118
Trade unions, 239, 245
Traditional artisans, 177
Traditional conservatism, 153
Traditional gender, 323
Traditional organizations, 220
Transitional process, 28
T-test, 293, 296–297

Unconscious process, 286
UNESCO Institute of Statistics, 326
Union Bank of India, 170
United Nation's Fund, 322
United Nations General Assembly Special Session, 327
Universalisation of Elementary Education (UEE), 163
Unplanned pregnancy, 146
Uterine artery resistance index, 194

Vedic period women, 2
Vedic religion, 2
Village Panchayats, 245
Violence alarm system, 329
Violence and Reproductive Health, 145

Violent relationships, 32

Wage employment, 172
War atrocity, 21
Welfare programmes, 259
Women cops, 119
Women development cell, 108
Women entrepreneurship, 161, 171
Women film-maker, 125
Women In the Public Sector (WIPS), 245
Women managers, 14, 96–97, 104–107, 242, 245–246
Women travellers, 118
Women wage earners, 9
Women's health movement, 141
Women's socialization, 150
Work load, 94, 145, 327
Work organization, 212
Work pressure, 97, 106–107
Work resources, 220
Work responsibilities, 97, 219
Work-at-home, 217
Work-family
  balance mechanisms, 108
  benefits, 224
  conflict, 6, 12, 95, 211–215, 218–221, 223–225
  literature, 213
  relationships, 221, 223
World Bank, 142, 152–153
World Economic Forum, 324
World Health Organization, 142, 145, 284
World Population Day, 328
World Report on Women, 143
World Values Survey, 186

Yoga, 108–109
Youths, 43, 116–117, 160, 251, 283
  traumatized, 37
  unemployed, 276